THE CRISIS
AND CHALLENGE OF
AFRICAN
DEVELOPMENT

THE CRISIS AND CHALLENGE OF AFRICAN DEVELOPMENT

EDITED BY

Harvey Glickman

Contributions in Afro-American and African Studies, Number 112

GREENWOOD PRESS

New York • Westport, Connecticut • London

Library of Congress Cataloging-in-Publication Data

The crisis and challenge of African development / edited by Harvey
Glickman.
    p.   cm. — (Contributions in Afro-American and African
studies, ISSN 0069-9624 ; no. 112)
    Bibliography: p.
    Includes index.
    ISBN 0-313-25988-7 (lib. bdg. : alk. paper)
    1. Africa—Economic policy. 2. Africa—Economic conditions—1960–
I. Glickman, Harvey. II. Series.
HC800.C745 1988
338.96—dc19   87-31792

Library of Congress Catalog Card Number: 87-31792
ISBN: 0-313-25988-7
ISSN: 0069-9624

First published in 1988

Greenwood Press, Inc.
88 Post Road West, Westport, Connecticut 06881

Printed in the United States of America

The paper used in this book complies with the
Permanent Paper Standard issued by the National
Information Standards Organization (Z39.48-1984).

10 9 8 7 6 5 4 3 2 1

Contents

v

Illustrations

FIGURES

TABLES

Preface

In 1983 the Economic Commission for Africa of the United Nations warned, "The picture that emerges from the analysis of the perspective of the African region by the year 2008 under the historical trend scenario is almost a nightmare."[1] It required television images of starving children to focus world attention briefly on rural black Africa in 1984–85. The world's political leaders reacted. Emergency food shipments arrived. The rains providentially returned. Farmers in Africa began to produce more food and returned from "the informal market" as prices for farm products rose — the result of a package of economic reforms pressed on twenty-four countries by the World Bank and the International Monetary Fund. Nevertheless, in 1985 Robert McNamara, former head of the World Bank, would still point out that Africa faced "a crisis of unprecedented proportions. The physical environment is deteriorating. Per capita production of food grains is falling. Population growth rates are the highest in the world and rising. National economies are in disarray."[2] For Africa the hope for development had turned into the prospect of decay. Survival rather than progress emerges as the dominant theme in recent collections of essays devoted to analysis and prescription.[3]

Television is impotent to dramatize an African continent under siege by forces more ambiguous than but in the long run as deadly as famine — political instability, economic stagnation, and international debt. Despite new loans and grants from the international donor community, based on conditions of "policy reform," there have been no sure signs of change. Although still beset by dispersed and limited food shortages, Africa also faces "financial famine."[4]

Can another collection of essays help? This volume was born in the conviction that Africa's problems must be addressed from several directions. The contributors to this volume believe that some basic questions have not been asked and that many of the issues can be framed differently. What can a bewildered reader look for? The volume is conceived as an inquiry in three areas — questions concerning Africa's development record, questions dealing with the present consensus on policy reform, and questions about the institutions presently available for enhancing the possibilities of development in Africa in the future.

The approach here is overtly interdisciplinary and transideological. We address matters from diverse perspectives. We recognize that economic decline is related to policy mistakes, but we place policy in a historical and cultural context (see especially the chapters by Abernethy and Washington). We are critical of Africa's economic performance, but we place it in a comparative perspective. Regarding the much-worried issue of exogenous versus indigenous forces as responsible for economic decline, we point to overlooked outside forces and to the effects of opening African states to even greater outside pressures in the future (see the chapters by Glickman, Schatz, and Diejomaoh). We note the value of the present emphasis on policy reform (chapters by Lyman and by Gulhati and Yalamanchili), but we also note the weight of an African political rationality in the face of liberal prescriptions for development (chapters by Glickman and Hopkins). Finally, we investigate certain key issues in the priority area of agricultural policy: decentralization, the role of women, and food subsidies. We suggest that factors other than the growth of markets and private enterprise can play important parts (see the chapters by Morgenthau, Lewis, and Hopkins).

Two analytical theses nevertheless emerge. The first deals with "images." Lyman makes specific use of this perspective in his chapter on U.S. policy toward African development, as does Glickman in his chapter on the impact of development problems on the role of the state. The thrust of analysis since the 1981 path-breaking "Berg Report" of the World Bank has been to emphasize the failure of the African state in economic management and mistakes in the strategies of economic development.[5] "Shrinking the state" is a phrase that captures prescriptions for reducing the public sector of the economy and concomitantly expanding private enterprise, decentralizing what remains of state activities, and privatizing many state ventures. As

Schatz, Glickman, and Hopkins clearly observe, some skepticism toward the potential gains of privatizing African economies remains in order.

A second analytical thesis is that Africa's crisis is institutional in addition to structural or volitional. At the present moment there is a disjunction between national goals and international goals. Donor organizations, foreign governments, and African governments must act together, but they do not yet act in ways that respond fully to Africa's preferences as well as needs. This thesis is perhaps best illustrated by the universal recognition that Africa's recovery requires great doses of foreign aid. Without massive and coordinated assistance from foreign donors, Africa's own efforts will fall short. Help for governments that are doing less in their own economies requires attention to two important matters: reciprocity in decision making and sustainability of the assistance effort. (The chapters by Lyman and by Gulhati and Yalamanchili deal directly with the evidence for this need.)

Political leaders have responsibilities. How to achieve an African state whose leaders act responsibly in regard to its economic needs; how to get the leaders of the international donor community to take responsibility for a long-term effort to help increase the capability of African states to wisely manage their resources — ultimately these are the overriding questions we raise by our contributions to this volume.

The chapters that follow originated in papers presented at the Colloquium on African Development of Haverford, Bryn Mawr, and Swarthmore Colleges, 1984–85, and at the Conference on the Crisis and Challenge of African Development at Temple University Sugar Loaf Conference Center, Philadelphia, September 26–28, 1985. The chapters by Glickman, Schatz, and Washington were also presented as papers at a panel at the Global Development Conference, University of Maryland, College Park, September 12, 1986. All papers were subsequently revised for publication in this volume. Sections of the chapter by Schatz have appeared in a different form in the *Journal of Modern African Studies* 25, no. 1, March 1987, no. 2, June 1987. Some of the material in the chapter by Morgenthau is included in the forthcoming volume, *Fighting Hunger in a World Full of Grain,* coedited by her and Leobardo Jimenez-Sanchez.

The editor expresses sincere gratitude for the generous support of the Heinz Endowment, the Ford Foundation, and Haverford College at various stages in the development of this volume. To contributor Raymond S. Hopkins, many thanks for inspiration and special efforts.

NOTES

1.   United Nations Economic Commission for Africa, *ECA and Africa's Development, 1983–2008, A Preliminary Perspective Study,* Addis Ababa, ECA, 1983, 93.

2.   Robert S. McNamara, *The Challenge for Sub-Saharan Africa,* Sir John Crawford Memorial Lecture, November 1, 1985, Washington, D.C., World Bank, 1985, 31.

3.   Robert J. Berg and Jennifer S. Whitaker, eds., *Strategies for African Development,* Berkeley, University of California Press, 1986; Reginald H. Green, guest ed., "Sub-Saharan Africa: Toward Oblivion or Reconstruction?" *Journal of Development Planning,* no. 15, New York, United Nations Department of International Economic and Social Affairs, 1985; Tore Rose, ed., *Crisis and Recovery in Sub-Saharan Africa,* Development Centre Seminars, Paris, OECD, 1985; John Ravenhill, ed., *Africa in Economic Crisis,* New York, Columbia University Press, 1986; Carol Lancaster and John Williamson, eds., *African Debt and Financing,* Special Reports, 5, Washington, D.C., Institute for International Economics, May 1986.

4.   Alwyn B. Taylor, director-general of the African Center for Monetary Studies, quoted by correspondent James Brooke, *New York Times,* June 21, 1987.

5.   World Bank, *Accelerated Development in Sub-Saharan Africa: An Agenda for Action,* Washington, D.C., World Bank, 1981.

Part One

Context

1

European Colonialism and Postcolonial Crises in Africa

David B. Abernethy

Sub-Saharan Africa in the 1980s is experiencing not one but several crises. Each crisis is extremely serious on its own account; each is also linked to other crises in complex and often mutually reinforcing ways. Perhaps most dramatic — and most readily quantifiable — is the situation in the economic arena. The region's per capita income rose by an insignificant 0.4% annually from 1970 to 1981 and, according to a recent estimate, may actually have fallen by 4% a year from 1980 to 1985.[1] Per capita food production declined by an estimated 2.3% annually during 1969–73 and by 1.7% annually during 1973–84. The disastrous 1983–85 drought, affecting thirty-five million people in over twenty countries, undoubtedly pushed this figure still lower.[2] The region can no longer feed itself, though two-thirds of its labor force works on the land. Sub-Saharan Africa's external debts ($80 billion as of 1984) are smaller than Latin America's in dollar terms. But Africa's far poorer and less diversified economies may face an even more intractable challenge than those of Latin America in servicing — to say nothing of repaying — debts already incurred. One can speak only euphemistically of Africa as an economically "developing area"; "dedevelopment" may more appropriately describe what is happening. "For the first time since World War II," notes a 1986 World Bank report, "a whole region has suffered retrogression over a generation."[3]

Africa has also experienced more than its fair share of political crises in recent years. The very existence of the territorial state has been at stake in prolonged civil wars besetting several countries, including four that account for over two-fifths of the region's population: Nigeria, Ethiopia, Zaire, and the Sudan. The legitimacy of political institutions and decision-making procedures, as well as the right of particular individuals to rule, have been repeatedly and often successfully challenged during the past quarter-century of independence. The most obvious signs of the legitimacy crisis are the frequency of military coups in such countries as Nigeria, the Central African Republic, and Benin (Dahomey) and the role of military officers as executive heads of over twenty countries as of 1986. Interstate conflicts, many with some degree of superpower involvement, have become more serious and protracted during the past decade than in previous years.[4] A tragic consequence of violent conflict within and among states has been the emergence of a large, rapidly growing refugee population. With one-tenth of the world's population, Africa now accounts for one-quarter to one-half of the world's estimated ten million refugees.[5]

Political crises have also been precipitated by the refusal of white minorities to cede power to indigenous majorities. This refusal produced sustained and violent preindependence conflicts in Kenya, Algeria, and Rhodesia (Zimbabwe), fuels a long-standing liberation struggle in South Africa–controlled Namibia, and is now generating sustained popular resistance at many levels within South Africa itself. What could rapidly become an open civil war in South Africa will quite likely have significant effects on the distribution and uses of power in all the countries of southern Africa, and not simply within the borders of the last bastion of white supremacy.

Africa is experiencing, as well, a "crisis of government performance" that both affects and is affected by the economic and political crises noted earlier. Ostensibly, governments are instituted in order to alleviate — and, if possible, resolve — many of the conflicts and problems faced by the members of a society. At the same time, the cost, the priorities, and the policies of governments can themselves constitute serious problems for citizens and may actually reduce a society's capacity for problem solving. In preindependence years African nationalist movements popularized the view of central government as problem solver once power was transferred to the colonized majority. As Kwame Nkrumah put it, "Seek ye first the political kingdom, and all else shall be added unto you." In rather sharp contrast, the post-independence years have seen widespread disillusionment with the political kingdom. Something seems rotten in the kingdom, and the king seems unable or unwilling (or both) to deliver to his people what had been promised.[6]

To the extent that the African state consumes scarce resources to maintain the lifestyles and further the ambitions of the political/ bureaucratic elites controlling it; to the extent that corruption diverts public resources to private ends and undermines the legitimacy of the political system; to the extent that public policies neglect or exploit the rural majority of the population, undercutting incentives for economically productive activity — to this extent the performance of the public sector becomes an obstacle rather than a stimulus to economic and political development. The crisis of government performance is particularly alarming because central governments are the only institutionalized means Africans have to cope with many of the problems within their countries, as well as with powerfully intrusive institutions from the international environment. If the capacity to cope with multiple crises is seriously reduced by the ineffective or counterproductive actions of governments, then the harmful effects of other societal crises are magnified.

Enumerating Africa's multiple crises and estimating their magnitude are necessary steps along the path leading to crisis resolution. But before one moves "forward" from description to prescription, it is important to take a few "backward" steps to consider the factors contributing to these crises. Implicit in policy recommendations for the future are assumptions about causes embedded in the past. Such assumptions deserve to be made explicit and their validity questioned.

Single-factor causal theories are emotionally appealing but intellectually deceptive. When crises are multiple, complex, and interactive — as Africa's are — it is not unreasonable to expect that their causes will have similar characteristics. Scholars and activists will continue to debate the relative importance of the following factors, but most analysts would probably agree that each has contributed in some measure to at least one of the crises noted:

Africa's physical/natural environment
Actors from the external (international) environment
Policies and practices of elites governing the populace
Institutions, values, and behavior of the populace

Each factor in turn affects developments in each of the three time periods of recent African history: the precolonial, the colonial, and the postcolonial or political independence eras.

Analysis of each causal factor during each time period is clearly beyond the scope of this chapter. My more modest goal is to focus on the role played by one of these factors — actors from the external environment — during one of the three time periods noted. My question is: In what ways and to what extent did the policies and practices of European colonial governments contribute to Africa's postcolonial crises? Attempting an answer to this "limited" question is itself grandly ambitious, if only because European colonial rulers were not only external actors but also, during the period in question, the elites governing the African populace. Two analytically separate causal factors were thus temporarily fused into one. Colonialism constituted the domestication or internalization of powerful forces whose base was foreign or external to Africa.

The essence of being colonized is the experience of powerlessness. To be sure, over time the power ratio between colonizer and colonized shifted more in favor of the latter. But the shift took place through structures and procedures and within territorial entities that were initially imposed by the colonizer. When Africans eventually gained formal political power, it was in large measure on the strength of nationalist movements whose idealized "nation" was the product of boundaries arbitrarily drawn by Europeans. The citadel of power Africans came to occupy — the executive and legislative institutions of central governments — had been constructed by foreigners employing foreign architectural designs. Thus both the "nation" and the "state" of the postcolonial "nation-state" are artifacts of European colonial rule.

The colonial situation produced by European rule in Africa may be defined as a system of multiple relationships of dominance and subordination in which the dominant group is racially and culturally distinct from the subordinated group and in which the latter is a substantial majority of a colony's population.[7] The several arenas within which these unequal relationships may be found — notably the political, administrative, economic, social, cultural, religious, and psychological arenas — are analytically distinct from and in some sense parallel with one another. At the same time, these unequal relationships are mutually reinforcing, so that dominance by the colonizer in one arena facilitates dominance in others. This situation is presented schematically in Figure 1.1, the arrows representing lines of influence. For instance, the activities of European settlers and of European mine and plantation managers in the economic arena provide important resources to finance the political (policy-making) and administrative (policy-implementing) activities of the

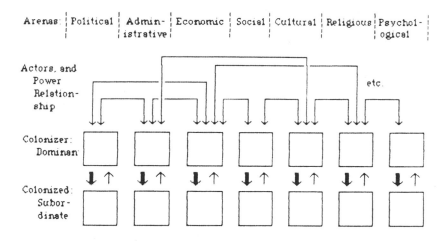

Figure 1.1 The Colonial Situation

central government. The educational and proselytizing work of Christian missionaries, which affects the cultural, religious, and psychological arenas, provides literate and numerate indigenous workers useful in the economic and administrative arenas. In turn, the dominance of the colonizer in the political and administrative arenas provides a setting of predictability, of protection for person and property, and of development of the vital infrastructure of transport and communications that facilitates the activities of colonizers in all the other arenas.[8]

This last point suggests that the political and administrative arenas are particularly vital for the ongoing operations of the colonial system as a whole. A colony's central government provides a "steel framework" or "grid," in Margery Perham's words,[9] underneath which the multiple relations of dominance and subordination can be most effectively formed and maintained.

THE LEGACY OF COLONIAL GOVERNMENT POLICIES

In examining the effects of colonial government policies and practices on contemporary African crises, we may take several complementary approaches. One is to identify significant differences in the policies of the European metropoles and then to speculate on the implications of these differences. An important distinction, for example, is between policies encouraging and those discouraging the arrival of European settlers. Territories with substantial settler populations — Kenya and Rhodesia under the British, Algeria and Madagascar under the French, Angola under the Portuguese — were most apt to experience violent preindependence conflict between colonizers and colonized. This conflict assumed particular intensity because not only political power but also control of the means of production (land) were at stake, and because power inequalities coincided with highly visible racial differences.[10]

Another distinction — between direct and indirect rule — provides some clues as to the extent of postindependence domestic violence among indigenous peoples. Ethnically heterogeneous territories where Europeans employed indirect rule policies — such as Nigeria, the Sudan, and Uganda under the British, Chad under the French, and for periods of time the Congo under the Belgians — seem particularly susceptible to postcolonial civil wars in which politically mobilized ethnic or regional groups challenge the very existence of the territorial state. Both these types of conflicts — interracial and interethnic — are particularly difficult to resolve, if only because the stakes are so high for winners and losers. The widespread resort to violence that such conflicts provoke obviously inhibits the savings and investment activities required for sustained development, hence magnifying the economic crisis.

Another approach is to identify significant similarities in the policies of the European metropoles and then to speculate on the implications of these common features. Two of many similarities will be discussed here: policies affecting remuneration of government employees and policies affecting the volume and composition of a colony's international trade.

To rule a colony is to administer it; a defining characteristic of the colonial situation is authoritarian rule by bureaucrats. Each metropole felt that the occupants of top generalist and specialist positions in the colonial bureaucracy should be Europeans, who would have a direct personal interest in maintaining metropolitan power and in affirming the general status of whites as superior beings.[11] In order to attract the desired quantity and quality of Europeans, each colonial power set salaries for the top positions at a level competitive with what well-qualified individuals would expect to earn in the metropole. Moreover, in view of Africa's reputation as a hardship post, perquisites relating to house rent, length of leave, travel, and children's education allowances had to be offered that, if anything, were more generous than those obtaining in the metropole.

The practice of paying Europeans according to European standards, begun at the very outset of colonial rule, continued throughout it. In particular, salaries and "perks" for European colonial administrators shifted upward after 1945 to reflect postwar improvements in European living standards and to compensate for the effects of inflation within Europe. Moreover, in the terminal phase of colonial rule metropolitan governments were anxious that salaries, pensions, and other forms of compensation for European administrators be set sufficiently high to induce these individuals either to stay on, if requested to do so by the new African government, or to return to the metropole in a reasonable financial state.[12]

If salary scales for Europeans at the top of the hierarchy were set with the metropole in mind, those for Africans at the lower and middle levels of the hierarchy were set with the colony firmly in mind. Europeans were generally prepared to pay Africans (especially those with post–primary school qualifications) wages above those a peasant might obtain from producing cash crops for export. Such wages were, of course, even further above the income equivalent of a subsistence farmer or herder. At the same time, the rulers were anxious that low-level civil service compensation not be raised "too much" above African per capita income. The concern was in part fiscal and in part political. Could the government cover its own costs if scales at the base were set close to those at the apex? Should not Africans be discouraged from comparing themselves with Europeans? If Africans made such comparisons, would they not aspire to positions of administrative responsibility that Europeans intended to reserve indefinitely for themselves?

The direct result of colonial remuneration policies was the emergence of two extraordinarily large income gaps. One was between the highly paid European bureaucrat and the low-level African functionary — that is, within the public sector but across racial lines. The other gap was between the low-level African functionary and the average African peasant — that is, between the public and private sectors but within the same racial group. Calculating the magnitude of these two gaps is, of course, a hazardous and inevitably arbitrary enterprise. The gaps varied from colony to colony; estimating the income equivalent for subsistence-sector peasants is problematic at best; and living expenses were obviously greater for urban dwellers (European and African alike) than for those living in the rural areas. A very rough guess, however, would be that in the period between World Wars I and II an unskilled laborer employed by an African central government could earn £15 a year. This was well above the average for rural farmers, yet it was less than 1% of the compensation level for the top civil servant advising the colonial governor or governor-general. In the 1945–60 period a literate African occupying a low-level teaching or clerical position could earn several times the average farm income yet receive only about 3 to 5% of the income — not to mention "perks" — at the top of the scale. The average salary of the African bureaucrat might be five to ten times that of the peasant yet one-fifth to one-third that of the average European bureaucrat.[13]

The income gaps produced by colonial rule had a number of significant consequences. The gap between low-level bureaucrats and peasants led many of the latter to reassess occupational options for their children. Instead of preparing the next generation to work the land, as in the past, peasants began to invest their meager savings in Western-style education for their children, for education provided the formal qualifications needed for access to well-paying and relatively secure government posts. African attention shifted, in short, from economic prospects in the indigenous private sector to far more attractive prospects in the externally imposed public sector.

The gap between Europeans at the top of the hierarchy and African employees at the base stimulated the rise of African nationalism and gave that nationalism a particular character. After 1945 increasing numbers of Africans earned the secondary and then university-level degrees that qualified them to compete for highly paid, high-level administrative positions. As they did so, it became increasingly clear that Europeans were opposed to rapid indigenization of the top positions and were unwilling to pay Africans who did make it into the top ranks on the same scale as whites. Understandably, the Western-educated Africans who formed the leadership core of growing nationalist movements across the continent made opposition to racially based "job reservation" and insistence on equal pay for equal work among the most central and powerfully articulated of their demands.

On both counts the nationalist movements were eventually successful.[14] With independence, therefore, the status quo in the racial or national composition of the hierarchy was overturned, while the status quo in remuneration levels at the top positions was retained. Ironically, the demands of African nationalism for equality — defined as equality with Europeans — carried over to the postcolonial period the highly inegalitarian remuneration patterns Europeans had developed during the colonial period.

In 1963–64, when Kenya, Tanganyika, Nigeria, and Uganda were newly independent, the ratio of top civil service salaries to the per capita gross domestic product of these countries was 82 to 1, 96 to 1, 118 to 1, and 130 to 1, respectively.[15] (The ratio in the United States, by way of contrast, is well below 10 to 1.) At the lower end of the civil service, salaries and perquisites have remained far more lucrative than the amount the average farmer involved in cash-crop production — to say nothing of subsistence — could expect to earn. As of 1980, according to an International Monetary Fund study, the average central government wage in a sample of sixteen African countries was 6.05 times greater than per capita GDP. Figures for other regions covered in the study were 2.94 in Latin America (n = 8), 2.90 in Asia (n = 5), and 1.74 for advanced industrial market economies (n = 16).[16] European colonialism thus created the pattern — which African anticolonial nationalism insisted on retaining — of high unit costs of administration relative to the income of the vast majority of a country's population.

Once the nationalist leaders gained political power, they embarked upon a rapid expansion in the size and functional scope of the public sector. This expansion was due primarily to political factors: for instance, party activists' expectations of patronage, demands for appropriate white-collar employment by growing numbers of secondary school and university graduates, and leaders' beliefs that an activist public sector was needed in view of the limited capacity or will of their countries' private sectors to stimulate economic development. Not to be ignored in the expansion of scale, however, was the sheer attractive power of government salaries and "perks" compared to what else was available.

When high costs per government employee are multiplied by an enormously enlarged number of employees in government ministries and parastatal agencies, paying for the day-to-day operations of the political kingdom becomes an expensive proposition. The ratio of general government consumption to gross domestic product rose in Africa from 9.7% in 1960 to 14.3% in 1981. The increase of 4.6 in this percentage was twice that for South Asia and for the Latin American/Caribbean region, and over four times that for East Asia and the Pacific. By the early 1980s government consumption took a higher portion of GDP in contemporary tropical Africa than in all other developing regions save the Middle East and North Africa.[17] African governments, moreover, spend an unusually large portion of recurrent costs simply covering wages and salaries of their employees: about 30% in the 1974–80 period, compared to roughly 20% in the Latin American/Caribbean region and about 15% in Asia and the Middle East.[18]

The combined effect of colonial remuneration policies and of postcolonial patronage policies is a public sector that may simply be too expensive to be sustained by the private-sector economic base on which it rests. At some point a conspicuously consumptive state ceases to become an engine for economic development. If it is an engine for development but if the engine consumes large amounts of scarce fuel simply to keep itself idling, then the engine's capacity to help the larger vehicle (the national economy) move forward is seriously impaired. It may be that in the 1980s the sheer expense of maintaining the African state poses a threat to the viability of the African economy.[19]

A second example of broadly similar policies is the strong encouragement colonial governments gave to international trade. In West Africa and the Sudan — areas termed by Samir Amin "Africa of the colonial trade economy" — peasants were coerced and induced to produce cash crops directly for export. In the Congo River basin — Amin's "Africa of the concession-owned companies" — local people were recruited to work on European-managed plantations whose products were exported. In the eastern and southern regions of the continent — "Africa of the labour reserves" — varying degrees of land alienation produced a pool of African migrant laborers to work in the export-oriented mines, farms, and ranches owned by white settlers.[20] That the means employed to shift African production patterns from the local to the international level varied from place to place should not obscure the fundamentally similar objectives of the colonial powers. The colonial economies were to be incorporated into wider trade and investment networks controlled by the metropoles and responsive to the requirements of advanced industrial capitalism.[21] African raw material exports were valued as inputs into a complex European industrial process that demanded large, predictable volumes of such inputs at low cost. At the same time, Africa was valued as a supplement to already-existing markets for Europe's manufactured goods.

In view of these metropolitan needs it is not surprising that, as P. Robson and D. A. Lury observed in the 1960s, "external trade is, after subsistence activities, the most important feature of the African economic scene." The two economists noted that as of the late 1950s the ratio of commodity exports to gross domestic product was higher in this continent than in others: 21% for Africa as against 17% for Europe, 13% for South America, 10% for Asia (excluding Japan), and 5% for North America.[22]

The colonial state played an important role in facilitating the trade-oriented activities of European private-sector actors. Of particular importance in this respect were public investments in transport and communications, which "opened up" large areas back of the coast to production for the world market; forced-labor policies; and land alienation favoring white settlers. It would be a mistake, however, to perceive the state as acting merely as the instrument of European private interests. It was very much in the colonial administration's own interest to encourage an economy oriented to international trade. A cardinal principle of colonial policy everywhere was that each colony pay for itself — that is, it should generate enough revenue to cover the recurrent expenditure of its own government. But it proved extremely difficult and quite costly to extract the required resources directly from a poor, physically dispersed populace whose members were engaged in a largely self-reliant, precapitalist mode of production. Moreover, direct methods of capturing this "uncaptured peasantry"[23] such as forced labor and head, hut, or cattle cesses were politically dangerous. The risks were demonstrated in the 1898 Sierra Leone Hut Tax Rebellion, the 1929 Aba "Woman's War" in Nigeria, and other less well publicized rebellions.

Administratively much simpler was a policy of getting peasants to produce (or to work for whites whose enterprises produced) commodities valued in the metropole but not consumed in raw form by the colonized people themselves. In such a case the bureaucrats would not have to disperse into the countryside to locate and then tax what was being produced; rather, they could wait for the commodities to come to them. As these commodities converged on a limited number of points within the colony, even a small administrative staff could readily assess their value and tax them before the commodities left for Europe. Similarly, policies encouraging local people to purchase imported consumer goods — and discouraging them from producing their own — made fiscal sense because of the ease with which the imported goods could be taxed. That such taxes were indirect also greatly reduced the political sensitivity of the operation, for the extraction of surplus could be disguised from the colonized population in a way that was quite impossible with forced labor or hut taxes. What the colonized people did not know would not lead them to revolt.[24]

In a study of twelve African economies, Robson and Lury estimated that 80% of government revenue as of the early 1960s was derived from taxation; of the tax revenue about half was generated by import duty, about 15% by export taxes.[25] Thus roughly half of government recurrent revenue was derived from the taxation of commodities crossing territorial borders. The public sector in the colony therefore had its own needs in mind when it encouraged an "open" economy focused on the export of primary products and the import of manufactured goods. A provincial commissioner in Tanganyika summarized both the problem and the solution to it when he wrote in 1928, "To help the revenue position we must get every nut we can out of the province."[26]

What is the link between this type of economy and Africa's postcolonial crises? I would not agree with the argument of those in the dependency school that an orientation to international trade is inherently bad for African development. Too much depends on available developmental alternatives for a particular territory and on world market demand for a particular commodity to permit acceptance of a generalization of this sort. I would argue, however, that in many places colonial government policies seriously undermined the capacity of African economies to satisfy basic food needs by stressing export-crop production and by directing male labor into mining activities. The virtually complete absence of scientific research on staple foods, in contrast to well-funded research on export crops, had serious long-term consequences when the continent began by the 1970s to devote increasingly scarce foreign exchange resources to the import of food grains. On the import side, official encouragement of the sale of metropolitan consumer goods frequently undercut the market for items produced by African artisans. The decline of artisanal activity seriously inhibited Africans' capacity to build on the small-scale, labor-intensive, self-reliant industrial base of the precolonial period. When independence-era regimes attempted experiments in structural change through industrialization, they looked to large-scale, capital-intensive, import-intensive industrial models developed in wealthy countries rather than building on models indigenous to Africa. The high cost of imported industrial models — like the high cost of imported administrative models — has in many cases had the unfortunate effect of depressing rather than revitalizing African national economies, of changing the form but not reducing the extent of dependence on the world economy.

The major consequence of developing trade-oriented colonial economies is, as noted earlier, that these economies became extremely vulnerable to market forces over which Africans had minimal control. When prices for African exports were buoyant, as in the Korean War commodity boom of the early 1950s, this vulnerability was in fact a source of strength. But when demand slackened, Africa's vulnerability was a source of profound weakness. Such has been the case in the past decade, which has featured both a global recession and the continuing development of synthetics to compete with many of Africa's raw material exports. Uncertainty over export revenue seems to make national planning imperative. Yet it is precisely this uncertainty that makes planning exercises potentially a waste of time if not in fact counterproductive.

THE COLONIAL STATE AND AFRICAN SOCIETY

We have seen that certain policies adopted by the colonial state, in large measure to satisfy the state's own financial and organizational needs, contributed in important ways to postcolonial economic and political crises. Colonial policies also contributed to the current crisis in government performance that in turn renders the resolution of other crises so difficult and problematic. In the final section of this chapter I focus not so much on what colonial governments cost or what they did as on how they related to the social and economic structures of the people they ruled. The colonial situation is, after all, a set of relationships: two unequally powerful parties, the colonizers and the colonized, interacting in complex and mutually dependent ways.[27] The effects of colonialism on a given society will therefore depend not only on the resources, interests, and institutions of the colonizer but also on the kind of society upon which external rule has been imposed. Two questions come to mind here, the answers to which are admittedly as speculative and abstract as they will be brief. What was the degree of fit, or congruence, between colonial state and colonized society? And what are the implications for the postcolonial period of the degree of fit that we have observed?

I would argue that there was a particularly poor fit between state and society in the colonial period. In the first place, colonial structures were imposed from above by non-Africans rather than developing out of the indigenous social and political environment. This meant that from the very start the colonial state faced a crisis of legitimacy. If Africans complied with the new rulers' dictates, this was primarily out of fear of the consequences of disobedience, not because Africans felt morally obliged to obey. There was good reason to fear the consequences of disobedience, because the state's coercive resources were so much greater than anything the colonized could deploy. But the Europeans' very dominance in the coercive arena may have made it more difficult for them to foster genuine loyalty to them and their imported institutions on the part of the masses they ruled. The legitimacy crisis thus persisted, unresolved, throughout the colonial period. This meant that although the colonial institutions and procedures African elites inherited were in some respects quite powerful, at the level of societal acceptance they were fundamentally flawed and weak.[28]

Second, there was generally a lack of fit between the political and administrative structures of rulers and ruled. The Europeans brought with them the administrative "output" structures of their home countries while proving quite reluctant to export political "input" structures. Bureaucratic hierarchies thus quickly sprang up in African soil. But not until much later, and under constant pressure from Africans, did indigenous professional associations, trade unions, political parties, and representative legislatures become significant in the life of the colony.[29] Precolonial African politics, in contrast, were not nearly so unbalanced in the direction of administration. Given the ease with which people unhappy with their ruler could move to available land elsewhere and the speed with which information about rulers' misdeeds could spread within a small-scale polity, African "traditional" rulers generally developed quite sensitive mechanisms for assessing and responding to the demands of their subjects.

The bureaucracies Europeans brought with them, moreover, were quite visible, functionally specialized, and hierarchical. These "Weberian" structures were imposed upon societies that relied far less on bureaucratic means for realizing public goals. The contrast was particularly striking when an African society existed without a state — that is, when its political, legal, and administrative functions were performed "invisibly" by a variety of organizations that carried out social, economic, and religious functions as well. These organizations included age-grades, secret societies, localized cults, and deliberative councils called on an ad hoc basis.[30] The ability of people to solve collective problems without resorting to a state structure is surely a fine art that in today's world of powerful public bureaucracies one can well view with genuine admiration and envy. But the Europeans who established the colonial order regarded a society without a state as a people without a civilization. The lack of congruence between the structures the Europeans imposed and the structures Africans had developed was to produce considerable misunderstanding on both sides. It further meant that the colonial state was suspended, as it were, over the colonized society, with very few linkages to the ways ordinary people in that society thought and acted and went about solving problems.

We can elaborate on this image: the colonial state was like a prefabricated house suspended above the ground by wires from a giant crane hovering above it (the metropole). The house was not supported from below by the building blocks of the indigenous social order. Nor could the colonial house be supported in this way, because the building blocks had been arranged for an edifice with different dimensions. If anything, the colonial rulers acted as wrecking crews of the foundations they came upon, either razing these foundations altogether (direct rule) or knocking them akilter (indirect rule) so that they could not support anything that would meet the internationally accepted "building code" of the modern state. With independence, the house was lowered to the ground. But because of the absence of solidly and appropriately built foundations, anyone observing this process would have to wonder how habitable such an unstable structure really was.[31]

A third problem, indirectly alluded to earlier, was the significant difference in scale of indigenous and colonial politics. One can think of Africa as a single unit in geographical and racial terms, as pan-African writers have done, in which case the besetting sin of the Europeans was to divide the continent into too many small, economically unviable units. On the other hand, one can think of Africa as the physical setting for hundreds or even thousands of indigenous entities defined in linguistic and cultural terms, in which case the Europeans were at fault for attempting to create states too few in number to reflect the continent's abundant diversities.

Paradoxically, both perspectives and both criticisms are valid. Measured by contemporary international standards of population, GDP, and GDP per capita, the fifty-plus states of Africa are unacceptably small. For example, thirty-one of the forty-one states of continental sub-Sahara have under ten million people; ten have under two million. In addition, many are microstates in the most obvious sense of being territorially tiny; eight occupy less than one hundred thousand square kilometers. (Offshore island nations are not included in these figures.) Except in the case of Nigeria, such limitations of scale pose almost insuperable obstacles to even a modest degree of industrialization. At the same time, the African state may be unacceptably large, attempting as it does to bring within a single political and administrative framework a large number of ethnically distinct peoples. European colonialism left Africa too balkanized politically to develop economically. It is just possible that colonialism also left Africa insufficiently balkanized to develop politically in response to the perceptions and demands of its diverse populace.

To raise this possibility is not necessarily to argue for the creation of still additional, ethnically less heterogeneous African countries. Such a recommendation would in fact be economically disastrous, not least because it costs so much per capita simply to maintain a legally sovereign state. It would also ignore the reality that ethnicity is itself highly fluid and that the particular way in which ethnic identities and objectives develop is highly dependent on the size and character of the polity within which people find themselves.[32] The suggestion is rather that more might be done than at present to devolve responsibilities currently monopolized by the central government down to regional and local government agencies. Devolution of public functions might proceed outward to the private sector as well as downward in scale in order to tap the organized energies of savings clubs, burial societies, football clubs, local churches and mosques, producer and consumer cooperatives, ethnic improvement associations, age-grades, and other manifestations of development activity at the grass roots.[33]

The colonial state in Africa was placed atop a host of small-scale, mutually insulated units of production, consumption, and political identity. The problem for the state when its status shifts from colonial to postcolonial is that relations between state and society are likely to be particularly unhappy for all parties concerned. On the one hand, small-scale units such as lineages, clans, and villages will have an interest in boring into the structure of the state in order to extract whatever can be taken from an institution at once relatively rich in resources and poor in legitimacy. The large number and small size of units of identity and the powerful moral obligations most public employees have to these units make it extremely difficult to protect the state treasury from the costly effects of nepotism and other forms of public-sector corruption.[34] On the other hand, state officials find it difficult to control a socially atomized and geographically dispersed peasantry. Officials are tempted to neglect the peasantry altogether or to establish large parastatal structures with ambitious mandates to regulate rural transport, staple and cash-crop marketing, credit, and the like. These parastatals tend to be effective and efficient in three respects only: absorbing public funds, stifling peasant incentives and opportunities to produce, and diverting private resources into illegal "parallel" markets that cannot be easily taxed by the government.[35] The postcolonial state is simultaneously too vulnerable to penetration by society (which leads to costly corruption) and too tempted to regulate society (which leads to reduced productive activity on the part of the small-scale private sector).

Thus in several respects there is a poor fit between the state structures Europeans established during the colonial era and the structures and problem-solving processes of indigenous African society. The lack of congruence becomes an even more serious problem in the postcolonial era. As the state expands in size and in functional scope, and as its personnel are localized, the public sector becomes increasingly vulnerable to societal penetration and inclined to overregulate society. In both instances, the consequence is the crisis of government performance noted at the outset of this chapter.

How to deal with this performance crisis is particularly problematic. The crisis stems from colonial policies and practices that were retained by the indigenous elites who inherited the Europeans' political kingdom. The crisis also stems from the relationship — in a sense, the striking absence of a meaningful relationship — between the importations of the colonial period and the home-grown characteristics of African society. Part of the solution to the crisis is simply to rein in a state that it is unclear how the developmental potential of small holder peasants can be tapped without significant government efforts to counter the effects of ecological deterioration and encourage higher crop yields. A leaner central government is hard pressed to improve its performance in delivering essential services or in resolving violent domestic or interstate conflicts.

NOTES

1.   The 1970–81 estimates are in World Bank, *World Tables,* 3rd ed., vol. 1, *Economic Data,* Baltimore, Johns Hopkins University Press, 1983, 485. The estimate for 1980–85 is in Economic Commission for Africa, "Second Special Memorandum," Addis Ababa, April 1985, cited in Lester R. Brown and Edward C. Wolf, *Reversing Africa's Decline,* Worldwatch Paper no. 65, Washington, D.C., Worldwatch Institute, 1985, 8.

2.   World Bank, *Financing Adjustment with Growth in Sub-Saharan Africa, 1986–90,* Washington, D.C., World Bank, 1986, 87, 7–8.

3.   Ibid., 9.

4.   Gerald J. Bender, James S. Coleman, and Richard L. Sklar, eds., *African Crisis Areas and U.S. Foreign Policy,* Berkeley, University of California Press, 1985.

5.   Estimates of the number of refugees vary widely. The International Conference on Assistance to Refugees in Africa (*Refugees in Africa: A Country by Country Survey,* Geneva, ICARA, 1981, 3) gives a figure of 5 million in 1980, up from about 750,000 in 1970. Tony Hodges ("Africa's Refugee Crisis," *Africa Report,* January–February 1984, 4) estimates over 2.5 million. See also Gaim Kibreab, *Reflections on the African Refugee Problem,* Uppsala, Scandinavian Institute of African Studies, 1983.

6. The theme of disillusionment with politics and government is powerfully expressed in the works of African novelists such as Chinua Achebe, *A Man of the People*; Ayi Kwei Armah, *The Beautyful Ones Are Not Yet Born*; and Ngugi wa Thiong'o, *Petals of Blood*, as well as in the film of Ousmane Sembene, *Xala*.

7. The literature on European colonialism in Africa is vast. Useful overviews offering widely differing interpretations may be found in Peter Duignan and L. H. Gann, general eds., *Colonialism in Africa, 1870–1960*, 5 vols., Cambridge, Cambridge University Press and Hoover Institution Press, 1969–75; Immanuel Wallerstein, ed., *Social Change: The Colonial Situation*, New York, Wiley and Sons, 1966; Michael Crowder, *West Africa under Colonial Rule*, London, Hutchinson, 1968; A. G. Hopkins, *An Economic History of West Africa*, New York, Columbia University Press, 1973, 168–282; Frederick Cooper, "Africa and the World Economy," *African Studies Review* 29, no. 2/3, June/September 1981, 1–86; Margery Perham, *The Colonial Reckoning*, London, Collins, 1962; Walter Rodney, *How Europe Underdeveloped Africa*, London, Bogle-L'Ouverture Publications, 1972; and Albert Memmi, *The Colonizer and the Colonized*, Boston, Beacon Press, 1965. On the concept of the colonial situation see G. Balandier, "The Colonial Situation: A Theoretical Approach," in Wallerstein, *Social Change*, 34–61, and Memmi.

8. Relationships among dominant groups in the political, administrative, economic, cultural, and religious arenas were not necessarily harmonious, but in the normal colonial situation there were enough common, overlapping interests among colonizers that one can speak of the overall dominance-subordination relationship as having systemic properties. For the classic instance of a "triple alliance" among state, church, and European economic interests, see Crawford Young, *Politics in the Congo*, Princeton, Princeton University Press, 1965, 10–32.

9. Perham, *Colonial Reckoning*, 58–59. Perham was referring specifically to the indirect rule policies of British governments, but the metaphor she employed is more broadly applicable.

10. In cases where whites have been present for so long that they no longer consider themselves settlers, and where they control a state internationally recognized as sovereign, racial conflict can be expected to be even more intense, and its peaceful resolution virtually impossible to envisage. This is the situation in South Africa. It is significant that the politically dominant white ethnic group defines itself as "Afrikaner" and refuses to apply the term "African" to blacks.

11. In some British West African colonies, for example Sierra Leone and the Gold Coast, Africans did hold high administrative posts in the nineteenth century, but this situation changed dramatically in the 1890s as whites came to monopolize the highest positions. Richard Symonds, *The British and Their Successors: A Study in the Development of the Government Services in the New States*, London, Faber and Faber, 1966, 158. The pattern was somewhat less restrictive in France's colonies, where a few West Indians and Africans from such territories as Senegal or Dahomey could assume relatively important positions in the years before World War II. Still, the European effort to link a white skin with power, authority, and status was a key feature of colonialism everywhere in Africa. On the allegedly race-blind policies of the Portuguese see Gerald J. Bender, *Angola under the Portuguese: The Myth and the Reality*, Berkeley, University of California Press, 1978.

12.   Referring to high-level administrative salary scales that were set by the preindependence Lidbury and Flemming commissions, an official Kenyan commission noted in 1971 that "while it might not be accurate to say that those basic scales were directly related to salary levels in the U.K., there is no doubt in our minds that the main consideration at the time was to devise scales which, with the overseas addition, would be attractive to expatriates and would encourage their recruitment and retention in the service for some years to come." Republic of Kenya, *Report of the Commission of Enquiry (Public Service Structure and Remuneration Commission), 1970–71*, Chairman: D. N. Ndegwu, Nairobi, Government Press, 1971, 47. A similar point was made in Gold Coast, *Report of the Commission on the Civil Service of the Gold Coast, 1950–51*, Accra, Government Press, 1951, 62.

13.   Data from three countries illustrate these gaps. As of 1962 in Kenya, an ungraded clerk with a Standard 6 "pass" started at £88 and 1 shilling, a trained primary school teacher at £113 and 16 shillings. A district officer started at £798, a provincial commissioner at £2,800. Kenya, *Opportunities for Employment in the Kenyan Civil Service*, Nairobi, Government Press, 1962.

In Mali as of 1959, the average nonwage agricultural worker received the estimated equivalent of $76 a year. The average African wage earner received $600, the average European (in the private as well as the public sector) $4,200. William Jones, *Planning and Economic Policy: Socialist Mali and Her Neighbors*, Washington, D.C., Three Continents Press, 1976, 44.

A survey of the Dahomean city of Porto Novo, conducted in the mid-1950s by Claude Tardits, indicates the following distribution of monthly incomes in francs CFA: Africans with private-sector wage income: 98% under 15,000, 2% 15,000–30,000. Africans in the public sector: 60% 15,000–30,000; 37% 30,000–60,000; 3% over 60,000. Europeans in the public sector: 10% 15,000–30,000; 47% 30,000–60,000; 43% over 60,000. Income for the average Dahomean peasant household at the time was probably between 5,000 and 10,000 francs CFA. Claude Tardits, *Porto Novo: Les nouvelles générations africaines entre leur traditions et l'Occident*, Paris, Ecole Pratique, 1958, 84.

14.   African representatives in the French Assemblée Nationale won a major victory for the principle of equal pay for equal work with the passage in 1950 of the Deuxième Loi Lamine Guèye. In the British colonies each territory moved at its own pace toward acceptance of the same principle, the pace accelerating as Africans gained control of the legislature and as the civil service's senior ranks were Africanized.

15.   Estimates based on data in the appendix to Martin Godfrey, "The International Market in Skills and the Transmission of Inequality," *Development and Change* 6, no. 4, October 1975, 23. These estimates do not include the monetary value of perquisites, which was considerable.

16.   Peter Heller and Alan A. Tait, *Government Employment and Pay: Some International Comparisons*, Washington, D.C., International Monetary Fund, Occasional Paper no. 24, revised March 1984, 18.

17.   World Bank, *World Tables*, 3rd ed., vol. 1, 501. "General government consumption" includes all current expenditures for purchase of goods and services by central, regional, and local government agencies, as well as capital outlays for defense. Outlays for public nonfinancial institutions (often termed parastatals), which are considerable in many African countries, are not included.

18.   International Monetary Fund, *Government Finance Statistics Yearbook* 6, 1982, 47–48. Nigeria is not counted as an African country in these figures; it qualifies for the "oil-exporting" category.

19.   For an elaboration of this argument, see David B. Abernethy, "Bureaucratic Growth and Economic Stagnation in Sub-Saharan Africa," in Stephen K. Commins, ed., *Africa's Development Challenge and the World Bank,* forthcoming, 1988.

20.   Samir Amin, "Underdevelopment and Dependence in Black Africa — Origins and Contemporary Forms," *Journal of Modern African Studies* 10, no. 4, December 1972, 503–25.

21.   For a summary and critique of different views of this incorporation process, see Frederick Cooper, "Africa and the World Economy."

22.   P. Robson and D. A. Lury, editors, *The Economies of Africa,* Evanston, Northwestern University Press, 1969, 52. The African figure excludes South Africa. The ratio of African commodity exports to the region's monetary product was higher still: an estimated 30%.

23.   This phrase and the reference to precapitalist modes of production are taken from Goran Hyden, *No Shortcuts to Progress: African Development Management in Perspective,* Berkeley, University of California Press, 1983, 6–24. See also Hyden, *Beyond Ujamaa in Tanzania: Underdevelopment and an Uncaptured Peasantry,* Berkeley, University of California Press, 1980.

24.   The secretary for native affairs in the Gold Coast informed the (British) Committee on Trade and Taxation for West Africa in 1922 that "he has never heard it put forward by the natives that the [cocoa] duty is unjust in its incidence. 'It is,' he says, 'a form of indirect taxation, to which natives do not object more than they do to any other form of indirect taxation, and they certainly do not object to indirect taxation in the way they certainly would if we replaced it with direct taxation.'" Quoted in G. B. Kay, editor, *The Political Economy of Colonialism in Ghana,* Cambridge, Cambridge University Press, 1972, 115.

25.   Robson and Lury, eds., *Economies of Africa,* 41–43.

26.   Quoted in D. M. P. McCarthy, *Colonial Bureaucracy and Creating Underdevelopment: Tanganyika, 1919–1940,* Ames, Iowa State University Press, 1982, 64.

27.   For a fine analysis of this mutual dependence in what initially appears to be the extreme instance of a colonizer unilaterally setting the terms of the relationship, see Steve Stern, *Peru's Indian Peoples and the Challenge of Spanish Conquest: Huamanga to 1640,* Madison, University of Wisconsin Press, 1982.

28.   See Peter Ekeh, "Colonialism and the Two Publics in Africa: A Theoretical Statement," *Comparative Studies in Society and History* 17, no. 1, January 1975, 91–112. David Apter in *The Gold Coast in Transition,* Princeton, Princeton University Press, 1955, 320–24, 329–30, asserts that a charismatic leader may legitimate these structures and procedures by working through them. But Apter's argument does not apply to noncharismatic leaders, nor does it sufficiently take into account the rapidity with which a leader such as Nkrumah can lose, through the very exercise of power, whatever charisma he may have possessed when out of power.

29.   On the imbalance between administrative and political structures in the colonial situation, see Fred Riggs, "Bureaucrats and Political Development: A

Paradoxical View," in Joseph LaPalombara, ed., *Bureaucracy and Political Development*, Princeton, Princeton University Press, 1963, 120–67.

30.   See, for example, Robin Horton, "Stateless Societies in the History of West Africa," in J. F. A. Ajayi and Michael Crowder, eds., *History of West Africa*, 2nd ed., vol. 1, New York, Columbia University Press, 1976, 72–113.

31.   One might argue that the state is still suspended above the ground in the independence period, this time by a new set of support wires provided by bilateral and multilateral aid donors. Foreign aid permits the state to appear stable, but only in the sense that the lack of fit between building and foundation is not a problem if the state does not in fact rest upon a foundation. But any building not placed on solid foundations is, quite clearly, not going to prove serviceable for long.

32.   These characteristics of ethnicity have been persuasively demonstrated for colonial Africa, and for many other parts of the world as well, in Crawford Young, *The Politics of Cultural Pluralism*, Madison, University of Wisconsin Press, 1976. See also Donald L. Horowitz, *Ethnic Groups in Conflict*, Berkeley, University of California Press, 1985.

33.   For an imaginative discussion of the possible developmental role of indigenous nongovernmental organizations, see Hyden, *No Shortcuts to Progress*, 114–33.

34.   Ibid., 100–03, and Ekeh, "Colonialism and the Two Publics in Africa," 104–11. F. C. Okoli notes that from the African perspective "bureaucracy is seen as a neutral institution, the white man's institution, and the bureaucratic process becomes the white man's job. In this conception, he is also a hero who can successfully defraud and appropriate public service resources. This notion of a white man's job has gained wide currency even among the bureaucrats themselves." F. C. Okoli, "The Dilemma of Premature Bureaucratization in the New States of Africa: The Case of Nigeria," *African Studies Review* 23, no. 2, September 1980, 12.

35.   On the costs and inefficiencies of parastatals, particularly in the rural development arena, see L. Gray Cowan, "Africa Reconsiders Its Parastatals," *CSIS Africa Notes* 33, September 4, 1984; David B. Jones, "State Structures in New Nations: The Case of Primary Agricultural Marketing in Africa," *Journal of Modern African Studies* 20, no. 4, December 1982, 553–69; World Bank, *Accelerated Development in Sub-Saharan Africa: An Agenda for Action*, Washington, D.C., World Bank, 1981, 37–40 and John R. Nellis, *Public Enterprise in Sub-Saharan Africa*, Washington, D.C., World Bank Discussion Papers no. 1, 1986.

2

The Present and Future
of the African State in an
Age of Adversity

Harvey Glickman

A way has to be found to reintroduce Western capacity for organization, *without old forms of domination,* if the cycle of degeneration is to be reversed. Aid money and business investment just aren't enough. The cold dreadful conclusion to be drawn from a generation of independence is that African governments are incapable of providing the frame work and services that development requires.[1]

OVERVIEW

Africa's continuing economic crisis raises both economic and political questions. Analysis must be interested not only in what economic steps are needed to avert further decline, but also in what political and

The author gratefully acknowledges the financial support of a Ford Foundation grant through Bryn Mawr College, a faculty research grant from Haverford College, and the encouragement reflected in a Heinz Endowment grant for research and travel. An earlier version of this chapter was presented at the Conference on the Crisis and Challenge of African Development, Temple University Sugar Loaf Conference Center, Philadelphia, September 26–28, 1985, supported by a grant from the Heinz Endowment. Research assistant Farshad Rezazadeh provided much background information and friendly argument. Raymond Hopkins proffered a careful reading and sound editorial judgment in the best traditions of scholarly collegiality. Despite their best efforts to improve my thinking, I alone am responsible for the outcome.

institutional steps must be taken. Proposed policy reforms, centering on reducing the role of the state in the economy, in effect narrow the political options for the future while making an attempt to strengthen the state's capacity for coping with social and economic problems today.

The major explanations for decay of the African state rest on the inherited weaknesses of state structures, a global structure of dependency, insufficient and incoherent international aid policies, and inappropriate domestic policies. The analytical implications and the policy reforms recommended by most donor organizations — exemplified and led by the World Bank — reflect something of a return by many Africanist experts to a liberal theory of development and the politics of modernization, that is, a renewed emphasis on limited government, private enterprise, pluralist competition, and integration into world markets (largely Western) on the basis of comparative advantage. These reforms may diminish administrative weaknesses by reducing the strain on governmental institutions. They may repair certain policy mistakes discerned over the past decade, yet the overall political cost in terms of future options for development strategies may be high. A slight increase in influence outside their borders for African states that comply with the advice of outside donors will further restrict long-term freedom of action. More overt opportunities for private accumulation in a divided society, while limiting government, can further reduce the chances of a popular consensus.

The implications of the reform advice that Africa is getting are that the over-developed state is to be pared down; market activity and private enterprise are to grow. By doing less, government should accomplish more. By further implication, an alternative sphere for material achievement should reduce corruption in government. The redirection of resources from urban to rural areas is supposed to expand support for government and broaden accountability.

Emphasis, however, on export-oriented growth increases dependence on major foreign markets and international lenders and advisers, thus diluting the accountability of national elites to domestic groups and to public enterprises. Expanded foreign-based influence further undermines domestically originated development objectives. While governments may be strengthened, the political spectrum narrows. Finally, a reduction in public services, reflecting austerity measures required for policy reforms, in the absence of breakthroughs for expanded interest expression, invites the possibility of increased use of police and military force to obtain compliance to unpopular measures.

This chapter surveys the analytical models drawn upon in explaining Africa's economic and political decline. It recognizes the special utility of middle-range, Africa-based theories that underlie present policy recommendations, while noting their ideological implications. Finally, the chapter suggests more attention to institutional weaknesses rather than policy failures over the long run.

ECONOMIC DECLINE AND THE CRISIS OF THE STATE

Economic decline sets back government plans for improvement, which undermines not only existing shreds of authority but the raison d'être of government itself. The overthrow of colonialism was perceived by African populations to mean the destruction of the barriers to development. African governments justified their forms and policies in terms of the need for developmental resources.[2] Today authoritarian forms hinge on the basic requirements of order, as development seems a forlorn hope. The future prospects of economic decline in the face of continued population growth have been described by the Economic Commission for Africa as "almost a nightmare. . . . At the national level, the socio-economic conditions would be characterized by a degradation of the very essence of human dignity. . . . Poverty would reach unimaginable dimensions. . . . The conditions in urban centres would also worsen. . . . The level of the unemployed searching desperately for the means to survive would imply increased crime rates and misery."[3] In the analysis underlying the dialogue with the four major reports of the World Bank and the programs flowing from them since 1981, bad policy and the soft state figure prominently. While recognizing external sources of difficulties, such as declining terms of trade and reductions in foreign aid, the Bank emphasizes domestic policy deficiencies as the major source of Africa's crisis.

The nature of the crisis is one of economies and public policy unable to meet the minimum needs of a people. What stands out is declining production in industry, where that sector is consuming resources rather than generating a surplus, but more emphatically in agriculture, where per capita production has fallen since 1960, where the share of African commodities in world trade has also fallen, and where, most obviously, food dependency has grown. In addition, the balance of payments of African countries has gone into rising public debt. All these factors have combined to reduce government services, which had expanded in the 1960s.

In the Bank's view the major source of difficulties can be identified as overvalued exchange rates, inappropriate agricultural policies, and an excessive role for the public sector. The major advice is to alter these domestic policies, but also for foreign donors to provide more aid, to be more flexible in their provisions, and to coordinate efforts to avoid duplication, overlapping, and waste. In brief, that is the analysis and the program of the "Berg Report" and the three follow-up reports.[4]

The fundamental weakness of the African state institutions was masked in Africa's first decade of postcolonialism, the 1960s. The world economic environment worked in favor of expansionist policies and government direction. An economic boom in Western countries, low oil costs, and a high-water era in foreign aid contributed to growth in a number of areas: infrastructure expanded, per capita agricultural production rose, export quantities rose, and per capita income went up, as did average life expectancy and literacy.[5] But this was also a period in which African governments assumed more tasks than they could manage efficiently. Governments rapidly dominated agriculture, finance, manufacturing, and the markets for agricultural and consumer sales. Governments also took on the tasks of increasing revenue as well as redistributing income. The overall development strategy of the 1960s — import-substitution industrialization — quickly exhausted its early gains. Its very operation, requiring extensive regulation of tariffs and quotas, proved inefficient and provided opportunities for political advantage. Access to political power became the basis for economic success.

Military coups of the 1960s initiated an expansion of military expenditures in many states. Increasing security problems of the 1970s drove arms expenditures from $175 million in 1970 to $2.3 billion in 1979. By the mid-1970s African governments had lost control of their economies. Production declines meant shortfalls in export and income taxes as well as in the proceeds of marketing boards. Vast overruns accrued to parastatal enterprises. In part to compensate for the "oil shocks" and the enormous jump in the price of fuel and petrochemicals, currencies remained overvalued, and external borrowing grew rapidly, as did interest payments. Inflation and black markets paralleled one another.[6]

Ironically, the politically inspired drive for independence and self-reliance wound up in policies that demanded greater reliance on foreign donors of food and other assistance, on foreign and international banks for credits, and on foreign export markets for revenue. It is clear that African states in the 1980s are more dependent on outside forces and are more vulnerable to outside pressures than at any time since formal independence.

STATE-CENTRIC POLICIES AND POLITICS

Triumphant nationalism in Africa promoted a vision of the omnicompetent state. While practiced with varying degrees of intensity, nationalist development strategy equated state direction of the economy with what was regarded as crucial to changing the balance of benefits, the creation of wealth at home rather than draining it abroad. The notion was that only the power of the state, recently fallen into the hands of its own citizens, could assume the monumental tasks of altering the trajectory of benefits of economic development. Differences in development strategies reflected variations in degree and type of connections with former metropoles and the United States, as well as rhetorical and actual ties to Communist powers, but these differences were marginal in terms of government intervention in economies. The actual machinery for government intervention in markets had been established in the colonial period, and the main beneficiaries of marketing boards, monopolies, licenses, and other regulatory devices were white settlers, private firms favored by the metropole, and, at the end of a long skein, metropolitan central banks. The private sector was either corporate foreign or non-African. Thus did capitalism in Africa reek of colonialism.

But capitalism in the West had also been recently saved by newly recognized planning and welfare functions of the state. Moreover, the Soviet achievement in industrializing a backward country and mobilizing to triumph against a foreign enemy impressed African as well as other Third World nationalists.

The colonial state was paternal as well as interventionist, especially with regard to the colonial — or urban and bureaucratic — sector, where it directed low-priced, subsidized services. Nationalists seized on this "consumptionist approach to public services"[7] and projected it to the rest of the country. In an important sense, the nationalist version of the postcolonial state was the social service state without the expansion of wealth and production to pay for it. The standard of African development was what had served colonial and settler standards of living.

The state-centered development strategy complemented mono-political authority systems. Governments swallowed parties soon after nationalist movement victories and decolonization. Party states proceeded to destroy alternative political influences via absorption or suppression.

In turn, they were stymied or terminated by the military, who seized governments and destroyed rival parties at one time or another in most African states.

While military regimes are often open to foreign private investment and are compatible with varieties of private enterprise, these trends generally do not lead to shrinking the state or pluralizing government. Indeed, the opposite occurs: an exaltation of the state, bureaucratized decision processes, and technocratic rather than democratic solutions to policy problems.

The perception by African leaders that development was an international problem and an international responsibility, ironically, also had the effect of exalting the role of the national state and its attendant symbolism. The external legalities of statehood, in the setting of international conferences and institutions, became a source of strength in bargaining for increased assistance and more beneficial relationships with developed countries. While the results of internationally bargained arrangements, such as the New International Economic Order, have not been notably successful, the process requires and reinforces the entity of the state. Indeed, it is contended that the recognition within and the opportunities afforded by the international arena are the primary support for the continuation of state entities in Africa today. States thus owe their continued existence to juridical factors rather than internal institutions.[8] In terms of institutional capabilities, African states have gone "soft," that is, "limited in control over society [with] low capability of implementing regulations effectively over the whole territory . . . and of achieving goals."[9]

The contention here is that both the state-centric and global explanations of Africa's present development crisis are useful, but extreme. We need to account for the "soft state" and therefore to understand Africa's internal impulsions. We also need to recognize the global (structural) constraints within which the African state must operate. In other words, after recognizing the utility of each type of explanation — internal and external — we need to turn to middle-range, Africa-based theories for policy orientations. But in turning to Africa-based political sociology to balance Africa-based political economy, we must be sensitive to the overall policy thrust of the advice that follows. The implications of the advice called "policy reform" (terms now used regularly by the U.S. Agency for International Development [USAID] and by the World Bank) are critical not only for programs but for the forces shaping the character of states in Africa in the future.

ACCOUNTING FOR THE SOFT STATE

While a number of African states have difficulty in maintaining obedience to central government over the full area of territorial sovereignty (for example, Uganda, Sudan, Chad, Mozambique, Angola), the power of central government at the grass roots level is often perceived as quite "hard." Bureaucracy and the military can act somewhat autonomously and arbitrarily in relation to society. The hegemonic state and the soft state are simultaneous phenomena. It depends on the point of view, center or periphery.[10] An increase in capricious action by state officials, however, signals a decline in the longer-run effectiveness of the state.

The inherited structure of the colonial state can be considered overdeveloped in relation to generating economic growth. The aims of the postcolonial state stretch it even further. The result is that the state simply takes on too many burdens. It consumes too many resources in terms of gross domestic product. Economic decline and reduced public confidence make matters worse.[11]

Parallel to this imbalance between administrative machinery and economic support is a transformation in the perceived ends of political and bureaucratic office. Political activity in Africa has taken on the characteristics of a zero-sum game for elite participants; it is a negative-sum game for those left out. Politics, rather than being a process of bargaining, comes to be seen as a matter of extraction.[12] Rules for group exchanges have low salience. Patron-client relations and ethnic competition skew the already-uneven distribution of rewards that flow from government expenditure. In the absence of significant reward alternatives outside the state and given the consequences of policies that flow from the state, disconnection from state-determined activity means severe economic costs. The concept of the soft state and suggested explanations focus attention largely on internal factors that could yield policy remedies. Global explanations do not immediately translate into policies, but they recognize the context within which policy orientations must be embedded.

GLOBAL EXPLANATIONS OF STATE DECAY

These explanations draw on theories of development of worldwide implications, holding that problems of state creation and effectiveness reflect deeper problems of structural imbalances. The overview is that of incomplete social evolution, with implicit liberal or socialist goals.

"World system" and "dependency" models center on the evolution of capitalism on a global scale, with intertwined core capitalist and periphery ruling elites combining to construct a world of a few autonomous states and a multiplicity of dependent states, divided into core, periphery, and semiperiphery. Ruling classes, linked to the spread of capitalist relationships throughout the world, are tied to one another in a string of dependencies from the core to the periphery. The contradictions between the needs of expanding capitalist elites through its state formations and those of the lower classes in all parts of the world determine the character of the struggle. But the dynamics of capitalism do not mechanically determine the fate of states, since the uneven development of capitalism in different parts of the world permits various degrees of autonomy to politicians and bureaucrats and other elements of class fractions. The neo-Marxist concept of the relative autonomy of the state permits characterization of the strength of the state apparatus and the direction of its policies free of a mechanical reflection of the interests of its major classes.[13]

In the liberal version of global development, the modernization of societies and economies set in motion by commercialization and secularization outpaces the reconstruction of political systems. Political institutions require strengthening, renovation, or invention in order to absorb and channel expansion of participation. Rather than the contradictions of class struggle, the liberal view sees imbalance between government and group demands or discontinuities between elite leadership and mass followings that promote disorders. A pluralistic balance, usually achieved by party competition amidst the free expression of ideas — parallel to a largely market economy — is regarded as optimally conducive to development. But the Third World is particularly prone to disorder. Thus the strengthening of the state is seen as a prerequisite to meeting the needs of development because the state must provide a necessary order prior to reform, but also because it must serve as a partial substitute for an autonomous entrepreneurial and enterprising elite. Until recently the free market liberal version of modernization was hardly heard. What is not clear yet is the extent to which it is actually voiced in Africa rather than outside.[14]

A version of the world-system or dependency models sees the present weakness of the African states as a continuation of the penetration of imperialist capitalism within the territorial envelopes taken over by African successor elites in the early period of independence. Western, especially American, multinational corporations have stepped into the role of colonial trading and investment monopolies and indeed have expanded upon those roles. The African state is thus a localized version, often led by the military, of the colonial state. Its leadership is the local but dependent bureaucratic bourgeoisie.

World-system and dependency models depart from orthodox Marxism by claiming that capitalism has underdeveloped Africa by reducing its economies to appendages of Western capitalism. The global, revolutionary implications depart from present reality. Peripheral areas supposedly detach themselves from capitalist core areas and develop self-reliantly. (The "modernization" program of present-day China shows that socialist self-reliance is not necessarily synonymous with development. Comparison with Japan, China, and the USSR might indicate that internal power precedes development.) It is no accident that the experience of the weak states of Africa shows no correlation between self-reliance strategies and development. To break free of capitalism and pursue some sort of socialist self-reliance not only defies present realities, but also ignores one of the great insights of Marx, that capitalist imperialism in its peculiar fashion develops its hinterlands.

This brings us back to development as consisting of certain necessary stages. A peasantry must be captured before it can be regulated. A people's attitudes must be modernized. As Marx might say, people have to be exploited before they are liberated. In this way the market liberal and the Marxist join hands.[15]

MIDDLE-RANGE AFRICA-BASED THEORIES

What may be lost by turning away from a primary concern with global development relationships is more than made up by attention to political processes themselves. While the explanations derived do not result in comprehensive recipes for reversing political fortunes, they tie together interest group politics and policy making. If the mantle of leadership at independence is seen to fall on an urban-based alliance of civil servants and political activists, policies favoring urban populations — of all ranks — will tend to be favored. This point of view has particular utility for understanding agricultural decline. States in which rural elites are more closely tied to policy-making circles will incorporate less disfavor toward agricultural interests. Such states would tend to be more politically stable and less insecure economically. Examples such as Kenya, Ivory Coast, and Malawi can be offered.[16] The direction of policy advice may be clear, yet discovering ways to transform the balance of advantages via coalition politics is not.

The addition of a cultural dimension expands analytical power. It also reduces the certainty of recommendations for change. Authority systems in Africa are dominated by patron-client relationships. Political processes ensue via interlocking, descending, and unbalanced reciprocities. Governing institutions are penetrated by such networks. The political struggle becomes a scramble to capture some piece of government-distributed largesse — licenses, scholarships, jobs, grants, loans, equipment, and so on. The character of leadership and the role and weight of foreign influences must be added to the balance of domestic interests in order to describe forces of possible change. The political culture variable projects systemic implications, warning that policy outputs may be only partially manipulated by recombining political inputs.[17]

Theories located in the middle range may seem more accessible to policy inferences. In turning inward they bring us back to concrete African circumstances. Africa trails Latin America and Asia in husbanding political resources mobilized at the time of independence. Yet Africa's small, weak states and dependent economies require favorable world circumstances to overcome their shortcomings. For Africa there is no immediate alternative to some form of dependent development. Many states in Africa will remain weak, vulnerable, and wards of international agencies and foreign donors. De-linking and self-reliance may be at best premature strategies (simplistically derived from global theories of the development of underdevelopment), although expressing an aspiration of enhanced political capabilities. Perhaps we can expect that while middle-range theories strive for objectivity, they are also sensitive to their implications for policy. In the kinds of analyses canvassed below there is a sense in which the expectations for change either follow assumed sequences of transformation in Western states or increase the necessity for direction from the Western powers.

DERIVATIONS FROM POLITICAL SOCIOLOGY
AND POLITICAL ECONOMY

In the realm of political sociology, concepts of the overdeveloped state, the patrimonial administrative state, and personalistic rule have been helpful in formulating much description. An overburdened bureaucratic structure run on the basis of patron-client relations points to the functional transformation of official roles. Institutions and rules are a cover for patronage, favoritism, fraud, and sometimes force. Foreigners who have worked in African administrations often will anecdotally confirm this sort of analysis.

In the realm of political economy, concepts of overrestricted markets, especially for agriculture, and development coalitions favoring urban interests permit observers to point to wrong policies as undermining support for the state. Although not discouraged by donors of outside assistance at their inception, development strategies that were based on low food prices and low-cost imports for manufacturing eventually drove peasants away from commercial production and paved the way for inefficient, high-cost industries.

To claim simultaneously that African government undermined themselves through bad policies and that any policy would have been ineffective due to inherent weaknesses in the state itself is contradictory. Compatibility can be attained by connecting state overdevelopment to excessive market intervention and state ownership of enterprises. The analyses of state effectiveness and appropriate policies converge as tools for understanding through the idea of overextension. It seems clear that some governments can attempt to do too much. But leadership can also learn from the mismatch of economic needs and state capacities. (Witness the shift from the Articles of Confederation to the federal Constitution in the United States.) In circumstances of fragile support, relatively undiversified economies, and external dependence, withdrawal from the state becomes a strategy for survival for ordinary people. It is also a guidepost for political reconstruction. Such withdrawal can begin a process of rebuilding authority from the grass roots, leading to an economy shared by private and public sectors and a diarchical state structure in the future.

If, on the other hand, the chief reason that the state is ineffective is that the ruling coalition operates at the expense of important elements in society, then shifts in the coalition can lead to optimism about state effectiveness in the future. Yet given a declining economy and the absence of freely floating political resources, the construction of new coalitions requires sacrifice on the part of previously favored populations. A dramatic solution to this problem in the context of a transformation from a national democracy to a socialist democracy was favored by the theorist-politician Amilcar Cabral. He called for the postindependence national bourgeoisie to commit political suicide. Less revolutionary writers call for political statesmanship on the part of the present group of African leaders.[18]

Because they both point toward the overdeveloped state from different directions, the models of the patrimonial-administrative state and the urban-biased development coalition merit discussion. They combine to illuminate the longevity of soft states in Africa. But the implication of accepting these models in combination is to restrict change to the lines of a liberal modernization model of development.

THE PATRIMONIAL-ADMINISTRATIVE STATE MODEL

As the label implies, two forms of authority overlap in this model. [19] Authority is shared between the postcolonial administrative structure and an ensemble of personalistic connections and loyalties. The enforcement of rules and the dispensation of patronage vie for prominence in what are public and official circles. More disciplined forms of government, reflecting this model, function via "bureaucratic centralism"; looser forms act via "hegemonial exchanges." [20] Political participation centers on clientage that penetrates party and administration. Rule is authoritarian by a political aristocracy of military or party leaders.

The public policy of development is neomercantilist: economic policy is in the service of power. Outward-oriented economies depend on the accumulation and use of foreign exchange. Access to foreign exchange means wealth; the major access is via high public office.

This model is really about state-society relations. It can reveal to us why notions of office and rules are far from neutral in present-day African states. The rules do not define a pattern for the fair play of interests, but rather differential outcomes for various groups arrived at by playing with loaded dice. While acceptance of the idea of patrimonial administration as a form of rule gains plausibility from the evidence of doing business and implementing public policy in Africa, it gains intellectual appeal from its derivation from Weberian universal categories of the evolution of authority in the modern era. In the context of economic insecurity and in the presence of few economic opportunities that can avoid state involvement, the sources of nourishment for these arrangements seem legion. Recent history has shown that military and civilian rulers govern in much the same ways, struggling to manage various group particularisms. Declining economies promote shrinkage of the government and its increasing separation from society, yet the approach to governing in practice does not seem to depart very far from the patrimonial pattern.

The patrimonial model invites comparison with the analytical stages of the development of bureaucratic authority in the West. It seems pre–rational-legal. In its policy implications for the present it invites outside assistance to break the shaky equilibrium of clientage as the dominant mode of authority. In a European time frame, patrimonialism grows weaker as private enterprise assumes more importance. Foreign assistance to secure an expanding private sector and to promote rational-legal bureaucratic authority in public administration is implied.

THE URBAN-BIASED DEVELOPMENT COALITION MODEL

In this case the model more overtly indicates an African leadership's policy inclination, based on a particular development ideology and a supporting alliance of interests.[21] The development strategy of import-substitution industrialization and its supporting fiscal policy favor urban folk: managers and workers in industries, administrators and clerks in public bureaucracies, and so on. Left out are the rural smallholders. Internal food prices are held down. Producer export commodities are artificially underpriced. Governments attempt to co-opt or repress or at least divide rural factions. Patronage and clientage are instruments important in dividing rural areas. Overall, the costs of this sort of development are borne by rural smallholders, who react eventually by adopting exit options or turning to black-market transactions or smuggling. The state is thus softened even further. Ruling coalitions now find power more costly. Food production drops, food prices go up. Governments must borrow heavily, with attendant inflation.

The immediate implication of this model is policy reform, and underlying that, the need to search for a new coalition. A reduction of government restrictions on producers of food and export crops, which would bring them back to market pricing, restores some support to government in the rural areas. Presumably increased production will raise revenue. In the near term, exchange rates need adjustment to reflect the real value of currencies, thus raising the cost of imports. Urban life will cost more.

The expectation is that the expansion of markets reduces the strain on government. Once again outside assistance is required, in the form of recycling (mostly Western) foreign loans and interest payments, in the form of agricultural extension grants, and in the form of public safety aid to maintain public order in a period of transition.

POLICY REFORM AND ITS IMPACT ON THE STATE

From the previous analysis we can plausibly account for the causes of weak and ineffective government institutions and the inefficiency of the public sector in a way that fits with the most influential economic analysis and advice that Africa is getting: the African state stifled its economy by getting its development strategy wrong, expanding into areas it should have left to private enterprise, and providing patronage rewards in areas it needed to operate efficiently. Thus the analysis of the state dovetails with the centerpiece analysis and policy statements of the World Bank in the 1980s. One would undoubtedly feel more comfortable with the analysis of the 1980s if the World Bank had not paid for the statist strategies of the 1960s and 1970s, underwriting the expansion of parastatal credit, regulatory, and production agencies now under attack. It is important that the process of policy re-evaluation now occurring maintain the premise of international responsibility.

The implications of the advice from the World Bank are apparent. The rhetoric as well as actual efforts in the direction of reduced dependence on industrialized countries in the world economy must diminish. An export orientation, especially with regard to primary products, is underlined, along with accompanying reductions in the protection of industry. Important questions follow. The answers are still not clear. How efficacious is a policy of export emphasis for all African countries simultaneously? If all were successful, the projected gains via increased production would be undercut by a fall in prices. Can "getting the prices right" alone regenerate needed production? Attention to employment policies that put money in the hands of consumers cannot be avoided. How far can privatization go in the African economies? Certainly there is room for denationalization of many services, but profitable private enterprise awaits expansion of an economic and financial infrastructure that requires a strong and interested state. Into what channels will private enterprise flow? Will a policy of privatizations mean more small African-owned businesses, or will it come down to an expansion of foreign private investment, in many cases in partnership with Africans? The implications for the character of future African governments are obvious.

It may be difficult to foresee the development of local political resources in a way that would indeed strengthen nonstate institutions as internal markets are freed of government direction. A wholesale retreat from considerable government involvement in the economy is probably not in the cards. It is not yet clear that denationalization and deregulation by government would stimulate a great deal of indigenous private enterprise. Instead, there might well be an increase in foreign investment and foreign ownership, although in some countries there would be more dispersed private activity than in others, for example, in Nigeria, Kenya, and Zimbabwe. Some people expect that reducing constraints on the private sector, such as reducing taxes, will result in increased domestic saving. But it seems just as likely that such reductions would lead to increases in the repatriation of profits in foreign-owned enterprises. Finally, a shift in basic public services to private resources, resulting in a greater reliance on user fees, will probably lead to an overall deterioration of services and to their availability largely to the well-off.

The priorities created by World Bank recommendations will reflect on the kind of states that will exist in Africa in the next decades. One can argue that "national development" will be succeeded by elite development. Political consolidation, infrastructure construction, and human resources development will all be reduced. On the other hand, to be fair, it can be argued that such priorities were also undermined by personal rule, corruption, and public-sector inefficiency.[22]

Nevertheless, national development objectives can be abandoned too easily. Tighter integration of African economies into the world markets will entrench the priorities of production for such markets and its prices as completely dominant over national development objectives. Second, the overall emphasis on market prices as more efficient reflects on the market for administrative and technical skills as well. It will be cheaper for African governments to employ international experts than their own, at least until public-sector revenues can support renewed training programs for African administrators and technicians. The World Bank expects international donors to increase their support when ineffective policies in African countries are reversed. Yet it may be easier for foreign donors to take refuge in the newer views that "less is more" and to wait for proof that African governments have indeed operated more closely attuned to market signals before gearing up new aid programs. In short, while the World Bank clearly wants to help African economies recover, it seems that African governments will have to take much more direction from the World Bank and from governments in their major markets.

The *1983 Progress Report on Sub-Saharan Africa* of the World Bank seemed to confirm early questions raised concerning the efficacy of policy recommendations. The global economic situation had not measurably improved, and Africa's exports for the most part continued to face falling prices. The increased donor support called for was not forthcoming. The previous projection of levels of disbursements and commitments for 1985 was seen as "extremely unrealistic."[23] Policy recommendations, such as exchange rate devaluation, were offset by inflation. Rising prices for farm produce have not exceeded rises in the cost of living for farmers.[24]

Doubts arise as to whether the private-sector alternative to state intervention is always simply an efficiency alternative. The level and form of government involvement in an economy require reference to the objectives pursued by governments. While turning away from issues of income distribution, poverty, and basic human needs, Africa's new advice influentials must not terminate the ability of African governments to restore more egalitarian objectives at some future time. The argument that African states in their present condition cannot afford sympathy toward policies designed to reduce inequality is somewhat vitiated by a reminder that the world's development advisers thought that reducing poverty was a priority in Africa not too long ago.

It seems clear that analysis and advice aimed at African governments mean a shift toward capitalism. It should be no surprise if some of the social consequences of capitalism spill over. Domestic class polarization effects usually parallel a thrust toward international consumption patterns, which in turn are a consequence of greater dependence on global markets, replete with a rise in imported technology and foreign finance capital. The potential for class formation and class-like conflict increases as African economies make financial adjustments that result in higher food prices, lower wages, and fewer government services. The price of the benefits promised by adjustment programs goes up as the benefits themselves remain uncertain. It is not clear why export-led growth should be more reliable in the future than it has been in the past in view of price fluctuations and downturns for African exports in the past decade.[25]

In 1983–84 fifteen countries in Africa devalued their currencies; sixteen increased food prices; sixteen reduced government expenditure and raised taxes. Fifteen countries rescheduled their foreign debt payments. A revival of agricultural production will require not just removal of excessive government restraints but also the provision of needed new inputs in training, management, and technology in the countryside. Yet it is transport and distribution mechanisms that are cut in reducing public expenditure.

A revived private sector may create new sources of supply and more efficient enterprise, but it must be recognized that it is also a threat to the present state formation — the pattern of authority — in Africa. It can become an alternate base of power to government leadership; it also becomes a target for charges of foreign exploitation. Unless carefully managed — perhaps a contradiction in terms when speaking of laissez-faire — a new or re-created private sector can provide the resources that reproduce ethnic group tensions or anti-Asian and antiwhite sentiments. At the very least, the vested interests of the public bureaucracy will be difficult to shunt aside without more attention to the institutions of public order.

The African revival and development recipe of the World Bank offers hope for a more effective government at the price of greater dependence on foreign donors and a shift in the allocation of resources away from the poor and away from government policies of reducing social inequalities. But even this cannot be accomplished without a rise in commodity prices, a rise in investment and lending from abroad, and a rise in foreign aid. The prospects for all these external trends occurring soon and simultaneously are not favorable. The government may indeed shrink, but its redeployment of resources will court a period of increased internal unrest. (In 1984 the governments of Tunisia and Morocco were in peril; the government of Sudan was overthrown in 1985.)

The question remains whether the price for establishing greater development capacity in African countries will be the solidification of the ties between external and internal leadership, that is, the strengthening of a modernization coalition of a technocratic elite supported by a new rural elite, influenced by foreign investors and military guardians. This appears to represent not a new way of governing but a new and more dependent incarnation of the patrimonial-administrative state. One suggested answer is that there really may be no policy choice in the present position of state weakness. At best, the decline of the state may turn into a positive factor, not by strengthening indigenous private enterprise, but by encouraging grass roots initiative and local responsibility.[26] Elsewhere, state-centric economies have exhibited this trend (China, Eastern Europe). In the long run, it is such a trend that contributes to a vision of a revival of African economies that would create the conditions for a pluralist society and perhaps a democratic polity. In the present context of an "uncaptured" African peasant or perhaps antipeasant economy the view may be clouded. In the short run, enhanced pluralism threatens a retreat into subsistence, a rise in ethnic and regional conflict, and polarization into class-type inequalities. That is why policy reform alone is inadequate in the absence of institutional transformations.

CONCLUSIONS

There are two critical problems that remain unaddressed by the present reigning analysis of Africa's difficulties and the policy dialogue conducted between international agencies and the U.S. government, on the one hand, and the African governments, on the other. Everyone agrees that the African state has grown overextended and that African governments have pursued failed development policies. If government is the problem, if the state needs to restrict its role in the economy, then the conventional funnelling of assistance, whatever the level, to present governments is doomed. That the instrument required for policy reconstruction and future development is itself suspect is a paradox thus far not fully explored.

The second problem is equally basic. If African states rest on patrimonial authority and personalistic rule, if these "structures" are what maintain existing legitimacy and capacity for enforcing compliance, then their shrinkage could be conflict inducing rather than conflict resolving. Existing forces of ethnicity and strengthened forces of class interest will break through to further weaken the state framework in which market forces are supposed to work. The prior, or at least parallel, need for institutional reform requires more attention if policy changes are not to rely on increasing coercion or permanently narrow the political options of a reconstructed African state.

NOTES

1. Bernard Koucher, founder of Doctors Without Borders, *New York Times,* March 18, 1985 (emphasis added).

2. See Colin Leys, "African Economic Development in Theory and Practice," *Daedalus* 3, no. 2, Spring 1982, 99–124; J. F. Ade Ajayi, "Expectations of Independence," ibid., 1–10; Richard L. Sklar, *Democracy in Africa,* Presidential Address to the Twenty-Fifth Annual Meeting of the African Studies Association, Washington, D.C., 1982, Los Angeles, UCLA African Studies Center, 1983.

3. United Nations Economic Commission on Africa, *ECA and Africa's Development, 1983–2008,* quoted in World Bank, *Sub-Saharan Africa: Progress Report on Development Prospects and Programs,* Washington, D.C., World Bank, 1983, ii.

4. World Bank, *Accelerated Development in Sub-Saharan Africa: An Agenda for Action,* Washington, D.C., World Bank, 1981.

5. Sayre P. Schatz, "African Capitalism and African Economic Performance," chapter 4 in this volume.

6.   Carol Lancaster, "African Development Challenges," *Current History* 84, no. 501, April 1985, 145–49, 183, 186; also Carol Lancaster, "Africa's Economic Crisis," *Foreign Policy* no. 52, Fall 1983, 49–66.

7.   Shankar N. Acharya, "Perspectives and Problems of Development in Sub-Saharan Africa," *World Development* 9, no. 1,1981, 109–47.

8.   Robert H. Jackson and Carl G. Rosberg, Jr., "Why Africa's Weak States Persist: The Empirical and the Juridical in Statehood," *World Politics* 35, no. 1, October 1982, 1–24.

9.   Donald Rothchild, "Hegemony and State Softness: Some Variations in Elite Responses," in Zaki Ergas, ed., *The African State in Transition,* London, Macmillan, 1987, 126–40; see also Donald Rothchild and Michael Foley, "The Implications of Scarcity for Governance in Africa," *International Political Science Review* 4, no. 3, 1983, 311–26.

10.   Crawford Young, "Patterns of Social Conflict: State, Class, and Ethnicity," *Daedalus* 3, no. 2, Spring, 1982, 71–98.

11.   For discussion of the meaning of "overdevelopment," see Colin Leys, "The Overdeveloped Post-Colonial State: A Re-Evaluation," *Review of African Political Economy* no. 5, January-April 1976, 39–48.

12.   Richard Hodder-Williams, *An Introduction to the Politics of Tropical Africa,* London, Allen and Unwin, 1984, 95–99.

13.   Claude Ake, "The Future of the State in Africa," and Aaron T. Gana, "The State in Africa: Yesterday, Today and Tomorrow," *International Political Science Review* 6, no. 1, 1985, 104–14, 115–32.

14.   The implications and shortcomings of the modernization school of development in the context of a review of a wider range of problems in Africa are revealed in Michael F. Lofchie, ed., *The State of the Nations: Constraints on Development in Independent Africa,* Berkeley, University of California Press, 1971, especially in the contribution by Lofchie, 9–18.

15.   While not suggested, this possibility emerges from the challenging analysis in Goran Hyden, *Beyond Ujamaa in Tanzania: Underdevelopment and an Uncaptured Peasantry,* Berkeley, University of California Press, 1980.

16.   Robert H. Bates, *Markets and States in Tropical Africa,* Berkeley, University of California Press, 1981.

17.   Aristide Zolberg, *Creating Political Order,* Chicago, Rand McNally, 1966; Jean-Claude Willame, *Patrimonialism and Political Change in the Congo,* Stanford, Stanford University Press, 1972; Richard Sandbrook, "Patrons, Clients, and Factions: New Dimensions of Conflict Analysis in Africa," *Canadian Journal of Political Science* 5, 1972, 104–19.

18.   Compare Amilcar Cabral, *Revolution in Guinea,* New York, Monthly Review Press, 1969, 150–58, with Bates, *Markets and States,* 110–13.

19.   This model's relevance for Africa emerges in Thomas M. Callaghy, *The State-Society Struggle; Zaire in Comparative Perspective,* New York, Columbia University Press, 1984, 32–46.

20.   Rothchild, "Hegemony and State Softness," 141–45.

21.   Bates, *Markets and States,* 81–132.

22.   See the opposing submissions by Elliot Berg and Robert K. Browne in U.S. Congress, House Committee on Foreign Affairs, Subcommittee on Africa, "Africa, World Bank, and the IMF: An Appraisal," *Hearing,* February 23, 1984, 98th Cong., 2nd sess., Washington, D.C., U.S. Government Printing Office, 1984, 1–39.

23.   World Bank, *Sub-Saharan Africa,* 6.

24.   Ibid., 8–10.

254.   See Institute for Development Studies (Sussex), *IDS Bulletin* 14, no. 1, January 1983, whole issue, articles by Manfred Bienefeld, Reginald Green, Martin Godfrey, 18–23, 30–38, 39–44.

26.   See Naomi Chazan and Victor Azarya, "Disengagement from the State in Africa: Reflections on the Experience of Ghana and Guinea," *Comparative Studies in Society and History,* 29, no. 1, January 1987, 106–31.

3

The Crisis of African Development and the Lagos Plan of Action

Vremudia P. Diejomaoh

INTRODUCTION

There is a growing consensus among development analysts both in Africa and in the rest of the international community that there is a crisis in African development. This view is reflected in reports and publications of the United Nations Economic Commission for Africa,[1] the World Bank,[2] the African Development Bank,[3] and several other international organizations and scholars.[4] Proposals for dealing with the African development crisis are being presented from many sources.

In this chapter we shall examine the dimensions of the crisis in African development and propose one possible way out of the crisis. Since the resolution of the African development crisis is expected to center on two major aspects — more effective domestic development policies, programs, and efforts, as well as greater and more effective economic assistance to Africa from the international community — one could focus either on aspects of domestic development policies and efforts of African countries or on aspects of the international dimension of the crisis for possible solutions. This chapter examines just one aspect of the latter dimension, the impact of foreign investments on capital formation in Africa. We relate our findings to the Lagos Plan of Action as a possible way out of the African development crisis.

The need for examining the impact of foreign investment on development in Africa is particularly relevant because major proposals for resolving the African development crisis are premised on substantial increases in the inflow of external resources for African development.[5] An analysis of past experience in the impact of foreign investments on African development could well provide useful clues as to the likely effectiveness of the proposals being put forward regarding increased foreign resource inflows and what changes in policy and direction are needed in order to ensure that foreign investments do in fact contribute in future to the resolution of the crisis in African development.

DIMENSIONS OF THE CRISIS

The dimensions of the crisis in African development are multifarious, but some key aspects could be highlighted in the areas of growth of gross domestic product and gross domestic product per capita, food production, population growth and its implications, declining net inflows of external resources, rising external indebtedness, which is reaching crippling proportions, rising political instability and social disorders, natural disasters and their implications, and, most importantly, the overall deteriorating position of Africa relative to other regions of the world, both developing and developed.

According to World Bank data,[6] the rate of growth of gross domestic product (GDP) for low-income countries in Africa, which consists of most sub-Saharan Africa, has declined from 3.5% per annum in 1960–73 to 1.4% in 1978–80 and to 0.5% in 1980–82. Although these rates were expected to increase in the 1982–85 and 1985–95 periods, the rates of GDP growth in low-income African countries would be considerably lower than those of other developing countries and even those of the industrialized countries (see Table 3.1).

The growth of GDP per capita per annum for low-income Africa has fallen from 1.0% in 1960–73 to –1.0% in 1973–79, an estimated –1.6% in 1980–85, and will continue to decline in the decade of 1985–95 at between 0.1% to 0.7%, depending on improvements in development policies. The low-income African countries as a group are the only countries in the world expected to experience declines in per capita GDP in the period 1985–95, while other regions are in fact expected to register significant gains in GDP per capita (see Table 3.2).

With respect to population and the food balance sheet, African population growth has accelerated from an average annual growth rate of about 2.5% in the 1960–70 decade to about 3.2% by 1983. In contrast, food production in Africa is estimated to have increased at an annual rate

TABLE 3.1
The World Economy: Past and Projected Growth of GDP, 1960–95
(average annual percentage change)

Country Group	1960-73	1973-80	1980-82	1982-85	1985-95 Low	Central	High
All developing countries	6.0	4.7	1.9	4.4	4.7	5.5	6.2
Low-income							
Asia	4.6	5.4	4.1	4.5	4.5	4.9	5.3
Africa	3.5	1.4	0.5	2.9	2.7	3.3	3.9
Middle-income							
Oil importers	0.3	5.2	1.2	4.5	4.4	5.7	6.9
Oil exporters	7.0	3.7	1.7	4.0	5.3	5.7	5.8
Industrial countries	5.1	2.5	0.4	3.0	2.5	3.7	5.0

Source: World Bank, *World Development Report, 1983*, Washington, D.C., 1983, 27.

TABLE 3.2
The World Economy: Growth of GDP Per Capita, 1960–95
(average annual percentage change)

Country Group	1960–73	1973–79	1980–85	1985–95			
				High case	Low case	Increased protection	Improved policies
All developing countries	3.7	2.0	0.7	3.5	2.7	2.3	3.1
Low income							
Asia	3.4	3.3	3.7	3.7	3.0	2.6	3.3
Africa	1.0	-1.0	-1.6	-0.1	-0.5	-0.7	-0.3
Middle-income							
Oil importers	3.8	3.3	-0.5	3.6	2.6	1.9	3.1
Major exporters of manufactures	4.4	3.6	-0.3	4.4	3.3	2.4	3.8
Other	2.6	1.7	-0.9	1.5	1.0	0.7	1.2
Oil exporters	4.3	2.3	-0.4	2.7	2.0	1.9	2.3
Industrial countries	3.9	2.1	1.5	3.7	2.0	2.0	2.0

Source: World Bank, *World Development Report, 1984*, Washington, D.C., 1984, 36.

of only about 2% in the 1970–83 period, leading to food deficits that have resulted in increasing food imports and aid, and increasing malnutrition and famine. The above situation is partly the result of policy failures, but it has been exacerbated by severe droughts, first in the early 1970s and again since 1982.

Africa's export trade and terms of trade have also deteriorated since the 1960s (Table 3.3). The declining rate of growth of exports and rising imports have been compounded by declining net inflows of foreign private capital. Although multilateral and bilateral grants and loans have increased in absolute monetary terms in the period 1960–82, this has been at a decelerating rate. When account is taken of debt amortization, net total foreign capital inflows fall by half, from U.S. $10.8 billion annual average in 1980–82 to U.S. $5 billion in 1985–87, while in the case of foreign private inflows there was a net outflow of about $1 billion annually in the 1985–87 period. These unfavorable developments in the external sector have resulted in severe debt service burdens that are constraining the development process.

On the political and social fronts internal dissension and open civil wars in many African countries and political instability have led to considerable disruptions in production and to an increase in the number of refugees, now estimated at about 2.5 million (about 25% of the world's refugees). The political will and determination to resolve the development crisis in Africa appear still to be lacking on the part of several African governments and major aid donors. All of these factors tend to add a sense of gloom and pessimism as to possible ways out of the crisis in African development. It is against this background that we turn to an analysis of the impact of foreign investment in Africa and how its linkage with the development strategy advocated in the Lagos Plan of Action could possibly lead us out of the crisis.

PATTERNS OF AFRICAN CAPITAL FORMATION, GROWTH, STRUCTURE, AND SOURCES OF FINANCING

It is important that in discussing the impact of foreign investment on capital formation, we start by having some understanding about the nature and pattern of capital formation in Africa. It is also important to stress that while it is desirable to have a satisfactory growth rate for capital formation, in the final analysis, what really counts is the contribution that capital formation makes to desired patterns of development. Whether capital formation makes a desired impact or not on development in Africa will depend partly on its growth rate, its structure (which is likely to affect its productivity), and the sources and methods of its financing.

A study of the African economy by the World Bank shows that the rate of growth of gross domestic investment declined from 5.7% in the decade 1960–70 to 3.2% in the decade of the 1970s (1970–79) for sub-Saharan Africa countries.[7] The world economic recession meant a further slowdown in the rate of growth of gross domestic investment in the early years of the 1980s. The rate of growth of gross domestic investment for African countries was slower than for the developing countries of Asia and Latin America during the decades of the 1970s and the early years of the 1980s. The pattern of growth of gross domestic investment in the North African countries was, however, different from that of the sub-Saharan countries, for there was a significant slowdown in the growth of gross domestic investment in the North African countries in the decade of the 1970s.

Although there has been a slowdown in the growth rate of gross domestic investment in sub-Saharan Africa since 1970 compared to the decade of the 1960s, there has been a very substantial increase in the rate of capital formation as measured by the investment ratio, that is, gross domestic investment as a percentage of gross domestic product. The investment ratio for the total of sub-Saharan Africa was 15% in 1960, but it had risen to 23% by 1979. Several countries, such as Mauritania, Zaire, Togo, Botswana, Mauritius, Ivory Coast, Nigeria, Gabon, Algeria, and Libya, had investment ratios of between 30% and 40% in the 1979–81 period. However, there were substantial declines in the investment ratios of a few African countries, such as Uganda, Ghana, and Angola, whose investment ratios fell to under 10% — in the cases of Uganda and Ghana, to under 5% — in the 1979–81 period. In spite of the relatively high investment ratios for the vast majority of African countries, the rates of gross domestic product growth for the gross domestic product of these countries were on the average rather low (less than 5% per annum) in the 1970s and early 1980s and were generally the lowest in the developing world. The implication of these relatively low rates of income growth in spite of the high rates of capital formation is that the productivity or efficiency of the capital formation has been relatively low during the period since 1960.

A partial explanation for the relatively low productivity of capital formation in Africa is the allocation of the capital formation between

TABLE 3.3
Key Macroeconomic Growth Rates in Sub-Saharan Africa, 1960–83
(annual average percent)

	1960–70	1970–80	1981	1982	1983a
1. GDP					
Low-income countries	4.0	1.9	1.1	0.5	2.7
Low-income semiarid	2.4	3.2	1.8	0.1	2.0
Low-income others	4.2	1.8	1.0	0.6	2.7
Middle-income oil importers	4.2	4.5	4.0	2.6	-0.1
Middle-income oil exporters	3.5	4.1	-3.7	-1.6	-4.1
Total sub-Saharan Africa	3.8	3.6	-1.0	-0.2	-0.7
All except oil exporters	4.0	2.9	2.3	1.4	1.9
2. Population					
Low-income countries	2.4	2.8	3.1	3.1	3.1
Low-income semiarid	2.5	2.6	2.7	2.7	2.7
Low-income others	2.4	2.9	3.2	3.2	3.3
Middle-income oil importers	2.7	3.3	3.4	3.4	3.6
Middle-income oil exporters	2.4	2.5	3.3	3.3	3.4
Total sub-Saharan Africa	2.4	2.8	3.2	3.2	3.2
All except oil exporters	2.4	2.9	3.2	3.2	3.2
3. Per capita GDP					
Low-income countries	1.5	-0.9	-1.9	-2.5	-0.3
Low-income semiarid	-0.1	0.6	-0.9	-2.5	-0.7
Low-income others	1.3	-1.1	-2.1	-2.5	-0.3
Middle-income oil importers	1.5	1.2	0.6	-0.7	-3.4
Middle-income oil exporters	1.1	1.6	-6.7	-4.7	-7.3
Total sub-Saharan Africa	1.3	0.7	-4.0	-3.3	-3.8
All except oil exporters	1.6	-0.4	-0.9	-1.7	-2.0

4.	Export volume b.c.d				
	Low-income countries	3.7	-2.2	-8.7	-1.7	..
	Low-income semiarid	6.6	10.5	-14.9	23.4	..
	Low-income others	3.5	-3.7	-8.0	-4.4	..
	Middle-income oil importers	6.8	1.4	-3.5	0.0	..
	Middle-income oil exporters	7.3	-0.6	-17.4	-10.4	..
	Total sub-Saharan Africa	5.5	-0.6	-12.8	-6.5	..
	All except oil exporters	4.9	-0.6	-6.4	-0.9	..
5.	Import volume b.c.d				
	Low-income countries	5.1	-1.6	2.9	-8.1	..
	Low-income semiarid	6.5	7.7	0.5	-5.0	..
	Low-income others	4.9	-3.0	3.2	-8.5	..
	Middle-income oil importers	5.9	3.9	1.9	-6.7	..
	Middle-income oil exporters	4.1	14.0	-2.5	-13.5	..
	Total sub-Saharan Africa	5.0	7.4	-0.2	-10.6	..
	All except oil exporters	5.4	0.7	2.4	-7.4	..
6.	Terms of trade b.v.e				
	Low-income countries	1.1	-0.4	-13.1	-1.5	..
	Low-income semiarid	0.0	-2.0	-2.4	-0.2	..
	Low-income others	1.2	-0.2	-14.3	-1.7	..
	Middle-income oil importers	3.2	-0.2	-6.8	-4.3	..
	Middle-income oil exporters	1.2	17.4	7.9	-6.1	..
	Total sub-Saharan Africa	1.8	10.2	-0.1	-4.6	..
	All except oil exporters	2.0	-0.4	-10.3	-2.8	..

Source: World Bank, *Toward Sustained Development in Sub-Saharan Africa: A Joint Program of Action,* Washington, D.C., 1984,

different sectors of the economy, particularly between the more directly productive sectors and other sectors. An analysis of the composition of capital formation in Africa by sectors of economic activity shows that for most African countries, capital formation in the agricultural sectors has declined significantly since the 1960s to a level of less than 10%.[8] Investment in manufacturing has increased in most countries since the 1960s, but in virtually all countries the level of investment was less than 20% of the total. Typically, investment in the transport sector was quite large, claiming between 25% and slightly over 30% in most countries, while the share of the service sector amounted to between 30% and 40% for most countries. The relatively low allocation of investment to the productive sectors of agriculture and manufacturing, given the fact that African countries are largely agricultural economies, must account in no small measure for the relatively low productivity of capital formation in Africa. Other factors such as inadequate skills resulting in poor management of enterprises, official corruption leading to looting of the enterprises, and poor physical infrastructures, as well as the negative aspects of foreign investment to be discussed later, also account for the observed low productivity of capital formation in Africa.

Although the productivity of capital formation may have been low in Africa, particularly since the 1970s, we have already shown that the investment ratios were relatively high on the average, approaching 25% for Africa by the end of the 1970s. It is important to understand how this level of capital formation was financed in order to appreciate in particular the contribution of foreign investment to capital formation. An analysis of World Bank data shows that most African countries increased their gross domestic savings rate (gross domestic savings as a percentage of gross domestic product) significantly between 1960 and the end of the 1970s, although it was still the lowest in the world.[9] For sub-Saharan Africa, the savings rate rose from 13% in 1960 to 20% in 1979, leaving a negative resource balance situation of 3%, since gross domestic investment was 23% of GDP in 1979. For North African countries there was also a significant increase in the gross domestic savings rate from about 10% in 1960 to about 20% or more in 1981, with the exception of Morocco, which had a drop in its savings rate from 11% in 1960 to 8% in 1981. Further analysis shows that by 1979 foreign resources constituted a significant proportion of the total of gross domestic savings for several African countries. For the semiarid low-income countries of sub-Saharan Africa, net official development assistance amounted to 77% of gross domestic investment; for other low-income countries the contribution of net official development assistance to gross domestic investment was 47%, while for middle-income countries it was about 25%. If account is taken of foreign private-sector contributions, it will become clear that the level of capital formation in most of the African countries was largely financed from foreign resources or investments. Let us now turn to a more detailed examination of the impact of foreign investments on capital formation in Africa, starting with private foreign investments.

IMPACT OF PRIVATE FOREIGN INVESTMENT ON CAPITAL FORMATION IN AFRICA

Although it is difficult to provide quantitative information on total private investments in Africa because of data gaps for several countries, it is generally agreed that private foreign investments have contributed a preponderant share of total investments in the productive sectors of manufacturing, mining, commerce, and finance in most African countries. For example, it was estimated that by 1970 foreign private capital accounted for 75% of total investment in the manufacturing sector of the Ivory Coast, while for the agricultural foodstuff industry the contribution of foreign capital was 78%.[10] In Nigeria at about the same time, foreign private capital dominated the entire private sector. Even with the Indigenization Decrees of 1972 and 1974, private foreign capital still accounts for 60% of total investments in schedule III activities, and 40% in schedule II activities. Only in the small business sector of schedule I is foreign capital now totally excluded. Even in schedule II activities, where foreigners hold a minority equity of 40%, they still dominate because of the bloc voting power of the foreign investors in the boards of directors and their control over the technology in use. In smaller countries, foreign investors predominate through largely wholly owned subsidiaries of joint-venture enterprises. While there are a few socialist-oriented countries in Africa, such as Tanzania, Angola, Ethiopia, Mozambique, Algeria, and Libya (and Egypt to a lesser extent), where foreign capital has been largely nationalized, foreign private capital by way of direct investment still dominates capital formation in Africa.

It can be said that direct private foreign investments dominate total directly productive capital formation in Africa; it should also be noted that portfolio investments in the form of private foreign loans to Africa have increased considerably since 1970. According to World Bank data, total gross disbursement of external loans from private sources to sub-Saharan Africa increased from $490 million in 1970 to $3.768 billion by 1978 and possibly to over $4 billion in the 1980s, an almost tenfold increase in about ten years.[11] These loans consist of suppliers' credits and bank loans both to private- and public-sector projects. From the foregoing, it is clear that private foreign investments have made very substantial contributions to total capital formation in the private sectors of African economies by way of direct and portfolio investments, as well as to several public-sector projects by way of portfolio investments and joint-venture projects. This contribution has made it possible for capital formation to rise to an average level of about 25% of GDP by the end of the 1970s for African countries.

Apart from the impact of private foreign investment on the rate of capital formation in Africa, foreign investments have also greatly influenced the composition of total capital formation. Private foreign investors have typically been interested in seeking new markets for their finished products or new sources of raw materials for their production at home or in other world markets. As a result, the preferred areas for foreign investors in Africa have been in mining and plantation agriculture for the purpose of obtaining raw materials for their home production or markets; in manufacturing (essentially assembly-type operations) for the purpose of promoting exports of their manufactured goods in intermediate or completely knocked-down forms as the market for finished products was being blocked by tariff walls erected to promote domestic industrialization; and finally in services, such as banking, insurance, commerce, shipping, and consultancy, in order to facilitate the two major objectives of obtaining raw materials and promoting sales of manufactured goods. These interests of private foreign investors therefore largely determined the composition and structure of capital formation in the private sectors of African economies. Capital formation in the private and more directly productive sector was largely biased toward foreign rather than the domestic African markets because of the dominant role of private foreign investors in capital formation in Africa.

Knowledge of the composition and nature of capital formation, as influenced by private foreign investment, is essential for evaluating the productivity or efficiency of capital formation in Africa. Three major schools of thought have emerged in evaluating the impact of private foreign investments undertaken by transnational or multinational corporations in Africa. The traditional school of thought, advanced by liberal mainstream Western economists and their adherents in Africa, is that the multinationals have made major contributions to development by providing substantial capital inflows and introducing new and modern technologies and products contributing to tax revenues, as well as modern management and skills, thereby helping to transform, modernize, and develop African economies.[12] The opposing school of thought, usually of Marxist persuasion, sees the transnational or multinational corporations in Africa essentially as neocolonialist or imperialist agents whose operations have contributed to the underdevelopment of Africa and the current crisis in African development.[13] The multinationals are accused of having introduced inappropriate technology to produce inappropriate products designed only for a small African elite, as well as having contributed to substantial widening of inequality not only among income groups but also between the urban and rural areas, thereby endangering political stability. The multinationals are said to have also tried to manipulate governments to bow to their wishes and through transfer pricing to have usually extracted more from the countries than they contributed. In the view of this school, so long as multinationals play a dominant role in African development and capital formation, so long will Africa remain underdeveloped. Accordingly, the abolition of multinationals with their foreign investments is advocated by this school.

However, a third school of thought, to which I belong, sees the past activities of the multinationals in less ideological terms but recognizes the adverse impact of the foreign private investment in Africa.[14] As we have seen, private foreign investors have dominated capital formation and directly productive activities in Africa since independence. Yet as we have shown, the rate of growth of GDP has been relatively low in Africa, especially since the 1970s, food production has been ignored, leading to increased dependency on food imports, manufacturing production has not been based on domestic resources or directed to the needs of the majority of the population, and inequality has definitely increased between income groups and between the rural and urban areas.[15] While it is true that a large modern African elite has emerged partly as a result of the activities of the multinationals in Africa, the patterns of consumption and tastes of this elite are not sufficiently linked to the African economy and cannot be sustained in the long run. Accordingly, the current pattern of capital formation in Africa, dominated as it is by private foreign investment, must be changed in order for it to have beneficial effects on the African economy. This can be done if African governments play a more effective and dynamic role to relate African production more to the needs of the African market itself than it has done so far, and adopt more vigorously a policy of collective self-reliance in all its ramifications as advocated by the Lagos Plan of Action.[16] The multinationals would probably be ready to reorient their activities to the African market itself if it were profitable for them to do so. However, so long as African countries operate individually in their individual small markets, the multinationals will continue to direct their activities to their home markets and the world market, which provide better prospects for profits. It has to be realized also that the individual small African countries are too weak to negotiate successfully with the giant multinationals. Accordingly, unless larger African markets are formed, as advocated in the Lagos Plan of Action, initially in the subregional economic communities and later in the proposed African common markets, the multinationals will be too large to be controlled by the individual small African countries. Furthermore, so long as the bulk of funds for capital formation is provided by the multinationals, it will be difficult for African countries to ensure that capital formation actually takes place in desired economic activities. Domestic policies aimed at increasing gross national savings and domestic entrepreneurship must be intensified. In all successful cases of development foreign private investments play a subsidiary and supplementary role, not the dominant one, as is currently the case in Africa. The interests of foreign investors do not always coincide with those of the host country. African governments must be more active in determining where foreign private investors are needed through the introduction and implementation of right policies rather than allowing private foreign investments to go into whatever activities they like. Unless steps such as these are taken, private foreign investments, even if they increase in volume in the future, as is now being advocated both by African and international bodies and major aid donors like the United States, will continue to have largely negative impacts on capital formation and development in Africa.

IMPACT OF PUBLIC FOREIGN INVESTMENTS ON CAPITAL FORMATION IN AFRICA

Grants from bilateral aid donors are not strictly economic investment, even if they are regarded as an investment for political goodwill. This argument can be extended to grants from multilateral aid donors (that is, from international organizations, mainly agencies of the United Nations, and other bodies, such as the British Commonwealth and its Francophone counterpart). While the loan element of official development assistance is more akin to a commercial and economic investment in the sense that the loans bear interest and are meant to be repaid, the loans are strictly not economic investment, since the motivation for them is not directly to derive an economic return. The loans are offered on concessional terms. However, apart from the political returns expected from official development assistance, some aid authorities are on record in regarding these loans as an investment in the stimulation of their domestic economies.[17] Hence it is not farfetched to regard official development assistance as part of foreign investments, which for the purpose of our analysis we call public foreign investments. We define public foreign investments to include bilateral and multilateral development assistance since, apart from the World Bank, the funds come from the budgets of the aid-giving countries.

An indication of the trend and magnitude of official development assistance to African countries is given by the disbursement of official development assistance (ODA) to sub-Saharan countries. Total ODA disbursement increased from almost $1 billion in 1970 to $5.9 billion in 1979 and an average of $8.9 billion in 1980–82. As already indicated, ODA in 1979 accounted for 77% of gross domestic investment of semiarid low-income countries of Africa, while for other low-income countries it accounted for 47% of total gross domestic investment. It is clear that official development assistance has been significant in increasing the rate of capital formation in Africa.

Official development assistance to African countries has typically been disbursed by African governments on social overhead capital projects, so that the impact of official development assistance has largely been to bias the structure of capital formation against the more directly productive sectors. This has had the effect of increasing the incremental capital output ratio of total capital formation with the resultant reduction in the rate of economic growth that we observed earlier, in spite of relatively high investment rates. The combined effect of the loans granted as public foreign investments and as private foreign investments has been a relatively rapid increase in the foreign debt of African countries. Outstanding external debt of sub-Saharan African countries rose from $5.7 billion in 1970 to $31.8 billion by 1979. The 1979 level must have increased further in the early 1980s consequent on the world recession. According to International Monetary Fund data, external debt outstanding for the whole of Africa (excluding South Africa) had reached a level of $70.7 billion by April 1984.[18]

The relatively rapid increase in African external debt outstanding has meant an increasing debt service burden for most African countries. This debt burden has now reached crisis proportion in so many countries that these countries have had to approach the International Monetary Fund for adjustment loans as well as to arrange renegotiation of their outstanding loans with other creditors. The implication is that foreign investments have not stimulated sufficient increase in foreign exchange or savings in foreign exchange expenditure to keep the debt service burden within reasonable proportions. The current debt crisis in many African countries, combined with budgetary and foreign exchange constraints, makes it increasingly difficult to increase the rate of capital formation. Accordingly, future economic growth is greatly endangered. Projections by the World Bank[19] and the Economic Commission for Africa[20] show a bleak economic future for African countries unless there are major shifts in the policies of aid donors and African governments.

The unsatisfactory outcome of the impact of public foreign investments on total capital formation in Africa can be rightly blamed partly on the policies of aid donors themselves due to their predilection for financing certain types of projects that have so far not proved productive, either in terms of economic growth and development or in the earning or saving of foreign exchange. It is therefore essential that some greater flexibility be adopted in the types of projects selected for financing by aid donors to ensure that foreign aid will be more productive and related to the real development needs of African countries. The future development scenarios of the World Bank[21] and the Economic Commission for Africa[22] count on substantial increases of foreign aid (the World Bank estimates a requirement for a fourfold increase in the decade of the 1980s).

While these agencies advocate a shift in aid policies, in type of projects financed, and in total volume of aid offered, a realistic assessment of prospects is that a development strategy based as heavily on aid as in the past is likely to be frustrated. Future aid volumes are not going to come close to the expectations of the World Bank,[23] the Economic Commission for Africa,[24] or individual African governments.

The African governments themselves also must take a large part of the blame for the past low productivity of capital formation because of their poor economic management records. It is in this regard that African governments have to place greater emphasis on internal resource mobilization, greater cost effectiveness in public expenditures, and more efficient allocation of capital.

CONCLUSION

We have shown that foreign investments, both private and public, have dominated the pattern and level of capital formation in African countries in recent decades. In the words of the World Bank, "In some countries, the public investment program has become little more than the aggregation of projects donors wish to finance. These projects have not always been consistent with the priorities necessary for achieving national development objectives."[25] We have shown that foreign investments have increased significantly since 1960, although their rates of growth have slowed since the 1970s. We have shown further that the interests of private foreign investors, as well as public foreign investors, have influenced significantly the composition of capital formation in Africa. The types of investments preferred by foreign investors have, however, been relatively low in productivity. So in spite of relatively high investment rates, the rates of economic growth in Africa have been low, in fact the lowest in the world, particularly when judged on per capita income growth basis.

African governments have in the past not been sufficiently dynamic and effective in mobilizing domestic resources for capital formation, in managing the available resources judiciously and efficiently, or in pursuing self-reliant development strategies as proposed in the Lagos Plan of Action. Since it is unlikely that foreign investors, both private and public, will change their pattern of operations in Africa in any significant way in the future, the burden of adjustment still rests heavily on African governments. Past policies pursued by African governments on capital formation will have to change significantly, since the past record is now generally judged to have been poor. The needed reorientation lies in greater self-reliance for African countries collectively, both at subregional and continental levels, as advocated in the Lagos Plan of Action. The pattern of consumption of the fast-increasing African elite has to be reoriented to the domestic market, and the domestic market needs to be expanded through regional economic groupings and continental economic cooperation. This situation would provide the setting for the pattern of capital formation to be related more closely to the needs of the domestic market. If clear guidelines and policies are set by African governments for foreign private investors and aid donors within the contexts of broader subregional and regional markets, they may yet be able to make a more positive contribution to capital formation and economic growth and development in Africa.[26]

The aid donors themselves, bilateral and multilateral, must take much greater initiatives to support the growth and development of economic activities on the basis of subregional markets. Development analysts need to pay much greater attention to how success could be achieved in this sphere. The skepticism and outright hostility or at best lukewarm support of Western scholars, countries, and institutions to schemes of subregional and regional economic cooperation in Africa are puzzling when judged by the huge economic successes achieved by the continental markets of the United States, the growing Economic Community of Europe, the vast markets of the Soviet Union and Comecon, Communist China, India, and, to a lesser extent, Brazil and Mexico. These postures lead many scholars and intellectuals in Africa to conclude that the West is not really interested in genuine economic development in Africa. The much-paraded export-oriented success stories of South Korea, Taiwan, Hong Kong, and Singapore can at best happen only in a few African countries but not for the continent as a whole. Unless, therefore, greater attention is given to how the entire continent can be developed as an integrated economic region and guided away from unsuccessful economic outcomes, the crisis in African development can be expected to continue.

NOTES

1.   United Nations Economic Commission for Africa, *ECA and Africa's Development, 1983–2008: A Preliminary Perspective Study*, Addis Ababa, ECA, April 1983.

2.   World Bank, *Toward Sustained Development in Sub-Saharan Africa: A Joint Program of Action*, Washington, D.C., World Bank, September 1984.

3.   The African Development Bank and Economic Commission for Africa, *Economic Report on Africa, 1984*, Abidjan, 1984.

4.   International Economic Association, *Proceedings of the African Regional Conference on Structural Change, Economic Interdependence and African Development*, Addis Ababa, August 1983.

5.   These proposals are presented in the publications and reports listed in notes 1–4.

6.   The statistics cited in this section are from the World Bank's Development Reports for 1983 and 1984 and from World Bank, *Toward Sustained Development*.

7.   World Bank, *Accelerated Development in Sub-Saharan Africa: An Agenda for Action*, Washington, D.C., World Bank, 1981.

8.   The analysis is based on data compiled from various issues of Economic Commission for Africa, *Economic and Statistical Bulletin for Africa*.

9.   World Bank, *Accelerated Development*, 17–18, 143–48, 159–66; *Toward Sustained Development*, 7, 16–20, 23, 47, 57–89.

10.   Jean Masini et al., *Multinationals and Development in Black Africa: A Case Study in the Ivory Coast,* West Mead, N.J., Saxon House, 1979, 32, 52.

11.   World Bank, *Accelerated Development,* 162; *Toward Sustained Development,* 70–72.

12.   A good summary review of this school is given by S. P. Schatz, "Assertive Pragmatism and the Multinational Enterprise," in *World Development* 9, no. 1, 1981, 93–105.

13.   There is extensive literature on this subject; see, for example, W. Rodney, *How Europe Underdeveloped Africa,* Enugu, Third Dimension, 1981; and T. J. Biersteker, *Distortion or Development? Contending Perspectives on the Multinational Corporation,* Cambridge, Mass., MIT Press, 1981.

14.   This school is well articulated by S. P. Schatz, "Assertive Pragmatism," 93–105; also see V. P. Diejomaoh, *The Role of the Private Sector in Nigerian Economic Development,* Henry Fajemirokun Memorial Lecture, Lagos, Nigeria, American Chamber of Commerce, March 1981.

15.   See H. Bienen and V. P. Diejomaoh, eds., *The Political Economy of Income Distribution in Nigeria,* New York, Holmes and Meier, 1981.

16.   Organization of African Unity, *Lagos Plan of Action for the Economic Development of Africa, 1980–2000,* Geneva, International Institute for Labour Studies, 1981, 128–29.

17.   U.S. and British authorities quoted in M. P. Todaro, *Economic Development in the Third World,* New York, Longman, 2nd edition, 1981, 416.

18.   International Monetary Fund, *World Economic Outlook,* Washington, D.C., April 1984, 102.

19.   World Bank, *World Development Report, 1983,* Washington, D.C., 1983, 105–9, 138–43.

20.   United Nations Economic Commission for Africa, *ECA and Africa's Development, 1983–2008,* 93–94.

21.   World Bank, *Accelerated Development,* 6–8.

22.   United Nations Economic Commission for Africa, *ECA and Africa's Development, 1983–2008,* 96.

23.   World Bank, *Accelerated Development,* 124.

24.   United Nations Economic Commission for Africa, *ECA and Africa's Development, 1983–2008,* 96.

25.   World Bank, *Toward Sustained Development,* 41.

26.   The proposed subregional economic groupings for sub-Saharan Africa as envisaged in the Lagos Plan of Action, the Economic Community of West African States (ECOWAS), the Economic Community of Central Africa (ECCA), and the Preferential Trading Area (PTA) for eastern and Central African states have now been established. What is needed now is for them to succeed and for them to be linked by the year 2000 in the proposed African Common Market.

4

African Capitalism and African Economic Performance

Sayre P. Schatz

AFRICAN ECONOMIC PERFORMANCE

It may be useful to review briefly the record of African economic performance. This record has not been one of continuous crisis. There have been two phases. The first, running from 1950 to 1977, was a long one of modest economic growth and development.[1] Performance was less than satisfactory but not really poor. The second phase, from 1977 to the present, has been one of crisis.

After 1977 economic growth fell off sharply. We take the simple average growth rate (unweighted average annual increase in gross national product) as our measure of growth. For low-income sub-Saharan Africa, growth was 3.0% during the 1950s, 3.8% during the 1960s, and 3.3% from 1970 to 1978. It then fell to 1.2% from 1978 to 1981, hardly more than one-third its previous level, and was even lower in the next two or three years. For middle-income sub-Saharan Africa, the growth rate was 4.9% in the 1950s and 1960s and 6.4% from 1970 to 1976. It then fell to 3.0% in the 1976–81 period and even lower in subsequent years. For sub-Saharan Africa as a whole, the growth rate was 3.7% in the 1950s, 4.3% in the 1960s, and 4.2% from 1970 to 1977. It dropped to 1.8% during the 1977–84 period. We can express the difference between the two phases in another way: real income per capita rose in sub-Saharan Africa from 1950 to 1977 and fell thereafter.[2]

These broad averages, which indicate continental trends, mask great differences in growth rates between countries and over time within countries. Thus Togo had the second-lowest growth rate of twenty-seven countries in the 1950s and the highest in the 1960s. Sudan had the second-highest in the 1950s, the second-lowest for 1965–70, and the very lowest for the 1970s. The top performer for 1970–81, Lesotho, was the fourth worst during 1965–70.

Broader indicators of well-being also show a long phase of limited but positive economic development until recent years. From 1950 sub-Saharan Africa experienced decreasing crude death rates, population per physician, infant mortality, and child mortality, and increasing life expectancy, primary and secondary school enrollment rates, literacy rates, per capita rates of energy consumption, radio receiver possession, and newspaper circulation. Calorie supply per capita was constant, but higher than in South Asia. Data for recent years are not available.

The long phase of positive, though lackluster, development was followed by a crisis characterized by a broadly experienced sharp decline in growth rates. One cannot account for the breadth of this decline by any continentwide domestic factors. Nor was the decline confined to Africa; developing countries throughout the world experienced substantial shocks in the 1970s and 1980s from two recessions and a slowdown of economic growth in the more developed countries of the capitalist world. Thus the crisis was caused externally by the impact of negative exogenous factors on economies that were already functioning in a lackluster manner.[3] The weakest part of the Third World — in geographical terms, Africa — was the most vulnerable; the African economics have been the most severely affected by the crisis.[4]

There have been many discussions of the causes of Africa's weak economic performance. They are formidable and deep-seated. It is not the function of this chapter to review or appraise these discussions. Rather, the chapter has a dual purpose. First, it sets forth another major cause of Africa's unsatisfactory economic performance, one that underlies a number of the causes often advanced, namely the nature of the capitalism that has developed in Africa. Second, it begins to examine the ability of African capitalism to generate the powerful development thrust needed to overcome the formidable difficulties. We start by considering the emergence of contemporary capitalism in Africa.

EMERGENCE OF AFRICAN CAPITALISM:
THE MISAPPROPRIATED STATE

The crucial period shaping the nature of contemporary African capitalism was the time, largely in the 1950s, during which governmental power was transferred to Africans. Governments played a central role in economic development, and development orientations at this time were malleable. Several characteristics of the orientations that emerged in most of sub-Saharan Africa were fundamental.

First, the new African-controlled political economies tended to be capitalist. Despite some nationalist antagonism toward capitalism, which was associated with imperialism, the modern sectors of the African economies had been capitalist in the colonial era, and the economies were part of the Western world system. The colonial powers then actively guided decolonization toward capitalism. Moreover, the new leaders, who were often those who had made their way in the modern, generally capitalist milieu, tended to embrace that economic orientation, despite frequent rhetoric to the contrary.

Second, this was a state-guided capitalism. The state was expected to play a major role in the economy for several reasons. Leaders, planners, economists, and the general public all desired accelerated development. After World War II and its shining slogan of the "Four Freedoms," one of which was "freedom from want," the widespread hope and even expectation was for an historic economic leap, a rapid narrowing of the gap between the rich and poor countries of the world. It was widely believed, however, that achieving such a leap was too great a task for a laissez-faire approach. The length, breadth, and depth of the great world depression of the 1930s had weakened confidence in simple capitalism throughout the world. Then the war provided an actual demonstration, unique in the social sciences, of the efficacy of wholesale government intervention. Massive military spending quickly converted depression into prosperity and deep unemployment into severe labor shortages. Moreover, the generally unexpected wartime success of the Soviet Union imparted considerable luster to the concept of economic planning. Among economists, the new field of economic development opened up, focusing on "deliberate development" in the less developed economies of the world. There was also the colonial legacy, with its paternalism and the importance of the state role in the modern economy.

Third, a point of fundamental importance, the state has been the dominant source of economic surplus, and control of the state has been the key means of private access to this surplus, that is, to private enrichment. The state has controlled relatively large revenues directly and has also been capable of bestowing strategic positions in the economy on favored individuals and companies. This point will be elaborated later.

Fourth, Africa's state-guided capitalism tended to be exploitive. Several conditions brought this about: (1) The African political class generally achieved power in an historical setting that was conducive to the abuse of that power. It perceived a colonial pattern in which government accorded primacy to metropolitan interests, that is, to the interests of those who controlled government, rather than to the general welfare.[5] (2) The new leaders tended to be men who responded to or shared this perception of power. They were men who had been successful in the modern, capitalist-oriented sector of society, and one of their objectives, though certainly not the only one, was personal enrichment. (3) The temptations the leaders faced, the rewards for the abuse of power, were enormous, especially as many of them sprang from humble origins. (4) The leaders, moreover, were functioning in transitional societies; the traditional patterns of morality did not fully apply, while new patterns take time to develop. (5) At the same time, countervailing forces limiting abuses of power were weak. Civil servants were not effective guardians of public morality. Instead, they were co-opted; they shared in the surplus through disproportionately high salaries and through more illicit means.[6] Nor did the political processes do much to inhibit abuse of position and influence. Those with power largely escaped accountability.

Thus because of the specific historical circumstances under which contemporary African capitalism was shaped, control of the state was used as the primary means of capital accumulation. There emerged the misappropriated state.

EMERGENCE OF AFRICAN CAPITALISM: THREE KINDS OF CAPITALISM

While African capitalism is typically characterized by the misappropriated state, not all states nor all African capitalisms are alike. To varying degrees in different countries, three different tendencies developed. These coexist in virtually every country. Depending upon which predominates, we can say that three kinds of capitalism developed.

We have said that the state has been the dominant source of economic surplus. Control of the state can be used in two principal ways to acquire substantial amounts of surplus. First, government can assist and nurture private productive activities. It can provide tariff protection, low-interest loans, subsidized industrial estates, technical and commercial advice and assistance, preferential government purchasing programs, and so on. Such programs, to the degree that they are successful, nurture the growth of production. The second is "piracy."[7] Piracy, in turn, has two major forms. State revenues can be directly tapped for corrupt private gain, as when kickbacks are paid on government contracts or when "loans" are made that need not be repaid. In Zaire, government funds are appropriated even more directly. The other major form of piracy involves the corrupt bestowal by the government of strategic economic positions upon favored private citizens. A license to import rice in foreign exchange-short Nigeria, for example, where the domestic price of rice has been a multiple of the international price, has been a license to make a fortune. Unlike business-assistance programs, piracy does not nurture the growth of production.

When assistance to productive activities predominates, there is nurture capitalism. When piracy predominates, there is pirate capitalism. Nurture capitalism, then, is an orientation in which the state undertakes to accelerate economic development by nurturing private businesses engaged in productive activities. The acquisition of state-controlled surplus is associated to a significant degree with such productive activities. (At the same time, piracy also exists to a greater or lesser degree.) Nevertheless, for reasons that will be discussed later, the record of nurture capitalism has not been a good one.

Pirate capitalism is also an orientation in which control of the state is used to increase private incomes and wealth, not primarily through subsidizing and aiding productive activities, but through corruption in one form or another. Under pirate capitalism, development is more likely to stagnate than under nurture capitalism.

Which tendency has predominated in a particular country, nurture capitalism or pirate capitalism, has depended upon several conditions. Perhaps the most important condition has been the prior existence or absence of a substantial bourgeoisie when the transfer of power to African leaders got underway. The bourgeoisie was a constituency, and a strong bourgeoisie could be a powerful constituency, for nurture capitalism as opposed to pirate capitalism. The common weakness or absence of an indigenous bourgeoisie in Africa at the time of power transfer was an important characteristic distinguishing African development from that of many other less developed areas.[8]

Another powerful factor determining which tendency has predominated has been the relative return, actual and potential, from productive activities and from piracy. What counts here is the return to the big actors, that is, those with power and influence. Where an indigenous private sector flourished, business-assistance measures were an already-accepted and growing practice. Moreover, profiting from activity in this sector was a familiar and viable way for the big actors to aggrandize themselves economically. Such circumstances strengthened the nurture capitalism tendency. Where substantial incomes from productive business ventures were neither common nor feasible, pirate capitalism tended to be stronger.

Other factors affect the relative strength of nurture and pirate capitalism. The capability of the government apparatus has an effect. If government capabilities are too limited, it is difficult to carry out programs that effectively aid private business, and this favors pirate capitalism. The integrity and ideology of the leaders also affect the degree of piracy.

In addition to nurture capitalism and pirate capitalism, I suggest that there is a third tendency: ambivalent capitalism. This is a form of capitalism with an overlay of anticapitalist rhetoric and feeling. There is both reliance upon and antagonism toward capitalism. Thus it is capitalism that shoots itself in the foot; little is done to promote private business in the directly productive sector of the economy, and government actions may even be impeditive. Ambivalent capitalism characterizes most of Crawford Young's Populist Socialist and Afro-Marxist regimes.[9]

LOW-POWERED CAPITALISM

The force that propels capitalist development — whether under auspicious circumstances or difficult ones — is a vigorous process of capital formation, that is, a high rate of successful investment, with all its consequences. High-powered capitalism nurtures and stimulates such investment in many ways, but African capitalism has been low-powered. It has impeded beneficial investment and hindered the development process, and it continues to stand in the way of the strong development thrust Africa needs. This section delineates some of the development-impeding characteristics of African capitalism.

1. Dissipation of surplus. Much of the government-controlled economic surplus and potential surplus — which under benign conditions

would be used for capital formation — goes into corrupt private pockets, into the financing of political parties and political activities concerned with maintaining control over the state, and into extensive clientelistic payoff networks for the same purpose. Actual and potential surplus is also wasted. Ineffective, wasteful, and even economically harmful programs and policies are adopted partly with surplus acquisition and distribution in mind. Sometimes economically unwise programs are adopted primarily because they serve as effective channels for corruption and patronage. Sometimes governments devote resources to policies that favor the dominant class even when such policies are less productive than possible alternatives, such as the policies in Ghana that have favored large farming interests even though these are "detrimental to smallholder farmers . . . [who have] proved relatively efficient under conditions of scarcity."[10] Policy deficiencies that waste government resources are often not a matter of mistakes but of deliberate choices. There may be a conflict between political and economic rationality;[11] a call for "policy reform" may actually be a call upon those with power to make changes contrary to their own interests.

The loss of surplus is the more painful because it often consists largely of foreign exchange, a particularly scarce and strategic resource. Lack of foreign exchange not only curtails investments, it also causes shortages of crucial imported inputs for existing enterprises, thereby forcing them to curtail production and employment. For example, it was estimated that Nigerian manufacturing was operating at only 23% of capacity in 1983, largely for this reason.[12]

2. Related to the dissipation of surplus is a waste of government capabilities. The point has just been made that government energies are often poorly directed. Even when sound policies are followed, however, a portion of government energies may be channeled into illegitimate efforts to acquire surplus, such as delaying tactics designed to elicit facilitating bribes in one form or another. Moreover, if programs do achieve some success, for example, in increasing agricultural production, they may be subverted by local "big men," who may use their strategic positions in the political economy to siphon off the gains for themselves. "Top-level support is often needed to prevent local 'big men' from diverting benefits from villagers."[13] The greater the degree to which the state is viewed as the principal means of acquiring surplus, the less likely it is that such support will be forthcoming.

3. Waste of entrepreneurship. Valuable African entrepreneurial energies and capabilities are often diverted from productive economic

activities and investments into efforts to participate in the corrupt distribution of surplus. "For the most vigorous, capable, resourceful, well-connected, and 'lucky' entrepreneurs . . . [in oil-boom Nigeria], productive economic activity, namely the creation of real income and wealth, has faded in appeal. Access to, and manipulation of, the government spending process has become the golden gateway to fortune."[14]

4. Foreign investment is lost. The difficulties of investing in low-income, relatively economically backward Africa are compounded by the problems of piracy. Multinational corporations and other potential foreign investors are discouraged from establishing or expanding their activities.[15]

5. The misappropriated state loses legitimacy; the misuse of government causes general disaffection and public malaise. The sag in public spirit, in turn, hampers development efforts in numerous ways.

Alexander Gerschenkron captures the importance of the public spirit in his discussion of nineteenth-century French industrialization under Napoleon III. Asking why such capitalist industrialization proceeded under a Saint-Simonian "socialist garment," which was "readily accepted by the greatest capitalist entrepreneurs France ever possessed," he answers:

> Under French conditions a laissez-faire ideology was altogether inadequate as a spiritual vehicle of an industrialization program. To break through the barriers of stagnation in a backward country, to ignite the imaginations of men, and to place their energies in the service of economic development, a stronger medicine is needed than the promise of better allocation of resources or even of the lower price of bread. Under such conditions even the businessman, even the classical daring and innovating entrepreneur, needs a more powerful stimulus than the prospects of high profits. What is needed to remove the mountains of routine and prejudice is faith — faith, in the words of Saint-Simon, that the golden age lies not behind but ahead of mankind. . . . [I]n an advanced country rational arguments in favor of an industrialization policy need not be supplemented by a quasi-religious fervor. . . . In a backward country the great and sudden industrialization effort calls for a New Deal in emotions.[16]

The malaise in Africa affects not only entrepreneurs but also employees, particularly public employees. They become worse than lethargic; they become impeditive and hostile. A businessman's response to a government survey captures the flavor of this problem. "Both internal and external business would be much facilitated if departmental staffs (particularly those in junior grades with whom the public has most contact) were to be made to understand the importance of business to the life of the country. The usual attitude at present varies between disinterestedness and deliberate obstruction. The question seems to be not 'How can I help this person?' but 'What can I do (exceeding the limits of my authority if necessary) to hold up this transaction?'"[17]

The malaise also raises the general level of petty corruption and peculation in both the public and the private sectors, exacerbates the general corrosiveness of relations, and impedes all government operations that require cooperation from the public. Consider tax collection, for example, a function performed badly throughout most of Africa. The striking success in this arena of Ghana's second Rawlings regime — a regime with a political style of tough-minded populism that elicited more than usual popular support — indicates the deadening effect of the prior malaise. By energizing the existing tax-collection agencies and by enlisting popular support, the government increased direct tax collections by a whopping 65.4% in 1982 alone and by another 19.8% in 1983.[18] The regime was also able to undertake, in its 1983 budget, some of the difficult IMF-supported reforms that had previously caused widespread, fierce opposition leading to an earlier coup.[19]

The weaknesses just delineated — dissipation of economic surplus, waste of government capabilities, waste of entrepreneurship, discouragement of foreign investment, and public disaffection and malaise with its broad consequences — should not be thought of as illnesses of African capitalism. Rather, they represent its normal functioning. They are not aberrations or distortions, but constitute its standard praxis. They are what makes African capitalism low-powered capitalism; the natural way it operates is inimical to the strong development thrust Africa requires.[20]

Perhaps the low-powered capitalism thesis can be elucidated by speculating about a recent transaction. A sixteen-year-old U.S. Steel Corporation rod mill, which had been idle for more than a year, was sold to China in August 1985. The mill was to be dismantled, shipped to China, and rebuilt there under the oversight of U.S. Steel. It was expected that production of steel rods for domestic use in China could start in two years.[21] One's expectation is that in China such a venture may run into difficulties yet will succeed and be socially useful, but in Africa it would not. Let us explore the grounds for the contrasting expectations.

In Africa the project would probably be surrounded by a level of corruption that would not be tolerated in China. This is not because of any moral inferiority; it is because acquisition of surplus in this way is part of the general ethos of African capitalism. Moreover, because of the public disaffection and malaise discussed earlier, and because the enterprise would in all likelihood be partly foreign-owned and largely foreign-controlled, government officials would be suspicious, uncooperative, and even deliberately obstructive. There would be a feeling of "them" against "us." Public opinion would be hostile. Regardless of the actual terms of the agreement, there would be populist agitation against "excessive concessions," as in the case of the Firestone agreement in Ghana, which Firestone eventually terminated, maintaining that production was crippled by government refusal to allow a sufficient foreign exchange allocation.[22] Hostility toward multinational corporations coupled with high expectations would produce a recalcitrant even though highly paid labor force and high unit labor costs relative to other parts of the world. In the absence of substantial subsidies in one form or another, the enterprise would be money-losing. Even if real social benefits should exceed real social costs, the enterprise would probably be judged on its profitability. Thus, given the nature of African capitalism, the enterprise would be considered a failure and its operations would face curtailment.

POLICY IMPLICATIONS: LAISSEZ-FAIREISM

Three major policy thrusts are advocated today to deal with the inadequacy of African economic performance: a movement toward laissez-faire ("laissez-faireism"), continuation of government activism, but with reform involving movement away from piracy toward the nurturing of private productive activities (nurture capitalism), and socialism. None of these orientations holds forth the prospect of easy gains or sure success. This chapter will consider only laissez-faireism.

Laissez-faireism is an economic orientation advocating movement toward laissez-faire. It iterates the belief that a retreat from government activism in economic affairs is the major means of improving the quality of a country's economic performance. It is frequently seen as "central to the solution of a lot of the problems we see around the world."[23]

The orientation stresses the benefits of reliance on markets, on the profit incentive, and on the growth of the private sector. Free market pricing is crucial not only in markets for products (in Africa, particularly agricultural products), but also in factor markets and in international transactions. Wages should be allowed to find their own level as determined by supply and demand. Exchange rates should also be allowed to approach their natural levels, for artificially overvalued exchange rates are especially damaging. Tariffs and other forms of protection of import-substituting industries should be cut back. The country should turn toward an outward, export orientation rather than an inward, import-substitution orientation.[24]

Correlatively, the laissez-faireist stresses the harm inevitably done by government activism whether via state-owned enterprises, regulation of business, or welfarist attempts to improve income distribution, alleviate poverty, reduce unemployment, and the like.[25] Even if well intentioned, and regardless of government capability, such intervention is the major remediable cause of poor economic performance.[26]

Laissez-faireism is advocated by the World Bank and the International Monetary Fund, by some other governments and institutions, and perhaps most strongly by the present government of the United States. It appears to have attained the status of mainstream doctrine. It is, for many, a fervently held belief, an ideology that is zealously and even aggressively promoted, particularly among Third World countries. If enthusiastic proselytization is insufficient, its advocates are ready to impose it or elements of it. "When we find a country . . . that has adopted a lot of economic reforms . . . [that is, laissez-faireism], when it comes to funding, we remember."[27]

What follows is a critique of laissez-faireism. It is not a complete catalogue of criticisms, but a presentation of four major problems of a laissez-faireist strategy for contemporary Africa: the difficulty of implementing such a strategy effectively; the indispensability for such a strategy (contrary to the popular impression) of an active and effective government; the reliance of such a strategy upon a powerful private engine of growth, a requisite that is lacking in Africa; and the inadequacy of the market mechanism in poor countries.[28]

Difficulties of Implementation

To adopt laissez-faireism is to adopt a strategy that is extremely difficult to implement effectively in contemporary Africa. As this is a complex point, it will be helpful to state it briefly at the outset. Laissez-faireism at best involves substantial interim costs. To cope with these costs, Africa requires two conditions: (1) an enhanced flow of resources from the world economy, and (2) ability to handle powerful political opposition.[29] Unfortunately, however, these conditions are unlikely to obtain.

There is general agreement that movement from a network of government controls and activism toward laissez-faire, no matter how desirable, inevitably involves "austerity," that is, a bundle of short- and medium-term costs. The exact nature of this bundle depends upon the particular circumstances being addressed. For most African countries, it would include most of the following: (1) higher prices for domestic foodstuffs (resulting partly from domestic measures, such as the removal of subsidies or price controls, and partly from devaluation, which is a major component of laissez-faireism); (2) higher prices for all imported goods and services (also caused by devaluation); (3) decreased consumption of imported goods and services (a complement of the increased prices); (4) curtailment of domestic production requiring imported inputs, with consequent reductions in employment and real national income; because of heavy reliance on imported inputs, this impact is substantial, especially in manufacturing; it was estimated that Nigerian manufacturing output in 1983 was down to 23% of capacity, primarily because of this factor;[30] (5) production cutbacks in heavily protected import-substitution industries when the high-protection approach, which is inconsistent with laissez-faireism, is dismantled; (6) curtailment of government services and possible imposition of user charges (resulting from cuts in government expenditures for the purpose of restraining the high levels of income and aggregate demand, which cause inflationary and balance-of-payments pressures, which in turn give rise to a network of foreign trade, foreign exchange, and anti-inflationary controls; and (7) a general economic slowdown or recession (caused by the preceding circumstances, especially the need to reduce aggregate demand).

The first of the two conditions required to deal with these costs is a favorable international economic environment. To soften the hardships, an enlarged flow of foreign aid — loans and grants — is widely believed to be necessary. The World Bank, for example, stresses "measures which increase the flow of external financial support . . . ; increased external financial support . . . is critical."[31] However, the governments and financial institutions of the more developed countries, because of their own exigencies, have been curtailing rather than expanding the flow of financial support. Thus while "major increases in financial support through concessionary assistance from the donor community are urgently required," says the World Bank, "unfortunately, this is an unlikely prospect."[32]

The need for external support has been heightened by a number of other international conditions. Africa's international debt-servicing obligations, for one thing, have become very burdensome. While real interest rates (adjusted for inflation) have declined since 1983, they remain extremely high, a multiple of the real rate at the time of the original loans. The high value of the dollar, though it too has dropped some, raises the real cost to debtor countries of dollar-denominated interest and principal payments. The short-term nature of much African debt further enlarges annual repayments. While a common rule of thumb is that less developed countries can typically afford a maximum of 25% of their export earnings for debt servicing, African debt-servicing requirements typically amount to 35% to 40%.[33]

Exports are particularly important for developing countries moving toward laissez-faire and thus toward freer trade, but here too conditions are unfavorable. African exports have been curtailed by low Northern economic growth rates. In 1979 the World Bank estimated Southern exports for the 1980s under alternate low and high Northern growth scenarios for the 1980s. In the low-growth scenario (Northern GNP growth rate of 3.5%), Southern export expansion was only two-thirds as great as in the high-growth scenario (Northern growth rate of 4.9%).[34] The fact is that actual Northern growth during the first half of the 1980s has been far below that of the low-growth scenario: 2.3% for 1980–85.[35] At this rate, according to a rough calculation in accord with the earlier World Bank assumptions, Southern exports (and, by extension, African exports) would grow at only about 40% of the rate projected by the optimistic scenario of just a few years ago. Moreover, despite rhetoric to the contrary, protectionism and restrictions on market access impede African attempts to increase exports.[36]

As a result of the unfavorable trade conditions, terms of trade for almost all African countries are at exceptionally low levels, making debt repayment still more costly in real terms and significantly reducing real national income. The poor terms of trade, moreover, are likely to continue; "this deterioration in the international trading environment of African countries is unlikely to be reversed in a major way during the 1980s."[37]

Thus propitious external circumstances are needed to mitigate the short- and medium-term difficulties of laissez-faireism, but limitations in external assistance, burdensome debt-servicing requirements, the slowdown in Northern importation rates (caused both by a reduction in Northern economic growth and an increase in protectionism), and the consequent deterioration in African terms of trade all exacerbate these difficulties.[38]

Successful laissez-faireism requires also the ability to cope with the often-explosive political opposition evoked by the strategy's short- and medium-term costs. The resistance to increased food prices is especially fierce, for the large numbers of urban poor are disproportionately affected. It is not simply that they can afford price increases less than others. Since they spend a larger proportion of their incomes on foods than more affluent groups, their real incomes are cut by a larger percentage, and they are pushed (further) into malnutrition.

The political resistance to laissez-faireism is often so potent that African governments cannot adopt such an orientation even if the leaders believe that it would make economic sense. In Nigeria, for example, it is probable that no government could have survived the adoption of the devaluation measures urged upon successive regimes by the IMF from 1981 on.[39]

When laissez-faireist policies have been adopted, the public outcry has often brought about reversals. Thus when General F. W. K. Akuffo became Ghanaian head of state in July 1978 and quickly initiated an IMF-approved economic stabilization program, "The general public saw few economic benefits emerging from these harsh economic policies. . . . [T]he situation deteriorated and strikes became commonplace," and the regime was toppled in less than a year by the first Rawlings coup.[40] Policy reversals have also been associated in recent years with food price-related coups or riots in Sudan, Egypt, Tunisia, and Liberia.[41]

When laissez-faireist measures have nevertheless been adhered to, public opposition has usually set in motion offsetting processes that substantively negate those measures. Workers have managed to win wage increases to offset the rise in the cost of living, and producers of goods unfavorably affected by devaluation have had enough market power to raise their prices. The consequent rise in the domestic price level then offsets the effect of the devaluation. "[M]ost of the exchange rate adjustments made in Africa the past several years have been ineffective because domestic prices increased by more than the currency was devalued."[42] Nicholas Kaldor's observation that "[t]he main objection to this approach is that it assumes that devaluation is capable of changing critical price and wage relationships that are the outcome of complex political forces and that could not be changed by domestic fiscal and monetary policies" has been proven correct for Africa.[43]

Reliance upon Active Government

A second major problem of laissez-faireism is that it does not reduce dependence upon effective government to nearly the degree that one might suppose. Even a getting-prices-right approach is not a matter of simply dropping government responsibilities and leaving things to the free market. A free market strategy imposes major domestic responsibilities on government; "Policy reform of incentive systems is only likely to be successful," says the World Bank, "if pursued in the context of more comprehensive policy packages."[44] The Bank specifically mentions the need for such major and difficult programs as development of a more effective system to provide inputs to agriculture, the daunting task of reforming the marketing system of the country, the enormously expensive program of improving transport,[45] and other measures that induce a quick supply response to price incentives.[46]

Let us ask, focusing on agriculture, why a free market pricing strategy must include such a major and difficult package of programs. The answer lies in the limited responsiveness of aggregate agriculture production in Africa to prices. While an increase in the price of a single crop, ceteris paribus, elicits a substantial supply response for that crop, this is achieved primarily by shifting productive resources from other crops. Aggregate farm production in Africa, however, does not respond strongly to price increases. The only study of aggregate supply elasticity in Africa known to me shows a median short-run elasticity for nine countries of 0.13.[47] Thus to increase agricultural output by 5% after one year would require a 38.5% increase in agricultural prices.[48]

Moreover, this must be an increase relative to other prices. Offsetting rises in the prices farmers paid would necessitate still greater increases in agricultural prices. And, as suggested earlier, prices farmers paid would inevitably rise substantially. Food price increases and the general price-increasing effects of devaluation would exert irresistible upward pressures on domestic wages, including farm wages, and also on the prices of domestic nonfarm goods purchased by farmers. Moreover, devaluation would directly increase the price of imports purchased by farmers. Taking these secondary repercussions into effect, a 5% increase in agricultural output, induced by price increases alone, might easily require a doubling of agricultural prices.[49]

Farm prices would not only have to rise sharply, they would have to do so well in advance of any increase in production. Because of agriculture's annual nature, increased food prices would have to be paid approximately a year before any significant augmentation of the supply of farm goods occurred.

Thus for several reasons free market pricing in agriculture needs to be complemented by a major package of government programs: because agricultural price increases alone would have a limited effect on production, because the production gains would be deferred for almost a year, and because even the limited production gains would require price increases of a magnitude that would impose severe hardships and provoke massive political opposition. Price increases constitute just one measure — and a politically explosive one — among the large number usually recommended to raise agricultural output.

The fact that even a getting-prices-right approach requires an active and effective government reflects the clear reality that government programs often serve real needs. It is perhaps because of a rough balance in Africa between the benefits from useful government activities and the costs of government ineptness and venality that Raymond Hopkins was unable to find any significant statistical relationship between a growing government sector and poor performance in the food system and in the economy more generally.[50]

It is striking that the World Bank's *Accelerated Development in Sub-Saharan Africa* is highly reticent about the crucial issue of aggregate supply elasticity. It mentions the responsiveness of aggregate supply to price only in an opaque footnote, in which it merely expresses an extremely cautiously worded opinion, presenting no evidence — an opinion that appears to say that higher agricultural prices will cause those increases in aggregate farm production that are prevented because prices are too low.[51]

Engine of Growth

A third problem is that Africa requires a powerful engine of growth, but the laissez-faireist engines — African entrepreneurship and foreign investment operating in the contemporary African economic environment — are weak ones. The aforementioned inelasticity of aggregate agricultural supply is one instance of this problem: the responsiveness of agriculture, unaided except for the removal of harmful government policies, is likely to be disappointing. The problem holds for nonagricultural private enterprise as well, whether indigenous or foreign.

There have been many studies of the operations of African business, some by this writer, and the conclusion that clearly emerges is that the shortcomings of African entrepreneurship are formidable. Deficiencies in education, skills, training, experience, and so on operate at all levels; in particular, they make it difficult for African entrepreneurs to negotiate the technological, organizational, and marketing leaps that must be made to graduate from small-scale to medium- or large-scale business organization. Situate these vulnerable entrepreneurs in Africa's adverse economic environment, where myriads of cost-raising and demand-limiting problems are encountered that do not arise in the more developed economies — problems of securing proper equipment in reasonable time and in good working order, of human resources, particularly at the supervisory and managerial level, of infrastructure, of supplies, of adequate markets, of repair, and many more[52] — and it is easy to understand why indigenous business has not been able to provide much development thrust in contemporary Africa. Even in Nigeria, a country in which the basic attributes of entrepreneurship are abundant, in which indigenous business has been significant for many decades, and in which conditions for such business have been relatively propitious, the contribution of indigenous business to economic growth has been marginal.[53]

Foreign investment has also shown itself to be an inadequate, even feeble, engine of growth in Africa. Impeded by formidable economic-environmental problems (slightly different from those facing indigenous business) and by the limitations inherent in foreign investment anywhere in the Third World, foreign firms have almost invariably sought to escape from laissez-faireist conditions by securing a broad range of favorable government interventions in the marketplace: protection against international competition, a variety of tax breaks, special arrangements regarding land and natural resources, government provision of capital and infrastructure, and other government-bestowed benefits. Even with these concessions, however, foreign investment in the aggregate has provided only limited economic impetus in Africa.

The consequence of the ineffectuality of the laissez-faireist engines of growth has been clear for all to see: private investment, indigenous and foreign, has provided little development thrust in Africa. One could argue that great increases in such investment would occur if only laissez-faireism were adopted, but the role of private nonagricultural investment in Africa has been so small and the reliance of many of the private investors upon government nurturance has been so great that the evidence points in the other direction. I submit, then, that there is little reason to expect that African countries that "unleash private enterprise" through a policy of laissez-faireism will initiate a significant surge of privately powered economic development.

Market Errancy

A fourth major problem of laissez-faireism is market errancy, a problem of much greater dimensions than laissez-faireism contemplates. While the market is sometimes part of the solution in Africa, it is often part of the problem. It frequently gives misleading and socially dysfunctional signals, particularly in the poorer developing countries. The market works well only when the money receipts from producing a product measure the social benefits of production (the full benefits of all kinds to society) and the money costs of producing it measure the social costs (the full costs of all kinds to society). Then monetary profitability and net social benefit coincide. When money receipts exceed money costs (the venture is profitable), then social benefits exceed social costs (the venture is socially beneficial), and vice versa. In fact, however, the divergences between the monetary and societal outcomes are often enormous, especially in less developed countries. Rather than explaining this point in general and therefore abstract terms, I will attempt to make it clear by considering one example — that of domestic food prices.[54]

The harm done by inept market intervention by African governments to hold down domestic food prices can certainly be immense and has been discussed often.[55] Such clumsy intervention has usually been attributed to simple policy or ideological error or to a conflict between economic and political rationality (government schemes provide opportunities for graft, political patronage, and mobilization of political support, and for the decision makers these benefits outweigh the economic costs).

However, the fundamental reason for government resort to such intervention in sub-Saharan Africa, and indeed throughout the Third World, is that in poor countries the free market food-provisioning process functions not merely imperfectly but cruelly. The demand for domestic food crops comes mainly from low-income Africans, while the demand for export crops comes mainly from higher-income foreign buyers. When buyer income is low (as in the case with domestic food crops), demand and prices are relatively low; conversely, when buyers are affluent (as is the case with export crops), demand and prices are relatively high. Stating this in terms of prices and social benefits, foodstuffs for low-income consumers are of high human utility and therefore high social benefit but have low prices, while export crops for high-income purchasers are of lower human utility and therefore lower social benefit but have high prices. The natural free market response is constricted supply of low-priced though high-utility domestic foodstuffs and expansive supply of high-priced though low-utility exports. Foreign purchasers are liberally supplied with goods of relatively low social benefit, but African buyers, rural as well as urban, find that quantities of foods of high social benefit are grossly deficient. Problems of malnutrition and hunger are intensified. It has been estimated that 25% of the African population was malnourished in 1970,[56] and for children the situation has been even worse. The World Health Organization has estimated that two-thirds of Third World children suffered from at least some degree of malnutrition.[57]

Given all that is required for the success of laissez-faireism — a favorable international economic environment and the ability to proceed in the face of powerful political opposition; an improved system for providing agricultural inputs, improved transport, a reformed marketing system, and other measures to hasten agricultural supply response to increased prices; powerful private engines of economic growth; and market signals that measure true social costs and benefits — it is not surprising that successful implementation "is proving to be extremely slow and difficult for administrative, technical and political reasons."[58] Laissez-faireism is not a promising orientation.

NOTES

1.   The first phase may have begun earlier than 1950; this was the first year for which World Bank data were available.

2.   World Bank, *World Tables,* 3rd ed., vol. 1, *Economic Data,* Baltimore, Johns Hopkins University Press, 1983, and other World Bank sources. Faber and Green also see a more unfavorable phase starting in the late 1970s. Using UNCTAD data, they date the crisis stage from 1979. Mike Faber and Reginald H. Green, "Sub-Saharan Africa's Economic Malaise: Some Questions and Answers," in Tore Rose, ed., *Crisis and Recovery in Sub-Saharan Africa,* Paris, OECD, 1985.

3.   "[T]he international environment had become less favorable to developing countries in the period after 1973 and became even less favorable after 1979–80. The

slowdown in industrial-country growth hurt all developing countries, although the effect was not the same for all. Those which were exporters neither of oil nor of manufactures suffered most." World Bank, *World Development Report, 1984,* Washington, D.C., 1984, 23.

4.   Any quantitative study that purports to show that the external impact was minor has simply failed to include all important facets of that impact.

5.   Sayre P. Schatz, *Nigerian Capitalism,* Berkeley, University of California Press, 1977, 151–52, and also the rest of chapter 8 on "The Political Environment." See also Harvey Glickman, "The Present and Future of the African State in an Age of Adversity," chapter 2 in this volume. In the colonial period "the main beneficiaries of marketing boards, monopolies, licenses, and other regulatory devices were white settlers, private firms favored by the metropole, and, at the end of a long skein, metropolitan central banks."

6.   African civil servants were concerned with "[t]he very first objective of any bureaucracy — to extract the resources needed to finance the salaries and perquisites of its own members." David B. Abernethy, "Bureaucratic Growth and Economic Decline in Sub-Saharan Africa," paper delivered at the annual meeting of the African Studies Association, Boston, 1983, 2. Relative to per capita GNP, government wages and salaries in Africa are extremely high, and much higher than in other parts of the Third World; Abernethy, 14.

7.   Sayre P. Schatz, "Pirate Capitalism and the Inert Economy of Nigeria," *Journal of Modern African Studies* 22, no. 1, March 1984, 45–58.

8.   John Iliffe, *The Emergence of African Capitalism,* Minneapolis, University of Minnesota Press, 1983, 1–22, 64–87.

9.   Crawford Young, *Ideology and Development in Africa,* New Haven, Conn., Yale University Press, 1982, 297–326.

10.   Donald Rothchild and E. Gyimah-Boadi, "Ghana's Economic Decline and Development Strategies," in John Ravenhill, ed., *Africa in Economic Crisis,* New York, Columbia University Press, 1986, 276.

11.   Robert H. Bates, *Markets and States in Tropical Africa,* Berkeley, University of California Press, 1981, and John Ravenhill, "Africa's Continuing Crises: The Elusiveness of Development," in Ravenhill, *Africa in Economic Crisis,* 11–13.

12.   Central Bank of Nigeria, internal memo, 1983.

13.   Ruth S. Morgenthau, "Institutionalizing Rural Development: Lessons from Evaluation," chapter 8 in this volume.

14.   Schatz, "Pirate Capitalism," 55.

15.   Not all would agree, of course, that discouragement of foreign investment would impede development. The literature is vast. For a new paradigm on the effects of such investment, see David G. Becker, Jeff Frieden, Sayre P. Schatz, and Richard L. Sklar, *Postimperialism: International Capitalism and Development in the Late Twentieth Century,* Boulder, Colo., Lynne Reinner, 1987. See also earlier works by Sklar, "Postimperialism: A Class Analysis of Multinational Corporate Expansion," *Comparative Politics* 9, no. 1, October 1976, 75–92; and *Corporate Power in an African State: The Political Impact of Multinational Mining Companies in Zambia,* Berkeley, University of California Press, 1975.

16.   Alexander Gerschenkron, *Economic Backwardness in Historical Perspective,* Cambridge, Mass., Harvard University Press, 1962, 24–25. Similar patterns obtained in Germany and Russia according to Gerschenkron.

17.   Sayre P. Schatz and S. I. Edokpayi, "Economic Attitudes of Nigerian Businessmen," *Nigerian Journal of Economic and Social Studies* 4, no. 3, November 1962, 262. This survey was conducted in 1962; there is virtually universal agreement that the problem has grown worse since then. See also Schatz, *Nigerian Capitalism,* chapters 6 and 13.

18.   Rothchild and Gyimah-Boadi, "Ghana's Economic Decline," 258–59.

19.   Ibid., 376–77. The reference is to the coup that toppled the Akuffo regime in June 1979.

20.   The author owes this formulation to Robert L. Heilbroner. See Schatz, "Pirate Capitalism" and references there.

21.   *Philadelphia Inquirer,* September 3, 1985, 1-B.

22.   See Rothchild and Gyimah-Boadi, "Ghana's Economic Decline," 259.

23.   United States Secretary of State George P. Shultz, speaking of "privatization," an important facet of laissez-faireism, at a U.S.-sponsored International Conference on Privatization, attended by participants from 40 nations. The administrator of the United States Agency for International Development, Peter MacPherson, stated, "Privatization can be the right step at the right time to finally liberate developing countries' economies from slow growth or stagnation." *New York Times,* February 20, 1986, A13.

24.   An important "lesson" that USAID propounds, printed in bold-faced type, is that "import substitution is appropriate and efficient if it is not linked to special Government policies distorting relative prices," in other words, if it has very little muscle behind it. Jerome Wolgin et al., *The Private Sector and the Economic Development of Malawi,* A.I.D. Evaluation Special Study no. 11, Washington, D.C., USAID, 1983, ix.

25.   Thus a USAID study of Cameroon stresses Cameroon's strong overall economic performance, attributed to laissez-faireism, although "improvement in social indicators since independence was much smaller than clearly could have been possible," and "whether or not health, social services, and considerations of personal income distribution were neglected." Salvatore Schiavo-Campo et al., *The Tortoise Walk: Public Policy and Private Activity in the Economic Development of Cameroon,* A.I.D. Evaluation Special Study no. 10, Washington, D.C., USAID, 1983, 51.

26.   Thus the "most striking" factor explaining strong economic performance in Malawi has been "a significant reliance on market performance," while weaknesses in that performance are explained by unwise deviations from free market policies: "The country did diverge from its market-oriented approach to development and the [negative] consequences were far-reaching." Wolgin et al., *Private Sector,* 45–46.

27.   Quotation from the director of the Bureau of Program and Policy Coordination, USAID. The director of the agency's Africa Bureau noted, "If a country is moving in that direction [toward privatization], it would affect their funding levels. Conversely, if a country is moving away from that direction, it also would affect their funding levels." *New York Times,* February 20, 1986, A13.

28.   The critique by no means implies that all cutbacks in government activity would be unwise. Especially since resources are severely limited, one would find in every country specific reasons for reallocating government efforts in various ways.

29.   World Bank, *Sub-Saharan Africa: Progress Report on Development Prospects and Programs,* Washington, D.C., World Bank, 1983, 7, 10; also noted in *Toward Sustained Development in Sub-Saharan Africa: A Joint Program of Action,* Washington, D.C., World Bank, 1984, 46–48.

30.   Central Bank of Nigeria, internal memo, 1983.

31.   World Bank, *Sub-Saharan Africa: Progress Report,* 10. The foreword of the subsequent report emphasizes that "progress will be achieved only if the international community provides strong and consistent support to the reform efforts of the Sub-Saharan nations. . . . There needs to be increased international support for Sub-Saharan development by the provision of both expertise and concessional funds." World Bank, *Toward Sustained Development,* 5.

32.   World Bank, *Sub-Saharan Africa: Progress Report,* 5.

33.   Faber and Green, "Sub-Saharan Africa's Economic Malaise," 20.

34.   World Bank, *World Development Report, 1979,* Washington, D.C., 1979, 17.

35.   World Bank, *World Development Report, 1985,* Washington, D.C., 1985, 138.

36.   A striking example is provided by the international Multi-Fibre Arrangement (MFA) under the General Agreement on Tariffs and Trade. Two of the three stated goals of the MFA were (1) to expand textile trade and reduce barriers to such trade and (2) to increase substantially the amount and the share of world textile export earnings going to developing countries. These goals have remained in the realm of rhetoric. The actuality of the MFA has been precisely the opposite. The operative clauses (which related only to a portion of a third goal, avoidance of disruptive effects) have been used almost exclusively to restrict imports by the more developed countries. World Bank, *World Development Report, 1981,* Washington, D.C., 1981, 28.

37.   World Bank, *Sub-Saharan Africa: Progress Report,* 3.

38.   For a number of reasons, African countries are more vulnerable to external shocks than most other less developed countries. See, for example, Gerald K. Helleiner, "The IMF and Africa in the 1980s," *Canadian Journal of African Studies* 17, no. 1, 1983, 28–30.

39.   Vremudia P. Diejomaoh, oral remark, seminar at Swarthmore College, Swarthmore, Pennsylvania, November 1, 1984.

40.   Rothchild and Gyimah-Boadi, "Ghana's Economic Decline," 266.

41.   See, for example, Raymond F. Hopkins, "Overburdened Government and Underfed Populace: The Role of Food Subsidies in Africa's Economic Crisis," chapter 7 in this volume.

42.   Elliot Berg, "World Bank's Strategy," in Ravenhill, *Africa in Economic Crisis,* 69. Berg continues: "It is the same with changes in agricultural prices paid to producers. In many, probably most cases, the impact on farmer income and incentives has been lost because prices of the things farmers buy have risen by as much or more." See also World Bank, *Sub-Saharan Africa: Progress Report,* 8.

43.   Nicholas Kaldor, "Devaluation and Adjustment in Developing Countries," *Finance and Development*, June 1983, 35.

44.   World Bank, *Sub-Saharan Africa: Progress Report*, 10. See also World Bank, *Toward Sustained Development*, 1: "Making the most of investment requires not only appropriate pricing policies, but also adequate management capacity in government."

45.   Transportation development is usually the most costly part of an economic plan.

46.   Ruth S. Morgenthau forcefully makes the point that effective measures are more likely to be chosen if farmers can be brought into the decision-making process through the formation of an effective farmers' lobby. "There must be ways that the rural population can participate in the exercise of decision-making power over matters that affect them." "Agriculture and State Formation in African States," paper for annual meeting of the African Studies Association, Boston, December 7, 1983, 45 and 49.

47.   Marian E. Bond, "Agricultural Responses to Prices in Sub-Saharan African Countries," *IMF Staff Papers* 30, no. 4, December 1983, 716–25. Bond calculates the mean supply elasticity (0.18) in this study of nine African countries, but as the mean is greatly affected by an extreme figure for one country (0.54 for Senegal), I have used the median figure. The long-run elasticity (over a period of years) would be a bit higher; the mean is 0.21 and the median is 0.15; Bond, 724. Inelasticity of agricultural supply is simply one manifestation of a broader economywide inelasticity of aggregate supply. See Schatz, "Pirate Capitalism," 47.

48.   Price increases might be somewhat smaller if it were possible to raise farmgate prices to some degree by lowering taxation of agricultural products.

49.   This follows directly from the fact, already noted, that domestic price rises in Africa have typically offset the effect of devaluation (see note 42 and relevant text). The text remark is in fact a conservative statement; if other price rises completely offset agricultural price increases, then no boost in agricultural prices, no matter how large, would suffice.

50.   Hopkins, "Overburdened Government and Underfed Populace." Hopkins discusses his statistical efforts at some length.

51.   "The literature and common observation indicate that farmers respond strongly to changes in *relative* prices. The question of *aggregate* supply is more nuanced. In the short term, farmers' possibilities are indeed sharply constrained, and they respond to changed incentive structures by switching to the more profitable crops. . . . In the long run, a more congenial set of marketing conditions [which includes higher prices] will motivate them to invest in equipment, to hire labor, to work harder and to find other ways of breaking those 'constraints' which derive from inadequate motivation rather than from inadequate technology." World Bank, *Accelerated Development in Sub-Saharan Africa: An Agenda for Action*, Washington, D.C., 1981, 55.

52.   On the nature of the leap and of Nigerian entrepreneurial shortcomings in attempting to negotiate the leap, and also on the positive attributes of Nigerian entrepreneurs, see Schatz, *Nigerian Capitalism*, chapter 5; on the economic environment, see chapter 6.

53.   Ibid., 8–19, 24–38, and 237–38, and Schatz, "Pirate Capitalism," 46–54.

54.   I have explained this matter elsewhere; see especially chapter 7, meant for noneconomists, in *Nigerian Capitalism.*

55.   Socialists can be just as critical of such malintervention as laissez-faireists. On the consequences of misconceived price control in socialist-leaning less developed countries, see, for example, Alec Nove, *The Economics of Feasible Socialism,* London, Allen and Unwin, 1983, 193–94.

56.   Sterling Wortman and Ralph W. Cummings, Jr., *To Feed This World: The Challenge and the Strategy,* Baltimore, Johns Hopkins University Press, 1978, 23, cited in S. Malcolm Gillis et al., *Economics of Development,* New York, Norton, 1983, 243.

57.   See Alan Berg, *The Nutrition Factor: Its Role in National Development,* Washington, D.C., Brookings Institution, 1973, 5, cited in Gillis et al., *Economics of Development,* 244.

58.   World Bank, *Sub-Saharan Africa: Progress Report,* 7, 10. See also World Bank, *Toward Sustained Development,* 39–40: "There are definite signs of greater willingness of African governments to consider policy reforms. . . . However, actual progress in reform and in performance has been very limited."

5

Contemporary Policy Responses to Economic Decline in Africa

Ravi Gulhati and Satya Yalamanchili

Official reports and some professional journals are full of accounts of severe economic stress in sub-Saharan Africa. The setback to the economic development of many of these countries has lasted the best part of a decade, in some cases even longer. The World Bank, for example, has published a series of reports that diagnose the evolving economic situation in Africa and propose policies and programs aimed at restoring healthy economic development.[1] These Bank reports on Africa have proved to be both controversial and influential. Criticism has come from development experts such as those at the Institute of Development Studies, Sussex,[2] and from official bodies such as the Economic Commission of Africa.[3] Despite this criticism, however, these Bank reports have helped in drawing attention to Africa's colossal problems and in stimulating a reconsideration of policies pursued for many years by African governments and by foreign donors and creditors active in Africa.

Our aim in this chapter is not so much to summarize these reports or reactions to them but rather to illuminate some of the issues and approaches discussed in these reports by focusing on a sample of twelve countries in eastern and southern Africa. We will (1) asses the magnitude and scope of the economic decline in this sample; (2) specify the main causes of the predicament of these countries; (3) characterize the nature and extent of their initial policy responses; and (4) make some observations about the policy process as it is unfolding in sample countries. In this way we hope to elucidate and suitably qualify broad generalizations at the pan-African level. Also, since some of the sample countries have adopted policy approaches that are broadly similar to the ones advocated in the series of Bank reports, we will be able to review the early results of these reforms.

MAGNITUDE AND SCOPE OF
THE ECONOMIC DECLINE

Growth rates in GDP, agricultural production, and exports over three periods suggest a general picture of deceleration (Table 5.1). GDP increased very rapidly in 1967–73 in four cases and much faster than population in all but two countries. The picture for 1978–83 was a sharp contrast; GDP per capita fell in most countries. Increase in agricultural production was much slower in the later period than in the earlier one in eight cases. The volume of exports declined during 1978–83 in the majority of sample countries.

Almost the whole sample experienced some economic decline, but the extent and duration of the decline differed very considerably. Bar diagrams show average GNP per capita at the end of the 1960s, at the close of the 1970s, and during the early 1980s (Figure 5.1). The sample can be classified into three categories. The first consists of four countries who have experienced a drastic decline over more than two decades. Countries are ranked according to the magnitude of the decline in GNP per capita. The second category includes three cases in which per capita GNP increased during the 1970s but then fell during recent years. Finally, there are five countries in which there was no decline or in which the decline was of modest proportions.

Deceleration in the rate of economic activity was accompanied by signs of financial stress (Table 5.2). Budget deficits, covered by government borrowing from central and commercial banks, expanded very rapidly. Peak ratios of such deficits exceeded 10% of GDP in five cases. Throughout the sample these peak ratios were a multiple of 1977–79 average levels. High budget deficits sparked correspondingly high deficits on the current account of the balance of payments as well as high rates of inflation. Peak balance-of-payments deficits exceeded 15% of GDP in four cases and 10% of GDP in nine cases. These growing external deficits were financed to a substantial extent by foreign borrowing on hard terms and a drawing down of foreign exchange reserves. Debt service payments absorbed a small share of export

TABLE 5.1
Average Annual Growth Rates of Real GDP, Agricultural Output, and Export Volume
(percent)

Country a/	GDP 1967–73	1973–78	1978–83	Agriculture 1967–73	1973–78	1978–83	Exports 1967–73	1973–78	1978–83
1. Mauritius	9.2 b/	7.5	1.0	8.6 b/	−5.4	−1.4	4.7	3.9	1.6
2. Kenya	8.4	4.6	4.1	5.9	4.6	2.8	3.4	−1.8	−7.3
3. Zimbabwe	7.2 c/	−1.5	5.8	5.0 c/	−0.3	2.1	10.1	−1.4	−0.8
4. Malawi	5.3	6.1	1.9	4.1	6.4	2.1	0.8	1.8	3.2
5. Sudan	0.8	14.7	0.9	4.0	11.6	−1.7	2.7	−1.1	−1.9
6. Uganda	3.2	−0.5	1.2	3.4	0.5	1.6	0.6	−15.9	5.0
7. Tanzania	4.5	5.5	0.4 d/	2.6	5.3	−2.8 d/	−0.6	−4.7	−3.8
8. Ethiopia	4.2	0.8	3.7	2.1	−0.1	2.4	4.7	−8.6	7.3
9. Zambia	3.5 b/	0.9	0.6	2.1 b/	3.5	0.4	0.7	−0.1	−1.6
10. Somalia	3.0 b/	7.2	0.4 d/	0.6 b/	10.5	2.2 d/	5.0	3.6	9.6
11. Madagascar	−0.1 b/	0.0	−0.9 d/	0.5 b/	−1.4	1.5 d/	4.6	−0.1	−10.9
12. Zaire	3.9 e/	−2.7	1.0	−1.6 e/	0.5	2.3	7.8	−6.6	−16.8 d/

aCountries are listed in descending order of their agricultural growth rate during 1967–73.
bRelates to 1970–73.
cRelates to 1969–73.
dRelates to 1978–82.
eRelates to 1968–73.

Source: World Bank data files; UNCTAD, *Handbook of International Trade and Development Statistics,* UN, 1985.

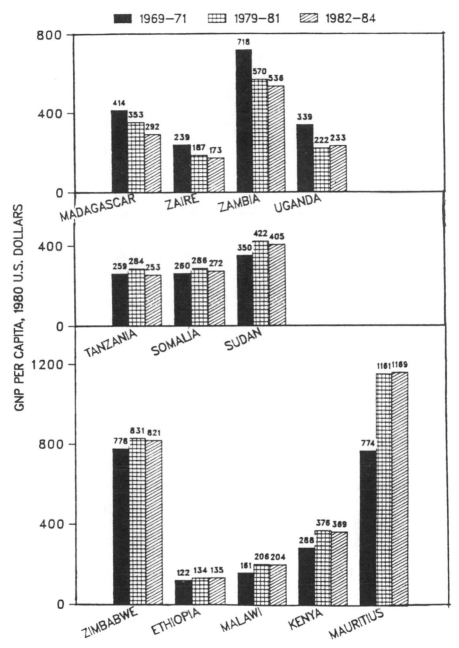

Figure 5.1
Changes in GNP Per Capita in Eastern and Southern African
Countries

TABLE 5.2
Selected Indicators of Financial Stress

Country	Budget Deficit as % of GDP a/		External Deficit as % of GDP b/		Average Annual Rate of Inflation (%)		Debt Service as % of Export of Goods and Services	
	1977-79 Average	Peak During 79-83	1977-79 Average	Peak During 79-83	1977-79 Average	Peak During 79-83	1970	1983
1. Ethiopia	2.5	7.8	4.2	7.0	15.7	16.6	11.4	11.5
2. Kenya	1.3	6.2	8.5	14.2	13.3	20.5	5.4	20.6
3. Madagascar	5.2	10.1	9.6	18.0	8.3	31.4	3.5	38.7 e/
4. Malawi	0.7	7.2	16.9	23.8	7.9	19.1	7.1	20.3 e/f/
5. Mauritius	8.4	10.6	11.9	13.9	10.7	42.7	3.0	16.5
6. Somalia	4.2	10.8	14.0	21.0	15.7	55.8	2.1	13.1 g/
7. Sudan	4.9	4.7	2.1	6.5	22.4	31.2	10.7	11.2 e/f/
8. Tanzania	4.7	9.7 c/	10.1	13.8	12.2	30.2	4.9	11.4 g/h/
9. Uganda	1.9	3.7	N.A.	N.A.	88.3	216.6	2.7	21.5 e/
10. Zaire	7.6	10.0	9.2	12.2	75.4	108.6	4.4	7.9 e/f/
11. Zambia	8.9	13.7	7.0	21.4	15.3	19.8	5.9	12.6 e/f/
12. Zimbabwe	N.A.	5.6 d/	0.7	11.5	11.3	23.1	0.9 i/	31.6

aGovernment net borrowing from domestic banks.
bDeficit on current account of the balance of payments. Official transfers are excluded.
cPeak during 1979–82.
dPeak during 1980–83.
eDebt rescheduled by Paris Club in 1980s.
fDebt to commercial banks rescheduled in 1980s.
gAccumulation of arrears in debt service.
hRelates to 1982.
iRelates to 1978.

Source: World Bank data files.

earnings in 1970, but the situation had changed dramatically by 1983. Not only was the debt service ratio above 20% in five cases, but many countries had found it necessary to go to the Paris Club (and some to foreign commercial banks) to obtain debt relief. Finally, double-digit inflation was already a characteristic feature of the sample during the late 1970s. This is still the case today.

MAIN ELEMENTS OF THE DIAGNOSIS

The economic decline and accompanying financial crises are the combined result of exogenous shocks as well as of policy and institutional distortions. The literature contains assessments that emphasize the predominant role of adverse shocks[4] or of policy and institutional failures.[5] We will try to sort out the relative contribution of these variables in our sample.

Exogenous Shocks

The measurement of shocks depends on the reference period for comparison, and this should be selected on the basis of expectations entertained by macroeconomic managers regarding exogenous variables, such as the terms of trade. Such expectations could be entirely simplistic (for example, that the exogenous variables will not change) or very sophisticated (for example, econometric forecasts of each exogenous variable based on historical experience). Our exercise assumes that macromanagers are aware of yearly fluctuations but expect that these are reversible and that over a three-year period they tend to cancel out. They also assume that no changes in trend values of exogenous variables are expected. Accordingly, we identify shocks during 1973–75, for example, by comparing this period with the average of the preceding three years, 1971–73. We also assume that the view of the trend taken by macromanagers is a rolling one, that is, they expect the 1975–77 average to equal the average of 1973–75 and not the average of 1971–73.

The impact of exogenous shocks can be assessed at different levels of aggregation, such as a single enterprise, an individual crop, a sector, public revenue, exports, or imports. Our focus here is at the macroeconomic level, and we will deal quantitatively with the following kinds of shocks:

— Changes in export and import prices. This procedure identifies repeated shocks generated by international prices of individual commodities, but in many instances adverse shocks of this kind are offset by simultaneous windfall gains accruing to other commodities. The terms of trade index picks up the net impact of all these micro disturbances, and we calculate the resulting loss or gain in income at the macro level.

— Changes in official development assistance (ODA), that is, foreign grants and concessional loans. Here again the focus is on aggregate ODA rather than on shocks resulting from the behavior of individual donors.

— Changes in net resource transfer (gross disbursement less amortization and interest) on account of foreign commercial bank loans, suppliers' credits, and International Bank for Reconstruction and Development (IBRD) loans. These changes reflect the shock emanating from the very sharp rise in international interest rates on loans from private sources from about 8% in 1976–77 to a peak of 14% in 1981. They also reflect the shock caused by the sharp decline in the flow of new commitments and gross disbursements of such loans in recent years.

— Since sample countries rely heavily on rain-fed agriculture, these economies are particularly vulnerable to changing weather conditions. Local production of cereals, other foods, and export crops are subject to sharp variations. In the absence of a reliable index of weather conditions, we have identified these shocks in terms of deviations of total crop output during the period under study from the average of the immediately preceding period.

This assessment of exogenous shocks does not take account of other disturbances such as armed conflict and civil unrest. Any comprehensive exercise at the country level should deal with these variables as well as others that are specific to that country. For example, in landlocked Malawi disruption of routes to the sea through Mozambique led to a very large increase in the transport cost of imports and exports.

If we start with the terms of trade, it is clear that this was the source of major disturbances throughout the 1970s and the early 1980s. The most catastrophic case is Zambia, which lost 17.5% of its gross domestic income through a deterioration in the terms of trade in 1975–77. This was followed by further losses in subsequent periods. On a cumulative basis, for the whole period 1971–73 to 1981–83 Zambia sustained a loss of 18%, Somalia of almost 7%, Malawi of 5%, Ethiopia of almost 4%, and Zaire of 3%.

The period of the second oil-price increase (1979–81) was particularly bad. Countries are listed in Table 5.3 according to the severity of adverse exogenous shocks in 1979–81. The severest shocks were generated from adverse changes in the terms of trade. Eleven of the twelve countries in the sample suffered a deterioration in their terms of trade; in three cases the loss exceeded 3% of Gross Domestic Income (GDY). The loss in GDY on account of terms of trade was offset or more than offset by rising ODA in five cases. It could be argued that our treatment of rising ODA as an offset to declining terms of trade misses some important elements of the real world situation. Foreign exchange derived from export earnings is a versatile resource that can be used flexibly for purchasing imports of food, intermediate goods, spare parts, or new capital equipment. The use of ODA, by contrast, is very much circumscribed by the specific preferences of donors regarding projects, commodities, and sources of procurement.

While ODA was a positive factor in all countries during 1979–81, this was not the case as far as loans on conventional terms were concerned. Mauritius, Malawi, Zimbabwe, and Madagascar had borrowed substantial amounts on a floating rate basis, thereby causing a sharp rise in the reverse flow of interest payments. In addition, the real flow of new commitments and disbursements of these loans was reduced to a trickle in most of these countries. The net resource transfer on account of such loans fell by more than 1% of GDY in Zaire, Malawi, Zimbabwe, and Kenya (Table 5.3). This fall occurred despite the fact that debt service was rescheduled in Zaire and Malawi during this period (Table 5.2, notes e and f).

Domestic harvest failures accentuated the impact of terms of trade and international capital market shocks in Mauritius, Zambia, Sudan, and Uganda. In all these cases the decline in crop output was more than 1% of GDY.

Altogether, taking account of all kinds of shocks, Mauritius, Malawi, Zaire, and Kenya experienced substantial losses in GDY during 1979–81. Similar analysis for 1981–83 is performed in Table 5.4. A large part of the sample incurred further losses on account of changes in terms of trade. While ODA was a positive factor in all cases during 1979–81, it became a negative one in Zaire, Zambia, and Malawi in 1981–83. Net resource transfers on account of loans on conventional terms continued to be a negative factor in even more countries. Altogether, Mauritius, Zambia, and Tanzania registered losses in GDY in excess of 1% on account of a variety of shocks during 1981–83.

TABLE 5.3
Impact of Exogenous Shocks during 1979–81 as Compared to 1977–79

(% of GDY)

Country	Terms of Trade	ODA	Loans on Conventional Terms	Crop Production	Total
Mauritius	-5.9	0.3	-0.6	-1.4	-7.6
Uganda	-3.4	..	..	-2.9	..
Malawi	-4.9	1.3	-2.1	0.7	-5.0
Zaire	-1.6	0.6	-4.0	1.4	-3.6
Kenya	-2.5	1.2	-1.0	-0.2	-2.5
Zambia	-0.2	0.7	1.1	-1.4	0.2
Sudan	-0.4	2.0	0.8	-1.2	1.2
Madagascar	-1.8	2.3	1.6	-0.1	2.0
Ethiopia	-2.6	0.7	0.3	4.6	3.0
Zimbabwe	1.1	1.8	-1.4	1.9	3.4
Tanzania	-2.1	2.2	0.1	4.3	4.5
Somalia	-2.5	5.3	-0.1	3.3	6.0

Source: World Bank data files.

94

TABLE 5.4
Impact of Exogenous Shocks during 1981–83 as Compared to 1979–81
(% of GDY)

Country	Terms of Trade	ODA	Loans on Conventional Terms	Crop Production	Total
Mauritius	-1.5	0.8	-4.5	1.0	-4.2
Zambia	-2.2	-0.5	-0.2	0.1	-2.8
Tanzania	-0.5	0.4	-0.3	-1.2	-1.6
Madagascar	-1.0	2.4	-3.5	1.4	-0.7
Sudan	-0.4	1.9	-0.4	-1.5	-0.4
Kenya	-0.7	0.5	-2.0	2.3	0.1
Malawi	1.0	-1.1	-2.5	3.9	1.3
Ethiopia	-1.2	0.4	0.2	2.5	1.9
Zaire	2.7	-1.1	-1.0	2.6	3.2
Uganda	-1.5	..	..	7.2	..
Zimbabwe	2.5	1.3	1.8	-0.2	5.4
Somalia	-0.7	6.0	0.9	6.4	12.6

Source: World Bank data files.

To summarize, while the terms of trade and developments in the world capital market were adverse factors in both periods for most countries, the rise in ODA in many countries tended to reduce the net negative impact of exogenous shocks. However, the fact that ODA could not be used flexibly complicated the situation. Policy-makers should have learned to expect a recurring succession of wind-fall gains and losses. Recent history suggests that such learning did not occur or at least that it could not be translated into effective macroeconomic demand management policies. The general tendency was for governments to adjust quickly public expenditures and imports to windfall gains but to resist or to delay retrenchment in the face of adverse shocks.

Policy and Institutional Distortions

Economic decline was also policy-induced to some extent. A characteristic feature of economic policy in the postindependence period was the leading role assigned to the state. This was reflected in sharp increases in total government expenditure relative to GDP in most countries in our sample, very rapid capital accumulation by government, the establishment of many parastatals, and numerous interventions by government in the marketing of agricultural inputs and outputs. Most countries also introduced price controls, restrictive licensing of foreign exchange, and import prohibitions. Table 5.5 lists these policy indicators. The rationale for the growing role of government and the heavy use of administrative policy instruments was the widespread view that market processes could not be relied upon to deliver economic expansion, technological progress, and structural change about which high expectations were entertained in the wake of political liberation.

In retrospect, the state also did not live up to expectations regarding its entrepreneurial role. We can offer the following generalizations about the outcome of the experiment with statist development:

— The volume of government investment increased at a rate of 10% per year in six countries. A very high proportion was financed with foreign aid and export credits. The pattern of investment did not reflect careful project preparation and screening based on economic criteria in many instances. Instead it reflected the preferences of diverse donors, the high-pressure salesmanship of foreign suppliers of equipment, patronage by political leaders to their supporters, and sometimes plain corruption. This resulted in rising incremental capital-output ratios and considerable inefficiency.[6]

— Government (including parastatals) tended to become the employer of last resort and thereby acquired overblown staffs, particularly after the economic decline began to diminish employment opportunities in the rest of the economy. Performance and productivity in the public sector declined sharply, reflecting weaknesses in public administration. A sharp decline in public-sector real wages, particularly for highly and moderately skilled workers, undermined incentives and reduced the capacity of the public sector to compete effectively in labor markets.

— The number of parastatals increased rapidly. At the end of the 1970s there were more than one hundred parastatals in eight countries. The functioning of parastatals was bedevilled by a whole host of problems, including lack of clarity in their mandate, conflicting instructions from controlling authorities, and the lack of autonomy or accountability. Discipline was undermined by the fact that parastatals faced in many cases a "soft budget constraint"; that is, they operated with the knowledge that if they got into financial difficulties, they would get support in the form of budget subsidies, loans, cancellation of debts, and the like.

The deceleration in the rate of growth of agricultural production pictured in Table 5.1 was policy-induced to a considerable extent. There was great interest in many sample countries to promote rapid industrialization, even at the expense of penalizing agriculture. This strategy was reflected in policies that extracted taxes or marketing board surpluses from export crops for use outside agriculture and made inadequate budgetary provisions for investment or current services destined for the agricultural sector.

Government interventions in agricultural pricing and marketing were particularly damaging (Table 5.5). Producer prices were controlled frequently at relatively low levels, and this policy went hand in hand with the requirement that farmers sell their surplus to government marketing parastatals. Where private traders were allowed to buy produce, they were hemmed in by a variety of restrictions, including transport barriers (such as roadblocks) across district boundaries. In addition, fertilizer was subsidized in many cases and marketed through parastatals in some cases. Consumer prices for major cereals were frequently

TABLE 5.5
Selected Policy Indicators: End 1970s

	KEN	MAD	MAL	MAU	UGA	ZAM	SOM	SUD	TAN	ZAIRE	ZIMB
A. Role of Gov't.											
1. Increase in Gov't expenditure as percent of GDP during 1970s	6	8	10	11	-16	-2	24	2	17	-11	8
2. Rate of growth of volume of Gov't Investment during 1970s: % per annum	6	36	21	24	-23	-11	14	13	18	-8	-15
3. Number of parastatals	176	136	101	N.A.	130	114	44	138	400	138	N.A.
B. Agriculture											
4. Gov't monopoly of major cereal marketing	Yes	Yes	Yes	Yes	Yes	Yes	Yes	No	Yes	No	Yes
5. Gov't control on producer price of major cereal	Yes	Yes	Yes	N.A.	Yes	Yes	Yes	Yes	Yes	Yes	Yes
6. Consumer price subsidy for major cereal	Yes	Yes	Yes	Yes	No	Yes	Yes	Yes	Yes	No	Yes
7. Gov't monopoly of major export marketing	Yes	Yes	No	Yes	Yes	Yes	Yes	Yes	Yes	No	Yes
8. Gov't monopoly of agricultural input marketing	No	No	No	No	No	Yes	No	No	Yes	No	No
9. Fertilizer Subsidy	Yes	Yes	Yes	No	No	Yes	No	No	Yes	No	Yes

C. Industry

10. Wide dispersion of import tariffs	Yes	N.A.	No	No	Yes	Yes	No	Yes	No	Yes	N.A.	Yes	No
11. Significant incidence of import prohibitions	Yes	Yes	No	Yes	Yes	Yes	Yes	Yes	Yes	Yes	Yes	Yes	No
12. Restrictive licensing of foreign exchange	Yes	Yes	No	Yes	Yes	Yes	Yes	Yes	Yes	Yes	Yes	Yes	Yes
13. Significant price controls on industrial and other items	Yes	Yes	Yes	Yes	Yes	Yes	Yes	Yes	Yes	Yes	Yes	Yes	Yes
14. Fuel subsidy	No	No	No	No	No	Yes	Yes	Yes	Yes	Yes	No	Yes	No

D. Macro

15. Real effective exchange rate (1970=100)											
(a) 1979	90	99	94	91	770	84	117	108	91	223	72
(b) Peak since 1979	91	116	96	93	1,351	94	270	108	178	223	85
16. Real interest rate on deposits:											
(a) 1979	-1	N.A.	4	-6	N.A.	-16	-4	-14	-1	-46	-9
(b) Lowest since 1979	-3	-15	-5	-14	-46	-16	-42	-14	-7	-46	-9

Source: World Bank data files.

subsidized. This kind of regime generated the following kinds of problems:

— Emergence of illegal or semilegal parallel markets or smuggling at prices much higher than government-controlled levels. These "free" prices varied from place to place and over the season. Operators in these unofficial markets were subject to the risk of harassment and arrest. Correspondingly, they incurred high transaction costs, and their insecurity inhibited investment in market development.
— Meanwhile, fixed, official, panterritorial and pantemporal prices undermined farmers' incentives to store produce or to transport it from surplus to deficit areas. Inflexibility and bureaucratization of parastatals led to rising costs and deterioration in the quality of marketing services provided to farmers.
— Fertilizer was subsidized with the objective of promoting its use and also to offset the impact of low producer prices or very high costs of locally manufactured fertilizer. These policies have seldom proved to be effective. The benefits of the subsidy did not reach the small farmer, or where it reached the farmer, it led to wasteful use of fertilizer.
— The widespread tendency to subsidize the consumer price of major cereals led to the emergence of black markets and budgetary pressures. The beneficiaries of such subsidies tended to be in the capital city, and they were not necessarily the underprivileged group, subject to high malnutrition. The availability of subsidized cereals in small towns and rural areas was much less, although the prevalence of malnutrition in these parts of the country was much higher than in the capital city.

Policies affecting the industrial sector were also a matter of some concern (Table 5.5). The main thrust was to replace imported manufactured goods with locally fabricated substitutes, except in Mauritius, which put the emphasis on export promotion. Another important strand of policy in Madagascar, Zambia, and Uganda was to reduce dependence on private foreign investors. These policies were reflected in the following:

— Extremely high tariffs on imported consumer goods (up to 300% in Uganda, 220% in Kenya, 100% in Zambia) with low duties on intermediate and capital goods, leading to a wide dispersion in the tariff structure

— A growing list of goods whose import was prohibited in several countries, thereby providing infinite protection to local manufacturers
— The spread of restrictive licensing of imports of competing goods as a result of pressures on the balance of payments, thereby providing high protection to local industry
— A growing number of parastatals to take over foreign private firms and to start new undertakings financed with external loans on conventional terms
— The spread of price controls on locally manufactured items to offset the impact of high protection against imports and to protect consumers against monopolists and speculators

This policy frame led to the development of manufacturing that catered mainly to the home market and was capital- and import-intensive. Investments were undertaken based on little technical, financial, or economic analysis, which added to external debt without commensurate economic benefits to the national economy. Delays in government decisions on changing controlled prices precipitated financial losses in producing firms. Furthermore, the policy of controlling prices on the basis of costs undermined the incentive for efficiency. As the foreign exchange situation worsened progressively at the end of the 1970s and in the early 1980s, it became more and more difficult to obtain imported inputs necessary for utilizing existing capacity in the manufacturing sector.

Although the state assumed a very forceful posture in spearheading economic development by expanding the public sector and by intervening at many points in agriculture and industry, government policy on exchange rates remained curiously passive throughout the 1970s.[7] Somalia, Zaire, and Tanzania experienced considerable appreciation in the real exchange rate, and in Uganda the official rate lost all touch with reality (Table 5.5). Although the exchange rate had not appreciated much in other countries, compared to 1970, the official rate in several instances did not reflect the scarcity of foreign exchange, which was rationed administratively. In turn, economic policies in these countries did not provide sufficient incentives for earning or saving foreign exchange by making investments and taking risks in new activities aimed at efficient import substitution and the diversification of exports.

INITIAL POLICY RESPONSES

To summarize our analysis so far, let us recall the following conclusions:

— The extent and duration of the economic decline in sample countries differed very considerably.
— The magnitude of exogenous shocks also varied a great deal. Mauritius, Malawi, and Kenya suffered sizeable adverse shocks during 1979–81, and Mauritius was the victim of further convulsions in 1981–83. Also, Zambia had been hit very hard earlier in the 1970s. Tanzania suffered notable losses during 1981–83. In the rest of the sample, terms of trade declines were largely or totally offset by rising ODA, although restrictions on uses to which ODA could be put proved to be a major obstacle in effective macroeconomic management. Furthermore, governments tended to behave asymmetrically with respect to windfall gains and losses, raising expenditures quickly in good times but failing to make downward adjustments in bad times.
— Most governments in our sample assumed a forceful, entrepreneurial role in promoting economic development that created a large number of policy and institutional distortions. These tended to impede agricultural and industrial growth as well as the efficiency of the public sector.

Demand Management

Given the substantial disequilibrium in both fiscal and external accounts (Table 5.2), it was very clear that governments had to restrain aggregate demand as well as to take measures to increase production and exports. In fact, the emphasis placed on demand management has dominated the policy scene. Many of the countries in our sample negotiated a series of agreements with the IMF, and some of those succeeded in reducing both budget and external deficits (Table 5.6). Surveying these stabilization efforts, Justin B. Zulu and Saleh M. Nsouli conclude as follows:

— Public revenues were close to targets while public expenditure targets were exceeded, so that government borrowing from the banks could not be restrained as much as expected.

— Targets relating to reduction of external deficit were achieved in about a third of the cases.
— The most important factor impeding implementation of stabilization programs was unforeseen developments, such as wrong forecast of commodity prices, adverse weather conditions, disruption of transport, and shortfalls in external assistance.[8]

The pursuit of stabilization meant a sharp reduction in the real rate of growth of gross domestic expenditure, both consumption and investment. Table 5.6 lists countries in order of the extent of retrenchment in 1978–83. Six countries recorded an absolute decline in GDE, and another three showed increases lower than the rate of growth of population. Per capita private consumption fell in ten countries, and the volume of gross investment declined in six. The volume of imports was curtailed in ten cases and real government expenditure in three. Primary enrollment ratios stopped rising in many cases as they had been doing during the postindependence period. These ratios actually declined in Somalia and Tanzania. Progressive trends relating to life expectancy were also interrupted. The quality of education and health services deteriorated substantially. To the extent that progress was achieved toward stabilization, it was mainly through a reduction of real demand rather than an expansion of supply. This outcome was inevitable insofar as excess demand had accumulated during preceding periods without much remedial action. Also, many countries encountered further exogenous shocks while they were trying to stabilize, and these added to the requirements for demand restraint.

It is worth considering, however, if a less traumatic outcome could have been obtained by giving greater recognition to structural constraints, specific bottlenecks, and policy distortions at the sectoral or micro levels. This would have implied (1) placing more emphasis on supply-side measures; (2) adopting a longer time frame for adjustment that allowed fully for lags typical of primary producing African situations; and (3) providing more external financing on suitable terms to support these policy reforms during the course of implementation. Such policy packages might have avoided or at least reduced substantially the underutilization of capacity that was a widespread occurrence in many sectors and many countries during the 1980s. Among the multiple causes for idle capacity was the unavailability of foreign exchange for imported intermediate goods and spare parts. There were instances in which foreign aid was available for new projects of dubious value but not for

TABLE 5.6
Impact of Demand Management Policies

Country	Number of Credit Tranche Arrangements with IMF in 1980's	Budget Deficit as % of GDP a/ Peak Ratio a/	Budget Deficit as % of GDP a/ 1983 Ratio	External Deficit as % of GDP a/ Peak Ratio a/	External Deficit as % of GDP a/ 1983 Ratio	Gross Domestic Expenditure b/ A	B	C	Imports b/ A	B	C	Government Expenditure 72/79	79/83
Uganda	4	4	1	c/	c/	3	1	-20	-4	-9	9	-19	22
Malawi	3	7	3	24	11	6	6	-4	8	5	-8	11	-6
Mauritius	4	11	6	14	3	3	11	-3	7	9	-9	27	2
Somalia	4	11	-2	21	20	3	9	-2	9	8	-3	20	4
Tanzania	1	10	8	14	9	6	6	-1	8	1	-13	14	1
Madagascar	5	10	4	18	11	4	-1	-1	0	2	-10	28	-19
Kenya	4	6	-3	14	6	10	5	0	6	3	-15	8	5
Sudan	3	5	0	7	3	0	17	1	5	8	0	8	-4
Zambia	3	14	7	21	8	1	-3	2	-1	-9	-4	-1	0
Ethiopia	1	8	8	7	7	4	4	3	0	6	-2	7	18
Zaire	3	10	9	12	10	7	-5	6	14	-18	-12	-5	9
Zimbabwe	2	6	-1	12	7	8	-2	9	6	-11	11	7	13

a Defined as in Table 5.2.
b A = 1967–73, B = 1973–78, C = 1978–83.
c The deficit in 1983 was $32 million compared to a peak of $143 million in 1978.

Sources: World Bank data files; UNCTAD, Handbook of International Trade and Development Statistics, UN, 1985.

critically needed imported inputs. Governments found it impossible to meet current foreign exchange requirements even for export activities. Furthermore, the austerity regime adopted in many cases prevented the full budgetary funding of nonwage recurrent outlays (on materials, petrol, drugs, textbooks, and so on) required to deploy effectively government extension workers, maintenance personnel, teachers, health workers, and the like. In addition, the cut imposed on government investment was so drastic in several cases that the implementation of high-priority ongoing projects was disrupted, thereby delaying the positive supply-side effects of investments on which considerable resources had been spent already.

Supply-Side Measures

Even though the initial policy response was dominated by efforts to curtail aggregate demand, a number of sample countries were able to take some measures to improve incentives and to ease structural constraints. To illustrate this process we present a sketch of recent changes in policies in Mauritius and Zambia.

Mauritius experienced rapid growth until 1980, when it faced a serious economic crisis resulting from the collapse of sugar prices and the effects of two oil-price increases. Increased fuel costs not only sharply raised the cost of fuel imports, but adversely affected the country's important tourist industry. The government's initial response to these events was to sustain employment through an expansionary fiscal policy; this did not prove to be workable, however. The government then agreed to adopt new policy and institutional measures in the context of a series of five IMF standby operations. Despite continuing exogenous shocks (Tables 5.3 and 5.4), Mauritius has succeeded not only in reducing sharply its financial disequilibria (Table 5.6) but also in securing a base for diversification in its production and exports.

Over the past several years, both consumption and investment in Mauritius have been reduced in real terms (Table 5.6). Public investment was cut by delaying large, ongoing, capital-intensive projects estimated to yield relatively low economic returns. The efficiency of resource use in the public sector (both capital and current outlays) was improved considerably, and consumer subsidies were reduced. In addition, the exchange rate was managed flexibly in combination with an effective policy of wage restraint. These measures helped to restore international competitiveness to the export of manufactured goods, and after stagnating or growing very slowly for several years, the volume of manufactured exports rose by 30% in 1984 and by 25% in 1985. Tourism receipts increased as well, by 10% and 8% respectively. These turnabouts in production and exports were encouraging, as the economy of Mauritius had to operate at a low level in the early 1980s during the years of stabilization. The rate of unemployment, for instance, rose from 7% in 1979 to 23% in 1982 before declining slightly in 1983–1984.

Even during the period of stabilization Mauritius took a number of steps designed to lay the foundation for renewed economic growth in the context of two structural adjustment loans from the World Bank. First, the government addressed the problems facing the sugar industry and adopted a program aimed at reducing production costs by centralizing and rehabilitating sugar mills, raising the productivity of small planters, and modifying the industry's fiscal and legal framework. Second, agricultural diversification was encouraged by reducing price subsidies on imported wheat and rice, promoting the production of potatoes and green vegetables (which is now meeting local demand, with a surplus for export), and designing policies to promote the production of livestock, dairy products, and fish. Third, measures were taken to strengthen the export-policy regime by establishing a scheme to guarantee export credit, an export development and investment authority, and a coordinating unit for industrial development. Furthermore, the government has removed twenty-two products from the list of prohibited imports and twenty-seven items from imports subject to quantitative restrictions; these instruments of policy will no longer be used. In addition, items subject to price control have been reduced from seventy-four to eight and those subject to control of markup from thirty-nine to nineteen. Fourth, an energy policy was formulated that aims at converting the generation of power from fuel oil and diesel fuel to bagasse; two sugar factories have already started projects in this field. While many aspects of policy need further adaptation, these four sets of measures provide considerable evidence that Mauritius is making serious efforts to design and implement a program of structural adjustment.

Zambia experienced a moderate rate of growth until copper prices collapsed in 1975. At first, the government tried to finance its way out of the difficulties, hoping for a recovery in copper prices. External debt rose sharply; payment arrears soon began to accumulate, and creditors tried to limit or reduce their exposure. Next, Zambia entered into a series of agreements with the IMF that were interrupted frequently. Financial imbalances were reduced sharply (Table 5.6), but only at the expense of very substantial contraction in imports, which undermined production. In retrospect, it must be admitted that both the acuteness and duration of the decline in copper prices were grossly underestimated by all parties; as a result, the scope and character of the policy and institutional reforms that were set in motion were never commensurate with the gravity of the crisis. Furthermore, Zambia had to cope with various other shocks, including the disruption of normal transport routes through Zimbabwe and, in recent years, drought in some of its major food-producing areas.

Among the twelve countries in our sample, Zambia probably represents the most difficult structural adjustment problem. Its economic decline is of extraordinary proportions. Copper has dominated the economy, contributing 30% to 40% of GNP and over 90% of foreign exchange. Known reserves will permit production at present rates for only seventeen years, new ore discoveries are unlikely, and mining conditions are expected to deteriorate gradually. Zambia needs to put in place a policy frame that will permit rapid diversification in production and exports. This diversification will take at least a decade to make a substantial impact on the economy. Meanwhile, the mining industry has to play a critical role in supplying the savings and foreign exchange needed to finance the diversification effort.

The government has recently made a fresh start in the reform effort in the context of a series of sector-adjustment World Bank loans. First, the real exchange rate was devalued by 27% during 1983–1984, thereby beginning a process aimed at restructuring the incentive system and dismantling onerous controls on the allocation of foreign exchange. Second, agricultural producer prices were raised from 1981–1984 by 30% in real terms, and the government is committed to the principle of pitching these at the level of export or import parity. Prices of maize, fertilizer, and tractor hiring are still subsidized, but the government is committed to phasing them out. The maximum tax rate on farm income was reduced from 80% to 15% during 1981–82. The government has agreed to introduce competition among official marketing agencies, cooperatives, and private traders, although this new policy has not yet been implemented. Third, the government decontrolled wholesale and retail prices for manufactures and other items, except for maize meal, wheat flour, bread, and candles, in December 1982. Controlled prices of these items were raised substantially. The government imposed a 10% minimum tariff on imports of many inputs that previously bore no duty in October 1984, thereby reducing to some extent the dispersion of tariff rates. INDECO, the parastatal holding company in the manufacturing sector, also has made some progress in systematically screening proposals for new public investment, and it is proposed to continue this work through the newly created Economic Evaluation Unit. Finally, the government has resolved to improve the competitiveness and efficiency of the mining sector. It has recognized that the emphasis on efficiency may require closure of uneconomic mines and a reduction of the labor force. A drastic cost-cutting program was initiated in May 1982, leading to a 17% reduction in operating costs and a 34% drop in capital costs by the end of 1983.

The road to Zambia's recovery will be a long one. Traveling on this journey will be very demanding of sustained economic and political discipline. It will also require extraordinary support from Zambia's donors and creditors.[9]

THE POLICY PROCESS: SOME THOUGHTS

The initial response of many African governments to the economic decline during the late 1970s was highly tentative. There was considerable reluctance to accept the irreversibility of some of the external factors causing the decline or to acknowledge that domestic policies were responsible for part of the difficulties. Time was lost while governments hoped that the terms of trade would improve or that the international community would organize a major initiative to provide relief. Later, as the conviction grew that the deterioration was proving to be durable and that no rescue effort was emerging, a body of opinion in favor of economic policy reform began to emerge. These reform managers had to contend with the following obstacles;

— Powerful forces of inertia and the fact that the economy did not occupy the center of attention of decision makers, particularly in countries plagued with war and civil unrest.
— Ideological predisposition in favor of the existing policy frame, typically characterized by numerous government interventions aimed at correcting "market failures."[10]
— The "practical political benefits of state-led development," in the words of Carol Lancaster,[11] which took the form of leaders giving jobs, import licenses, subsidized food, and cheap credit to their supporters. Such ways of building support for the regime would have to be sacrificed on the altar of economic reforms if these implied greater use of impersonal market-oriented allocation processes.

— Acute scarcity of professional skills and of institutional capacity for (1) clarifying policy objectives; (2) diagnosing policy distortions; (3) defining options for policy reforms; (4) detailing specific measures and taking legal or administrative action to implement them; and (5) monitoring the results of the new policies with a view to obtaining feedback for the next installment of reforms.

Notwithstanding these obstacles, several countries have managed to carry out a measure of reform that in some cases goes beyond the adoption of short-run austerity measures. Some have managed to live with a more or less uninterrupted series of reform measures for almost four years. Malawi and Mauritius can be placed in this category. Others have initiated a number of major reforms during the past several years but in a manner that is neither smooth nor uninterrupted. Kenya, Somalia, and Zaire should be put in this second category. These countries have described a zigzag routine with two steps forward and one step back. Finally, there are countries, such as Zambia and Madagascar, in which the perceived need for reform has been translated only within the past year or so into significant new adjustment measures. Too much should not be read into these intercountry differences. The policy-making enterprise in most countries in our sample remains in its infancy. It will require much nourishment and protection in the years ahead to cope with continuing economic difficulties.

Some economists have visualized policy making in a highly scientific framework using quantitative techniques, optimizing models, and game-theoretic approaches. This literature is of little relevance to Africa not only because of the scarcity of data and of professional economists but also because policy making has many dimensions that cannot be analyzed in the special, rational framework of economics. We agree with Amitai Etzioni that while analytical economics has an important contribution to make, we need to think of a separate policy discipline.[12] This would have the following characteristics:

— It would draw on analytical insights from economics, political science, social psychology, and other fields.
— It would rely on past experience and practical knowledge.
— It would recognize that policy has to be made on the basis of partial knowledge and under considerable uncertainty, thereby requiring trial-and-error types of approaches.

Recognizing that policy making is more an art than a science, we want to discuss two issues that are of concern to present-day African policymakers. The first relates to the trade-off between comprehensive and sequential reforms, and the second concerns the matter of the appropriate speed of adjustment. Clearly the two issues are interrelated.

While the political and technical capacity or willingness to undertake policy reform is limited anywhere and particularly in Africa, the need for reform is large. Despite some progress toward stabilization, major problems in this area remain to be solved. We can also expect further exogenous shocks that will add to such problems. Furthermore, we have already suggested the desirability of combining demand management with medium-term supply-side measures to a much larger extent than in recent years. Finally, the policy agenda also needs to accommodate measures to deal with longer-run concerns, such as environmental stress,[13] rapid demographic expansion, the acute scarcity of professional and technical skills, and the fragility of institutions. Given this dilemma, how broad should be the scope of the reform effort?

In principle, policy packages should include all measures required to deal with key elements of the diagnosis of economic difficulties in an individual country. This is the main message of general equilibrium approaches that emphasize the interrelationships among different parts of the economic system. A comprehensive policy package would internalize all these linkages and thereby maximize the benefits of the reform. This conclusion does not stand serious scrutiny, however, when we view the reform problem from a broader standpoint. Historically, policy change has tended to be incremental rather than all-embracing, except in revolutionary situations. History teaches that policy is seldom tackled in a rational framework of maximization or optimization. In any event, optimization would necessitate taking account not only of the benefits but also of the costs of reforms. Comprehensive policy packages (frequently described jestingly as the "Christmas tree syndrome") can be very demanding of professional, managerial, and administrative skills. They require a great deal of coordination across ministries and across different levels in the bureaucracy. There is a real danger, therefore, that while economywide comprehensive blueprints of reform look attractive on paper, they may not be translatable into reality. This conclusion is reminiscent of the recent history of integrated rural development projects. It was fashionable in the early 1970s to advocate such schemes on the basis of patently convincing sets of arguments, but subsequent experience with implementation of these models has demonstrated their impracticality in many country situations.

The calculation of costs of reform must include disturbances in the equilibrium of political coalitions that characterizes the status quo. Present policies bestow wealth, income, status, and power on certain strata at the expense of other segments in society. To the extent that stabilization implies a retrenchment in aggregate expenditures, it involves at least a temporary loss in income to most segments of society. Supply-side measures will hurt particular groups and benefit others, perhaps for a considerable time. The political leaders have to manage the reform process so that policy changes do not precipitate effective countervailing action by vested interests. The implications of these political economy considerations for the scope of the policy package are not altogether clear, but it would be surprising if reforms on a wide front turned out to be sustainable, except in very special situations.

If comprehensive policy packages are ruled out on historical, public administration, and political economy grounds, then the question of appropriate sequencing of economic policy reform becomes critical. This is a large topic, largely unresearched. It is possible, nevertheless, to offer a few comments.

It might be tempting to postpone action on the longer-run issues, such as reducing fertility, and to focus on stabilization and medium-term structural adjustment. Even a vigorous population policy would yield very few tangible benefits over the next five or ten years, while the political and administrative costs can be heavy.[14] Such considerations notwithstanding, we would press for not omitting this issue from even the first policy package, given its crucial importance for the long-run future.

What should be the proper sequence of stabilization and structural adjustment measures? Recent history of reform in many countries in our sample is largely that of stabilization without much structural adjustment. Of course, some instruments of policy, such as exchange rates and interest rates, affect both aggregate demand and the incentive system, thereby promoting stabilization and structural adjustment simultaneously. In our view, a better balance between the two than actually prevailed recently would reduce welfare losses and enhance the sustainability of progress toward stabilization.

It is possible to make progress in structural adjustment while macroeconomic imbalances between aggregate demand and supply persist, as long as these disequilibria have not become chronic. For example, we can visualize rationalization of taxes, subsidies, and tariffs, as well as improvement or dismantling of price controls and import licensing, even though the economy is experiencing substantial inflation and rising external indebtedness. Beyond a certain threshold, however, macroimbalances tend to accelerate dangerously and jeopardize progress at sector and micro levels.

Some research is under way on sequencing of economic liberalization, that is, the process of decontrolling the domestic financial sectors and the trade and capital accounts of the balance of payments.[15] Although no definite conclusions are forthcoming at this stage, and although the context for the research is not Africa, it may be useful to summarize some of the tentative findings. The first is the need to reduce budget deficits to manageable proportions before reforming the policy regime governing the domestic financial sector. If domestic interest rates are raised before the budget deficit is under control, it can complicate greatly the fiscal problem. The second tentative finding is that liberalization of imports requires a substantial adjustment period during which local firms have to improve their productivity and thereby enhance their competitiveness. The research does not discuss the proper sequence of import liberalization on the one hand and export promotion on the other, but this remains a pivotal issue. The third tentative finding is that dismantling controls on the capital account of the balance of payments should follow reforms of policy regimes governing external trade and domestic finance.

We have noted that policy distortions exist in several major sectors in most sample countries. If simultaneous reform in all these sectors is not feasible, structural adjustment can proceed sequentially. The first policy package should aim at removing distortions of strategic importance so that its implementation can have a beneficial multiplier effect through the relaxation of a number of key constraints. In all likelihood, such a policy package in sample countries will focus on agricultural strengthening. This can be followed by subsequent policy packages focusing on other problem areas in agriculture or in other sectors.

The removal of specific distortions or families of interrelated distortions usually requires a simultaneous change in a number of policy instruments. For example, the strengthening of agricultural production incentives may require a depreciation of the exchange rate, raising of producer prices, lowering of export taxes, increased allocation of foreign exchange for agricultural inputs, and the introduction of competition in the hitherto single-channel marketing of both inputs and outputs. Additional measures may also have to be taken to phase out budget subsidies on the consumer price of cereals and fertilizers or to strengthen research, extension, and credit. It may not be feasible to move on all these fronts at once, but an effective policy package will have to include a critical minimum subset of such measures in order to secure significant progress in this problem area.

Finally with regard to the emotive subject of the appropriate speed of adjustment, some have argued for the "quick fix," while others see virtue in dragging out the adjustment phase. Debate on this topic is confused because "adjustment" means different things to different commentators. To some, adjustment simply means reduction in budget and balance-of-payments deficits, but this interpretation is not acceptable to us. We should emphasize the need to move toward macroeconomic equilibrium at a reasonable level of real economic activity, that is, a combination of financial balance and resumption of economic development. Despite its imprecision, we believe that our definition provides more guidance in assessing how much progress a country is making in terms of genuine adjustment that stands a good chance of not being aborted.

Recent experience leads us to believe that attempts at a "quick fix" have a low probability of succeeding in our sample countries. We have already said that all-embracing, economywide reform is ruled out by historical, public administration, and political economy considerations. Progress is likely to be along the route of a succession of policy packages dealing in sequence with many different types of problems. Furthermore, while we do not share the extreme elasticity pessimism of some observers, it is quite clear that production and export responses to "getting the prices right" will not be as big as they are in mature and flexible economies of the OECD or even the newly industrializing country (NIC) type. Empirical estimates of these supply elasticities (both short- and long-run) in Africa are low.[16] Action to remove price distortions has to be combined, therefore, with supportive measures aimed at reducing organizational, institutional, and information constraints. These policies take considerable time to yield results.

Also, "quick fix" reform efforts often suffer from lack of preparation, consultation, and involvement of all authorities concerned, parastatals, and political party organs. They are typically engineered by the Finance Ministry alone, in collaboration with such external agencies as the International Monetary Fund and the World Bank. This lack of involvement of others, as well as the perception that it was largely designed abroad, can make the reform effort vulnerable to the criticism that it is not sufficiently adapted to local circumstances or not sufficiently responsive to unfolding events.

For these reasons we doubt the wisdom of "quick fix" approaches, but we are equally not in favor of dragging out the adjustment process. Slow adjustment is not a good prospect unless external aid in growing amounts can be obtained for a very long time. In the absence of such unconditional foreign subsidy, slow adjustment probably means sluggish production, stagnating per capita income, and rising economic stress for a considerable time. A slow pace of adjustment may also imply halfhearted reform that fails to build up the momentum required to tackle the economic situation. Given the interlocking elements that precipitated the economic crisis in sample countries, marginal changes in policy might not produce perceptible improvement and thereby might undermine the credibility of the reform effort. Such a weak reform impulse may enable vested interests to organize themselves to resist further government attempts to carry out policy changes. We conclude, therefore, that both "quick fix" and "drag out" approaches will be counterproductive in all likelihood and that governments in Africa should search for the optimal pace of adjustment, an elusive but useful concept.

It is also in the interest of foreign donors and creditor governments active in Africa to support adjustment at this optimal pace. They can do this by providing sufficient external finance to buttress the efforts of African governments undertaking intensive reform. Let us illustrate by recalling the critical importance of not neglecting the longer-run goal of birth control in the context of short- and medium-term stabilization and structural adjustment programs. Provision of basic needs services (such as education, health, and the water supply) to poor households is a key component in a broadly conceived program aimed at triggering fertility reduction. Measures can be taken to reduce per unit costs and to recover at least a part of these costs from the beneficiaries without impeding access of poor households to these basic needs services. African governments can protect public expenditures on critical economic and basic needs services and concentrate cuts required for meeting stabilization objectives on other budget items. It has to be recognized, however, that even if all these measures are taken, it may not be possible to reconcile the imperatives of stabilization, structural adjustment, and fertility reduction in the face of budgetary rigidities (such as debt services and defense and security needs) and stagnating or declining volume of new external resources. Under these circumstances, some flexibility on the part of foreign donor and creditor governments can break the logjam.

NOTES

This chapter reflects conditions prevailing in late 1985. The section entitled "Initial Policy Responses" should be read in that light.

1.   World Bank, *Accelerated Development in Sub-Saharan Africa: An Agenda for Action*, Washington, D.C., World Bank, 1981; *Sub-Saharan Africa: Progress Report on Development Prospects and Programs*, Washington, D.C., World Bank, 1983; *Toward Sustained Development in Sub-Saharan Africa: A Joint Program of Action*, Washington, D.C., 1984; *Financing Adjustment with Growth in Sub-Saharan Africa, 1986–90*, Washington, D.C., 1986.

2.   Institute for Development Studies (Sussex), "Accelerated Development in Sub-Saharan Africa: What Agenda for Action?" *IDS Bulletin* 14, no. 1, January 1983, whole issue.

3.   See United Nations Information Service (ECA), "The World Bank and Africa's Development Strategy," Information Sheet no. 4, September 29, 1982.

4.   Douglas Wheeler, "Sources of Stagnation in Sub-Saharan Africa," *World Development* 12, no. 1, 1984, 1–23.

5.   World Bank, *Accelerated Development*, 4–6, 16, 132.

6.   Ravi Gulhati and Gautam Datta, "Capital Accumulation in Eastern and Southern Africa — A Decade of Setbacks," *World Bank Staff Working Paper*, no. 562, April 1983.

7.   Ravi Gulhati, Swadesh Bose, and Vimal Atukarala, "Exchange Rate Policies in Eastern and Southern Africa, 1965–1983," *World Bank Staff Working Paper*, no. 720, February 1985.

8.   Justin B. Zulu and Saleh M. Nsouli, "Adjustment Programs in Africa: The Recent Experience," *IMF Occasional Paper*, no. 34, April 1985, 26–27.

9.   For a discussion of donor and creditor response, see E. V. K. Jaycox, R. I. Gulhati, S. Lall, and S. Yalamanchili, "The Nature of the Debt Problem in Eastern and Southern Africa," in Carol Lancaster and John Williamson, eds., *African Debt and Financing*, Special Reports, 5, Washington, D.C., Institute for International Economics, 1986.

10.   Crawford Young classifies several of our sample countries as follows: (1) Afro-Marxist group: Ethiopia, Madagascar, Somalia; (2) Populist Socialist group: Tanzania; (3) African Capitalist group: Kenya, Malawi. Despite significant differences, all three groups share a predilection for numerous government interventions. See Crawford Young, *Ideology and Development in Africa*, New Haven, Conn., Yale University Press, 1982.

11.   Two extracts from Carol Lancaster might be useful:

Patron-client relations are important elements in politics throughout the world. But since independence, they have come to play an especially prominent role in many African countries, where leaders are less reliant on open political competition and periodic elections to maintain their position and more on the continuing support of key groups and individuals.

A number of experts, both African and foreign, have begun to explore the role of traditional values and obligations in the African political economy.

... African government officials, Ekeh argues, will be judged by their associates in primordial groupings on whether they "channel part of the largesse from the civic public to the primordial public. . . . The unwritten law of the dialectic is that it is legitimate to rob the civic public in order to strengthen the primordial public. . . ." Another long-time observer of the continent, Goren Hyden, describes an "economy of affection" as influencing Africans at all levels of life, "a network of support, communications and interaction among structurally defined groups connected by blood, kin, community or other affinities. . . ." Hyden goes on to describe the economy of affection as imposing "social obligations on individuals that limit their interest and capacity to support public concerns outside their community, however defined. It tends to perpetuate a locale-specific outlook which often comes into conflict with the principles on which national development is based."

See Lancaster, "Thoughts on Policy Reform in Africa," typescript, Georgetown University.

12.   Amitai Etzioni, "Making Policy for Complex Systems: A Medical Model for Economics," *Journal of Policy Analysis and Management* 4, no. 3, 1985, 383–95.

13.   L. R. Brown and E. C. Wolf, *Reversing Africa's Decline,* Worldwatch Paper no. 65, Washington, D.C., Worldwatch Institute, June 1985, 65–72.

14.   Rashid Faruquee and Ravi Gulhati, "Rapid Population Growth in Sub-Saharan Africa — Issues and Policies," *World Bank Staff Working Paper,* no. 559, February 1983.

15.   S. Edwards, "The Sequencing of Economic Liberalization in Developing Countries," Country Policy Department Trade and Adjustment Division of the World Bank (CPDTA), Policy Note no. 1.

16.   M. E. Bond, "Agricultural Responses to Prices in Sub-Saharan African Countries," *IMF Staff Papers* 30, no. 4, December 1983, 703–26.

6
Images and Realities of Responsibility toward Africa

Princeton Lyman

There are several very different images of Africa. Each of them gives a different sense of what its problems are and how we see and respond to them.

One image of Africa, perhaps held by many long-time Africanists, was drawn particularly well by C. Payne Lucas and Kevin Lowther in an article for the *Washington Post*. In a continent with some of the planet's harshest environments, Lucas and Lowther see a stirring struggle of noble and sensitive people. "Africa is not a place for the weak and lazy," they write. "Africans are survivors — by necessity." Reporters may focus on coups, corruption, and disasters — "the quick and dirty story" — but those stories do not tell of the accomplishments achieved through painful trial and error. "We do not learn much about the evolution of political systems appropriate to African conditions, about the ability of African farmers to coax food from the soil or about the 'soul' of Africa — the people's understanding of their place in the cosmos."While Africa needs help from abroad, Africans, in their deep consciousness of nature, inhabit, in the words of Kenneth Kaunda, "a larger world than the sophisticated Westerner." This is their gift to mankind.[1]

The views expressed here are those of the author and do not necessarily represent the opinions of the U.S. government.

117

Africa's popular image, however, especially in recent times, is quite different. It is an image of disaster, of drought, starvation, and death. It is the picture of millions of helpless people clutching stick-figured babies to dried breasts, without hope unless outside help arrives. We are vaguely reminded that this is a recurrent phenomenon (one organization in its fund-raising used films of the 1974 drought right up to the more recent disaster). As the drought fades from our television screens, Africa recedes from our consciousness back into its incomprehensible sea of woes, to emerge again only when its misery becomes truly catastrophic. It is an image that calls forth our sympathy, indeed brings forth incredible acts of generosity and giving. But it is not an image that creates admiration, nor is it one that conjures up much hope.

There is yet a different image, put forward most often by Africans and by sympathetic intellectuals. It is of a continent buffeted by external factors over which it has no control: not only weather, soil, and disease, but terms of trade that have reduced Africa's purchasing power by more than half in recent years, imposed by commodity exchanges that determine prices of Africa's principal exports in London, Chicago, or Tokyo. Africa is caught up in an international system of economics, science, and technology that seems to make catching up with the rest of the world a futile dream. This system makes leaps — in computers, product substitutes, and satellite communications — that render African resources increasingly irrelevant and the tasks of modernization all the more expensive. Africa, with vast reserves of oil, copper, timber, iron ore, and rubber, finds itself the last continent to "modernize" at a time when these once-valuable resources are in surplus, when newly discovered sources of supply leave Africans to run their mines and plantations at a loss just to maintain employment and a small inflow of foreign exchange, victims since the 1970s of a seemingly unending buyers' market.

There is, however, another image, more brutal and cynical. In a series in the *Wall Street Journal* entitled "Road to Ruin," Africa's and Africans' own errors are considered to be as significant as anything that nature or international markets have inflicted. Against the promise that was present at Africa's early days of independence, when Zaire's economic development was comparable to parts of southern Italy and Senegal's to South Korea, Africa has witnessed since then "tribal warfare, coups, butchery, corruption, mismanagement and a seemingly endless list of man-made misfortunes." State intervention robbed the economy of incentives, swelled bureaucracies, and spawned decay.

Hundreds of millions of dollars went for prestige projects or investments that had no chance to succeed. After $60 billion of foreign aid, Africa was more dependent than ever. "Cities have grown shabby as the people have become poorer." Politics drove out economics; schools have expanded but are now without books or pencils; carpenters graduate from technical schools without ever having used a hammer. "Mismanagement" is the word and the tone that resound throughout the series. The image leaves one in the end without either hope or pity. "It's not only Africans that cannot make it work," a banker is quoted, "it's something about Africa itself."[2]

IMAGES AND THE ISSUES OF POLICY REFORM

These several images, sometimes contrasting, sometimes overlapping, shape not only popular perceptions of Africa but informed opinion as well. They have clearly had an effect on the debate over economic policy reform that has become central to much of the development discussion on Africa. Today there is much greater consensus on the need for policy adjustment in Africa than just a few years ago. Still, the debate over the importance or relevance of policy change, as opposed to other, more traditional approaches to African development, has taken on the coloration of these images and is not entirely over. Africa as "victim" made policy adjustment seem cruel; Africa as hopeless made it seem irrelevant; Africa as mismanaged made it sound like retribution.

None of this has made policy adjustment any easier to analyze or implement. Nor do these images promote strong support for long-term development assistance — as opposed to humanitarian aid that might be given in large amounts — because they do not promote confidence that such aid would produce results. Yet images are not drawn wholly from imagination. All of these images, especially when stripped of any mean-spirited or pejorative character, contain seeds of the "problem." They can help us see the relevance of and indeed critical need for policy adjustment. Policy adjustment is, or should be, a response to reality, whether that reality is externally or internally caused, whether by nature or man.

The realities of Africa do demand change. Africa faces a hostile environment. Painful experience tells us that weather vagaries are not an aberrant phenomenon but an integral part of the African environment, placing finite limits on reliable cultivation of Africa's semiarid lands, putting down markers about the wisdom of some of the larger irrigation schemes, and reinforcing the urgent need for new, better-adapted technologies. International markets for Africa's traditional exports will not likely recover for a decade, perhaps never to their former levels. One can rail against the "system" as one might against nature. But world markets are not any longer, if they ever were, easily controlled or managed. Diversification and rationalization of exports is not only sound policy, it is virtually a prescription for survival in today's world. There is, finally, a new generation growing into maturity in Africa, one that is looking critically at those human imperfections, those too-easily claimed privileges, all those elements of gross corruption that have no place in a truly modernizing society. These too are seeds, and political imperatives, of policy change.

THE EMERGENCE OF A NEW IMAGE

African leaders are acutely aware of the images, mostly unfavorable, that occupy the minds of Westerners when they think of Africa. More important, they are painfully conscious of the realities that confront their countries and of the imperatives for change. It was with awareness of both these facets of international attention to Africa that the African leadership, after long and painstaking preparations within the Organization of African Unity and the UN Economic Commission for Africa, approached the UN General Assembly's Special Session on the African Economic Crisis in May 1986. The special session was extraordinary in several ways. It was the first time that the UN General Assembly had devoted a session to the problems of one region. It was also the first time since the devastating drought of the 1980s, which had caught so much of the world's attention, that the African leaders were in a position to state their view of the continent's problems before international opinion.

The session may have witnessed the emergence of a new image of Africa. Spurning older approaches or excuses or supplication, the African leaders laid out their own program for recovery and growth. It contained many aspects of courageous policy adjustment, voiced strong support for agriculture and for more free market determination of prices and exchange rates, and called upon the African nations to raise most of the capital needed to achieve both recovery and growth. It was a statesmanlike and serious approach, and it did not go unnoticed.

Every major newspaper ran articles and editorials highlighting the new image that Africa portrayed at this UN session. Africa was commended for its courage, its honesty of analysis, and its dedication in addressing the critical problems it faced. The *Wall Street Journal,* which had run perhaps the harshest series on Africa's economic problems, referred to the "truly serious special session" that had just occurred. It spoke of a "new bargain" between Africa and the industrialized countries, one based on "realism."[3] The *New York Times* entitled its editorial "Something Better out of Africa" and said that a new generation of African leaders had made their voices heard.[4] The *Washington Post* spoke of a moment of "rare promise."[5] Nearly every account concluded that this spirit of determination and courageousness by Africa deserved strong international support if the new policies were to have a chance of success.

The new image, however, is in its infancy. So far, it is confined to the few who read those editorials and who follow the course of African events most closely. Popular images still retain the earlier pictures.[6] They will not fade easily. They are the images that may still control the extent of popular response to the new degree of African determination displayed at the UN special session and in policy adjustments taking place all across the continent, even when new responses are in order. The older images, in the end, will only be removed over time as different realities begin to predominate, repeated in the reports that filter back about Africa until they replace earlier ones.

THE U.S. RESPONSE: BILATERAL VERSUS MULTILATERAL AID

Africa's embrace of difficult policy adjustments and dedication to market-oriented growth strategies come at the precise time when the United States faces one of its own most serious budget crises. Foreign aid, which is one of the most important tools by which the industrialized countries can lend support to policy change, is in trouble. Caught between demands for budget restraint, efforts to hold down taxes, and struggles over the degree of domestic versus defense-related cuts, foreign aid is being sustained at historic levels only for countries of great and immediate strategic importance to the United States. The Africa program in fiscal year 1986 declined for the first time in a decade. Africa's share of future aid is in question.

Part of the outcome will be shaped by "images" — not only the images of Africa described above, but our images of the role of aid in support of such sensitive matters as policy adjustment, now perhaps the number-one priority in Africa. One of the "images" popular in some quarters is that policy adjustment is so delicate and controversial that it is best left to multilateral rather than bilateral aid agencies. The debate over multilateral versus bilateral aid, related not only to policy adjustment but to growth and development strategies generally, has been played out in Congress and among development professionals for years. It is a debate, unfortunately, that often lends itself to distorting the subtle relationship that actually exists between multilateral and bilateral donors.

The argument that multilateral agencies, particularly the World Bank and the IMF, should remain in the forefront of assisting countries with policy reform is persuasive. Policy reform involves changes that are, domestically, politically explosive in their impact — removal of subsidies, shifting internal terms of trade and shares of income, eliminating sources of patronage and profit, and inducing periods of austerity and, for some, unemployment. Multilateral agencies are deemed to be apolitical, objective, professional. Their ability to persuade leaders of the necessity for reform and to negotiate such reforms as conditions of assistance is therefore believed to be greater than that of bilateral donors and to carry less onerous overtones of "political pressure," neocolonialism, or interference in sovereign affairs.

Multilateral agencies also have built up professional staff expertise in macroeconomic and financial matters, more so than any single donor. Dialogue with individual countries on delicate issues such as these is part of their ongoing mandate and takes place on a regular basis even outside negotiation of assistance of standby programs, as in the Article IV consultations of the IMF and the regular economic reports of the World Bank.

These assumptions are all true, but not as categorically as some would assert. Above all, the international institutions do not act in a vacuum. They neither are nor are perceived in Africa to be totally "apolitical" even if they do not reflect the political interests of any one member. Furthermore, precisely because policy reforms are politically controversial, the multilateral agencies can only be as effective as political conditions permit. Those conditions must be present within the country being assisted. But they must also be present in the international community.

Specifically, the strength of the multilateral agencies in these difficult situations comes often from the degree to which they are backed up by their "owners." When it leans into more delicate and controversial issues, the World Bank looks over its shoulder to be sure that its principal creditors are supportive, not only in the board, where direct responsibility can be diffused, but in bilateral actions. Put another way, like any bank, the World Bank seeks to share the risks — and in the case of policy reform we are talking of politically high-risk ventures. The World Bank is always more comfortable in a controversial area of reform if key bilateral donors are taking the same line; at a minimum when they will not offer the country in question an easier alternative, thus in effect shutting the Bank out of real leverage; at best when they put their own bilateral aid on the line in back of the same reforms.

Moreover, in individual country situations the political weight of a key bilateral donor can be telling, precisely because that bilateral relationship carries so much political importance. If Sweden in Tanzania, the United States in Liberia, the Belgians in Zaire, the French in Senegal are all placing political weight on the need for policy adjustments, the opportunities and effectiveness of the multilateral agencies are greatly enhanced.

There is also need for diversity in analysis. The multilateral agencies do indeed have depth in economic expertise that goes beyond that of any single donor. But this expertise does not make them infallible. They can be wrong, or insensitive, or simply lacking enough experts on the site to understand the full implications of policy changes being advocated. By contrast, the United States has perhaps the largest permanent overseas development staff of any donor, multilateral or bilateral. It has insights into policy issues that headquarters-based analysts may well miss. Other donors have this capacity in particular countries. In sum, policy adjustment is too central, too important in Africa in the coming decade to be left to the multilateral agencies alone.

Finally, the implications and costs of reform are so great that the resources of the multilateral agencies will not be sufficient to cover the transitional costs such adjustment requires. Under these circumstances, the bilateral donors cannot enjoy the luxury of putting their funds into other activities, expecting the multilaterals alone to finance these costs. In time of scarcity all donor resources become relevant. Bilateral aid will continue for its own "political" reasons. To the extent that it is joined with the multilaterals in support of reform, therefore, the resources problem is eased. Thus a more complex, symbiotic relationship exists, and must exist, between bilateral and multilateral agencies in the area of reform. If all the responsibility for support of policy adjustment is placed with the multilateral agencies, the momentum of adjustment will, without question, be weakened.

The United States moreover, plays a unique role. We are the largest single donor in the world community, and even when our resources are not telling in a particular situation, our voice is great. It is illogical, therefore, to expect that if the United States' own bilateral program is not geared to support of policy adjustment, not only in words but in the form of aid most needed to back such reform, we can lend full support even within the multilaterals to this effort. We have a tendency toward uniformity in approach between our own and the other programs — witness the strong role of the United States in the 1970s not only in shifting its own program toward what were called "basic human needs" but urging the multilaterals as well as other bilateral donors to do the same. If there develops a serious bifurcation between how we allocate our own resources and what we urge the multilaterals to do, eventually there will be dissonance. We will find arising from our bilateral program voices that hearken to older images, that find policy reform too demanding, among other things, of balance-of-payments aid, when what Africa needs is "humanitarian" aid. If that happens, we will have failed to learn one of the most important lessons of the 1970s, namely that health, education, and agricultural programs cannot be sustained without a sound economic foundation.

The United States has played an active role in recent years in support of policy adjustment, utilizing its bilateral and multilateral voice in reinforcing ways. In fiscal year 1985 the United States initiated, on the bilateral side, the Economic Policy Reform Program, a multiyear effort involving additional, quickly disbursed balance-of-payments aid — the type the World Bank argues is most relevant in support of these reforms — for African countries undertaking difficult but important policy adjustments. The EPRP was a precursor and later a parallel effort to the World Bank's Special Program for Sub-Saharan Africa.

In late 1985, at the annual meeting of the IMF and World Bank in Seoul, U.S. Treasury Secretary James Baker proposed a more active multilateral effort for this purpose, involving a closer collaboration between the IMF and the Bank in support of growth and providing for more concessional funds for poorer countries such as those in Africa. Both institutions adopted the principles of this proposal. In early 1986 the IMF created the Structural Adjustment Facility, which will make available close to $800 million more in concessional financing to Africa than would otherwise have been the case, and specifically in support of policy adjustments that will lead to greater growth. The World Bank will work closely with the IMF, adding resources of its own for this purpose. A

substantial replenishment of the International Development Agency —
IDA VIII — should enable the Bank to play a very active role in this
collaborative effort.

It is significant that Secretary of the Treasury Baker urged at the same
time that bilateral resources be used to complement these programs. If
such resources were not used, not only would the total effort be deprived
of needed resources but the total political impact would be weakened.
Secretary Baker offered to devote more bilateral U.S. resources to this
effort if other donors would do likewise.

Policy adjustment is, of course, not the end of development. We still
need to understand the pathways to greater diversity, efficiency, and
quality of life in Africa that go beyond policy change. There is need for
the strengths of bilateral agencies and those outside government dedicated
to programs of improved health, education, and welfare. Somehow we
must harness these to the difficult but crucial tasks of policy adjustment,
not set them against each other. And we must find the resources to back
both those efforts, not cling to images that enable us to duck these
responsibilities.

NOTES

1.   C. Payne Lucas and Kevin Lowther, "Is Africa Going Under?" *Washington
Post,* July 14, 1985.

2.   "Road to Ruin," *Wall Street Journal,* July 15, 26, 29, and 31, 1985.

3.   "New Game in Africa," *Wall Street Journal,* June 5, 1986.

4.   "Something Better out of Africa," *New York Times,* June 5, 1986.

5.   "Partnership with Africa," *Washington Post,* June 3, 1986. See also
editorials in the *Baltimore Sun,* June 5, 1986, and the *Christian Science Monitor,* June
2, 1986.

6.   In the August 28, 1986, edition of *Washington Post,* one found the all-too-
familiar picture on page 1 of an emaciated, starving African boy — this time in Sudan,
due to civil war. Five sections back in the same edition, one found an article on the
resurgence of the Ghanaian economy due to sweeping policy measures taken during the
last several years and a picture of two happy, quite healthy Ghanaians who were re-
establishing businesses that had formerly collapsed. When such placements are reversed
on a regular basis, popular images will begin to change.

Part Two

Issues

7

Overburdened Government and Underfed Populace: The Role of Food Subsidies in Africa's Economic Crisis

Raymond F. Hopkins

African states experienced not one but a number of economic problems during the 1970s and 1980s. Most dramatic among them was a food "crisis." Per capita food production declined in a majority of states during the 1970s, and in spite of growing cereal imports the per capita availability of calories appeared to be lower than it had been a decade earlier.[1] This increase in African hunger stands in sharp contrast to trends in every other region of the world, where food availabilities have grown.

What lies at the heart of Africa's food problem? A number of explanations have been offered. Prominent among these are: (1) the continuing effects of colonial and capitalist exploitation; (2) the exigencies of the current international economic situation (particularly declining terms of trade and high interest payment obligations); (3) the rapid growth of the population and its shift to urban areas; (4) weather-related production shortfalls principally caused by drought; (5) changes in production practices that have led to soil depletion and desertification; and (6) disincentives to production and marketing caused by government policies.[2] International and weather-related factors are difficult to control. Domestic policies, however, do seem correctable. I therefore focus on them.

Food price policy, in particular, has been criticized by economists. African states' attempts to establish control over producer and consumer prices of food have been blamed for causing disincentives to production, high and unproductive administrative costs to the state, and heightened inequality, particularly between rural and urban incomes. These policies have been cited by the FAO and the World Bank as a significant cause of Africa's food shortages. Some agencies that provide foreign assistance to Africa, notably the IMF and the World Bank, have made changes in the price and market intervention policies of particular African states a requirement for them to continue to receive aid. Determining the "true" role of state price and marketing actions therefore is very important to African governments, both as a guide for better policies and as a basis for engaging in policy discussions with international assistance agencies.

National food policies, especially price and marketing policies, emerged in African states in response to important political and economic forces. Often consumer subsidies were not the major aim of policies. Rather, policies were introduced to generate government revenue, dampen short-term price variations, reduce marketing risks, and eliminate possible exploitation by traders who frequently were not Africans. As a result of the way policies evolved, however, urban consumers came to expect cheap foods and held the state responsible for providing it. The pattern of intervention to subsidize food consequently cannot be easily abandoned, at least not without risking urban protests.

Even reducing food subsidies, let alone ending the state's role in controlling prices, is politically dangerous. President Numeri of Sudan was overthrown in April 1985 following protests in Khartoum that took advantage of anger over higher bread prices. In the last decade political instability and violence has occurred in Egypt, Tunisia, Liberia, and several other African states after sharp increases in the formal price of food and other key staples. These lessons, together with leaders' own readings of the mood of their relevant publics, indicate that reducing food subsidies entails significant political risk to a government.[3] In this chapter I review criticisms of government consumer food subsidies and marketing controls, offer an appraisal of government food subsidies and the machinery required to provide them, and discuss evidence and arguments concerning their desirability. My purpose is to clarify the considerations relevant to future policy on these issues in Africa and to suggest what further evidence would improve judgments as to the effects of policy.

CRITIQUES OF FOOD SUBSIDIES AND GOVERNMENT INTERVENTION

Intervention by state authorities to control the price of key food items has a long and often erratic history in colonial Africa. During World

Wars I and II, for instance, food prices in many countries' urban areas were subsidized, and rationing systems were temporarily used. Food prices and urban wage rates have frequently been explicitly linked, and food subsidies have been used as a way to reduce upward pressure on wages.[4] In Zambia, for example, consumer subsidies on maize from the 1930s to the 1950s went "almost exclusively to mining and urban workers" and overall served "not so much to aid workers as to provide the industry with a steady supply of labor."[5]

Since the time of independence, food subsidies in African states have grown. Governments have generally increased the number of food commodities over which they attempt to establish official production and retail prices. The cost of subsidies doubled in Sudan, for example, between 1981 and 1983.[6] Because residents of urban areas are the principal beneficiaries of subsidies, and because urban population has grown, the potential cost of subsidies and the political salience of food prices have risen concomitantly. Similar historical shifts occurred in Europe.[7] Sales from government marketing boards reveal the familiar urban "bias" of the beneficiaries of subsidies,[8] although where local production is high-priced, as in the case of rice in Senegal, lower urban prices are a bias relative to the country and not to external prices; indeed, consumer subsidies do not always occur.[9]

Emergency relief is one major aspect of the African food crisis that I will not examine. It does, admittedly, involve state intervention, or at least tolerance for international intervention, and does provide subsidized food. Moreover, the target of subsidies is usually rural populations. I exclude it, nevertheless, because it is such a highly variable phenomenon, because it is relatively new as a major factor in black Africa, and because the criticisms of emergency aid are quite different from those of subsidies.

Food production shortfalls in 1983–84 were brought on by droughts in the southern and Sahelian regions. The resulting need for emergency feeding to prevent or at least reduce famine is the major explanation for the dramatic rise in food imports and food aid after 1982. The food emergencies occurred, however, not simply as a result of production shortfalls. The key factor was the adaptive ability of African societies that had eroded during the earlier years and was dangerously low. Many governments were near bankruptcy, and many people's household stocks had already reached low levels.

From 1970 to 1980 estimates of food production indicated a per capita decline in most African countries. With less production, average caloric intake had also declined for most countries. With the notable exception of the Ivory Coast and the several oil-exporting states, during the 1970s residents of black African states had on the average fewer than the minimum recommended calories available for consumption (Table 7.1). Even in states that have adequate *average* caloric availability, this aggregate statistic can easily mask a growth in those who are

TABLE 7.1
Calorie Supply as Percent of National Requirements, 1967–82

(Selected African Countries)

	FAO Requirements Calories/per capita/per day	Calories supplied: % of national requirements		
		1967–69	1975–77	1978–80	1982
Algeria	2,400	77	94	100	110
Angola	2,350	83	91	90	87
Benin	2,300	95	92	100	101
Botswana	2,320	85	88	94	96
Burkina Faso	2,370	85	85	85	79
Burundi	2,330	95	92	92	95
Cameroon	2,320	90	105	106	91
Cent.Afr.Rep.	2,260	93	96	96	97
Chad	2,380	97	75	76	68
Congo	2,220	94	100	99	113
Egypt	2,510	101	114	118	128
Ethiopia	2,330	87	77	74	93
Gabon	2,340	93	113	122	88
Gambia	2,380	95	91	95	86
Ghana	2,300	96	93	88	68
Guinea	2,310	88	87	84	86
Guinea-Bissau	2,310	88	99	102	68
Ivory Coast	2,310	111	107	114	115
Kenya	2,320	97	93	89	88
Liberia	2,310	98	102	107	98
Libya	2,360	101	135	145	152
Madagascar	2,270	105	109	107	114
Malawi	2,320	92	97	96	97
Mali	2,350	88	84	85	74
Mauritania	2,310	89	81	89	97
Morocco	2,420	98	109	110	110
Mozambique	2,340	89	84	81	79
Niger	2,350	90	86	94	105
Nigeria	2,360	92	95	99	104
Rwanda	2,320	84	92	95	95
Senegal	2,380	99	97	100	101
Sierra Leone	2,300	97	91	92	85
Somalia	2,310	96	96	92	91
Sudan	2,350	84	95	101	96
Tanzania	2,320	88	91	87	101
Togo	2,300	96	88	92	94
Tunisia	2,390	93	111	115	111
Uganda	2,330	95	84	80	78
Zaire	2,220	99	102	96	98
Zambia	2,310	93	95	86	89
Zimbabwe	2,390	87	88	80	89

Source: World Bank, *World Development Reports,* various years, including 1985, 220.

malnourished (as the case of Brazil illustrates).[10] In the 1980s caloric intake has remained at only about 90% of recommended levels.[11] Furthermore, the figures from 1984–85 show a slight decline, which would have been much worse without food aid to the twenty-five states that experienced emergency needs during this period.

To review, the major trends in sub-Saharan Africa over the last fifteen years include declining per capita food production; increasing imports; increasing reliance on market purchases or emergency feeding programs; and consequently, given high population growth rates, little change in the aggregate availability of food. In spite of some skepticism as to the accuracy of the reported slow growth or actual declines in production, the deterioration in the food supply systems in Africa seems clear from the rise of imports.[12] Cereal imports to sub-Saharan Africa grew from 2.3 million metric tons in 1969–71 to an estimated 11.9 million for 1985 (Table 7.2). Even more dramatic is the rise in food aid from less than half a million tons in 1970–71 to over 6 million tons estimated in 1985. During the 1970s food aid to sub-Saharan Africa averaged about one-fifth of imports; in 1985 it covered about half of all cereal imports to the region. For some countries, notably Sudan, Ethiopia, Somalia, Tanzania, Niger, Mozambique, Mali, and Burkina Faso, food aid has come to constitute the bulk of imports. A few other countries, especially ones with an important urban population and foreign exchange resources such as Senegal, Kenya, Zaire, and Zambia, have managed both to receive large amounts of food aid and to import significant amounts of cereals commercially.

Table 7.3 reports the 1984 and estimated 1985 cereal imports and food aid for selected African states. Some data are for the marketing year, that is, 1984 refers to July 1983 through June 1984. The major increases for Ethiopia, Sudan, Mali, and Kenya represent "variable" responses to drought. In the Kenyan case the emergency need arose in 1984 and by mid-1985 had been met, so that 1986 aid commitments to Kenya were down.

Much of the aid, however, is "structural"; that is, the food is provided to fill an ongoing food deficit. The structural food deficit is caused by increased demand for cereals, often wheat, rice, or maize, the so-called "preferred cereals." When such demand, usually concentrated in urban areas, cannot be met from domestic production, at least not efficiently, import demand rises. Given the lack of foreign exchange in most African states, food aid has become an attractive vehicle to fill this import need.

TABLE 7.2
Cereal Imports and Food Aid to Sub-Saharan Africa
(Millions of Metric Tons)

Year(s) (average)	Total Imports	Year	Food Aid	Food Aid as % of Total Imports
1961 - 63	1. 18			
		1971	. 41	
1969 - 71	2. 35			
		1975	. 96	
1977 - 79	4. 86	1977	. 87	17. 9
		1979	1. 12	23. 8
1980 - 82	8. 71	1981	2. 35	27. 0
		1982	2. 17	24. 9
1984	9. 23	1984	3. 45	37. 4
1985	11. 922*	1985	6. 13*	51. 4

*Estimated.

Sources: World Bank, *Accelerated Development in Sub-Saharan Africa,* Washington, D.C., 1981, 171; World Bank, *Toward Sustained Development in Sub-Saharan Africa,* Washington, D.C., 1984, 79; and FAO, *Food Crops and Shortages, Special Report,* Rome, August 1985, 37–39.

The growth of a structural deficit and the forward planning of food aid or commercial imports to meet it are closely linked to national food policies. Let me sketch out the scenario of government food pricing policy that critics argue has resulted in growing deficits. Projections based on trends from this scenario point to import demands that are four or more times recent levels by the year 2000. Paulino projects a change in net demand in sub-Saharan Africa from minus 6 million metric tons of grain in 1980 to over minus 45 million tons in 2000.[13]

A typical African government sets the retail price for one or more key food staples, most often maize meal, wheat bread, milled rice, and sorghum flour. (Governments seldom set prices for more "traditional" foods such as millet, cassava, or yams.) Such foods are most widely used in urban areas. For the urban poor and middle class these foods constitute anywhere from one-third to two-thirds of their caloric intake. Once the consumer retail price is set, a government marketing board is usually expected to stand behind it. To be effective, this requires providing millers or retailers a product sufficiently below the announced price to compensate their costs in processing or marketing it. Alternatively, parastatals can run their own milling and even retailing operations at a loss. Government boards thus enter domestic markets to purchase from producers unprocessed grain or paddy. If the government

TABLE 7.3
Cereal Imports, Food Aid, and Growth in Per Capita Food Production
(Selected African States; Thousands of Metric Tons)

Country	1970–82 Average annual growth in food production per capita	Total Imports	1984* Food Aid	%	Total Imports	1985* Food Aid	%
Angola	-2.0	285	68	23.9	351	101	28.8
Burkina Faso	0.4	163	103	63.2	143	171	120.0
Chad	0.4	127	77	60.6	207	203	98.1
Egypt	-1.1	8,725	1,677	19.2	7,952	1,749	22.0
Ethiopia	-0.3	511	459	89.8	1,317	1,166	88.5
Ghana	-3.1	288	117	40.6	195	127	65.1
Guinea	-0.5	181	67	37.0	41	33	80.5
Ivory Coast	1.0	610	0	0	124	0	0
Kenya	-1.9	185	180	97.3	896	412	46.0
Liberia	-0.5	106	47	44.3	63	48	76.2
Mali	-0.2	292	-159	53.8	301	273	90.7
Mauritania	-0.9	270	192	71.1	184	151	82.1
Mozambique	-5.1	468	358	76.5	598	536	89.6
Niger	0.8	31	20	64.5	323	294	91.0
Nigeria	-0.1	2,508	8	0.3	824	0	0
Senegal	-1.2	682	199	29.2	530	101	19.1
Sierra Leone	-0.8	43	23	53.5	24	22	91.7
Somalia	-1.8	297	233	78.5	361	269	74.5
Sudan	-0.3	402	374	93.0	1,492	1,426	95.6
Tanzania	-1.3	355	181	51.0	410	161	39.3
Uganda	-1.0	24	17	70.8	15	15	100.0
Zaire	-1.7	224	121	54.0	158	130	82.3
Zambia	-1.3	205	77	37.6	302	220	72.8

*Estimated and actual as of July 1985; some figures in 1984 are for 1983/84 and in 1985 are for 1984/85.

Source: FAO, Food Crops and Shortages, Special Report, Rome, August 1985, 37–39.

wants the board to operate at a break-even level, the board's purchase price to producers must be set sufficiently below its selling price to cover the board's costs for purchasing, transport, storage, and handling. Seldom are producer prices set this way, however. Rather, decisions to pick a price above estimated producer operating costs, or to never lower prices, or to encourage (or not) additional production, are political decisions. The top cabinet officials and president are involved, and their calculations rest heavily upon likely political reactions of salient constituencies.

Economic costs may be entailed by these political decisions. For example, the difference between buying and selling prices for a board may be too small to cover costs; it may even be negative. The producer price is often below international prices, especially if the food crop is widely consumed (say maize rather than wheat) and is grown by many producers.[14] As a result the board may be faced with great uncertainty as to how much it will be offered for purchase. In years of favorable weather it may be offered three or five times more than in a bad year.

Over the years, as the board is faced with greatly fluctuating local supplies, its costs rise on overcrowded or underused storage and transport. It faces a stable and constant wage bill, but its tasks expand and contract. This forces the government to (1) lower producer prices, (2) absorb board deficits, or (3) withdraw from market control efforts. If food production or at least board purchases are down, governments have invariably chosen the deficit route. This may in fact entail especially large deficits if producer prices are also raised to encourage future production. By creating a price wedge the government is backed into subsidies. Governments may be selling food for as little as one-third the price of similar commodities on the parallel market. Access to government-sold food in this situation is a privilege that can benefit clever retailers, civil servants, and others with an ability to demand the right to purchase at the official retail price. Demand for government food rises; to meet this, governments turn to imports as cheaper than domestic production at higher producer prices. Imports are especially preferred when they come partly or entirely as aid. In addition, government effort to buy more cereals locally through competition in the market has several negative effects. First, it will not expand the current year's domestic food supply, but it will drive up real rural food prices. This is true whether or not the government uses legal tactics, such as quotas, to secure additional supplies or simply pays more. Second, it is likely to provide unfair windfall earnings either to those lucky few with local surpluses for sale or to those who eventually get the grain, groups likely to be already well off. Third, it will be more inflationary if the money for purchases comes from government debt. Finally, the higher price will be hard to lower in future years. If next year there were a bumper harvest, the marketing board might be overwhelmed with high-priced purchases. When this happened in Kenya in 1978, the board had to stop buying, forcing those farmers who had not sold to go to a parallel market. Parallel market prices swing more broadly as a result of the government's role in marketing food crops because the "free" market has been thinned.[15]

The scenario thus depicted reflects the first priority of African governments, which has not been to stabilize producer prices, but rather to stabilize official retail prices in urban areas.[16] This often reflects interest-group power whereby unions, the military, and civil servants are given more importance in government policy making than rural producers. These groups, urban based and organizationally powerful, can command more targeted benefits from African governments. Indeed, they are widely blamed not only for cheap-food policies but also for economic policy distortions generally.

The failure of food policy is not only a function of the priority given to fixed prices for urban groups; it is also related to government capacity. Market boards often lack the capacity to carry out the tasks assigned. Production is hard to secure except for that from state farms and government projects, and the task is almost impossible because boards lack the funds or staff to effectively carry out government price policies nationally, that is, in rural and informal sectors as well as in the formal, urban sector. This is not to say that marketing boards are efficient. Often they are very inefficient, having high operating budgets compared to the work done by their staffs, and using money for salaries rather than trucks and maintenance costs. This only exacerbates their weakness compared to the efforts required to make policy effective. Thus boards seldom stabilize national food prices, even where a substantial portion of the food crops never enters any market — formal or informal. Sometimes boards cannot even succeed in the much less demanding task of buying and selling to stabilize some urban food prices. Whatever the explanation for government and marketing board behavior, the frequent results have been high costs for the marketing tasks, subsidization of privileged consumers, and, occasionally, withdrawal by producers from dealing with marketing boards.[17]

These outcomes are criticized for their negative consequences on the economy, both on growth and equity. The 1981 World Bank Report, after acknowledging that some advantages were possible from guaranteeing low food prices, argued that

> the price policies described above have proved self-defeating. The policy of attempting to control prices and supplies of foodstuffs has, by and large, succeeded in securing only a limited supply of low-priced (and often low-quality) foodstuffs for a relatively small group of urban consumers. It has increased farmers', and traders', risks in producing and marketing food surpluses. It has failed to stabilize and indeed has actually destabilized supplies over the course of the year. Further, through its effects on farmers' supply response, it has probably resulted in a higher overall level of food prices than would have pertained without government attempts to control supplies. Reliance on imports, moreover, is creating a potentially very costly structural dependence on wheat and rice.[18]

In its 1984 report on Africa, the Bank pointed to the need to reduce public-sector expenditures, which had become "unmanageably large."[19] It applauded the elimination of parastatal control of food marketing in Sudan, Uganda, and Zaire and its reduction in Mali, Senegal, Somalia, and Zambia. While private traders were given more of a role in these countries, government price policy and elements of subsidization still exist. By 1986 even greater reform and adjustments were under way, but not without continuing long-term declines in the economy and many remnants of excessive government effort to regulate food prices.

There are four major potential costs of food subsidies: the direct fiscal cost of the subsidy, the cost to producers passed on through low prices, the management costs, if any, that result from public-sector management, and the increased government burden from having the public associate management of food prices and availabilities with its support for a government. The first element is based on the difference between government costs and the selling price. This fiscal cost is a direct government expenditure that in Sudan was estimated to be $38 million for wheat in 1982. In Zambia maize subsidies amounted to 10% of government expenditures in the 1970s and in Tanzania to $8 million for 1985, or about 6% of government expenditures.[20] In Egypt food subsidies reached the $1 billion level in 1984–85 and have led to massive grain imports — over 8 million tons of wheat and corn in 1984 compared to 1 million a decade earlier. The subsidies have led to much larger food availability, however. Thus subsidies in Egypt, in contrast to some sub-Saharan states, have not led to less food for the rural and poorest populations.[21]

The second and often larger costs of subsidies may be those borne by producers. Producers often receive low prices for their food compared to an import parity price. When the burden of cheap consumer prices is borne by producers, rather than as a fiscal cost to the state, it becomes a disguised subsidy. It nevertheless has real effects on incomes, demand, incentives, and equality. Lower production and a growth of smuggling often result. These are both real and negative economic secondary costs and could be added to the initial producer income loss.

The third cost of subsidies would be any estimated expenses from government or parastatal administration, including those resulting from the inefficiencies or lack of incentives of government operations. This assumes that private-sector efforts would be more efficient, an assumption often borne out. Finally, once people come to expect governments to be responsible for cheap food supplies, failures to provide these can generate resentment, even if the subsidies become extremely expensive. Fulfilling a "social contract" on subsidies may crowd out alternative government spending that would prove more beneficial in the long run.[22] In summary, subsidies may cost the government (and producers) real wealth and raise political exposure. Of course, subsidies can also provide a political resource to officeholders because they yield support from those benefitting from them. Indeed, if subsidies proved critical to maintaining political stability, especially during a structural adjustment situation, they might "pay" for themselves.

The second basic criticism of subsidies is their effect on consumer and producer behavior. Consumers getting subsidies shift their spending to the subsidized commodity, thus lowering demand for nonsubsidized food and other goods, often domestically produced. Since the "benefits" of subsidies usually are not available in rural areas — Egypt may be an exception — there is an extra attraction to urban life that can further accelerate rural to urban migration. It can also increase income inequalities, especially when the subsidized food is wheat or rice, foods that are less important in the diet of poor people than to those in middle-income or above categories.

A frequently cited example of a country where subsidies have had negative effects is Tanzania. During the 1970s the National Milling Corporation (NMC) bought, processed, and made available basic cereals, most prominently maize, but also rice and wheat, for retail sales, principally in Dar es Salaam (about half its sales were there) and other major cities. As demand rose, the NMC turned to food imports, first commercial and then as aid, to meet food needs. Prices were set annually by cabinet-level decisions. The NMC ran up millions of shillings of debt. It has been decreasingly able to purchase domestically its grain needs, even after producer prices were raised on several occasions. In part the NMC did not have enough grain because of bad weather that reduced crops, but also purchases were lost to parallel-market and cross-border sales. Given an overvalued exchange rate, imported grain prices were artificially low, and this reduced pressure to raise domestic prices. Government officials had priority access to NMC. The cornerstone of food security policy became having adequate stocks to feed the populace of Dar es Salaam. At times rice sold for one-third its price on the parallel (illegal) market, and the NMC only had imported rice available. In 1985, in response to past criticism, state subsidies of wheat and rice were eliminated. Instead, a "tax" on wheat and rice sales was calculated to help pay for the continuing subsidy on maize.[23] The operating debts of the NMC after "earnings" from the spread between official buying and selling prices are used to offset its costs accumulated in the 1970s and have been estimated to be in the range of a billion Tanzanian shillings (about $50 million). The control over marketing gave large income to those willing to enter into black- or parallel-market activity. There has been a sharp rise in "economic crime" in the 1980s, and government campaigns have led to the arrest of civil servants and prominent Tanzanians, eroding the civic pride that had long distinguished Tanzania among African states. Of course, much of the economic distress of Tanzania is independent of its food policies and NMC management, but high costs to the government in this area, coupled with declining food availability, have made it a prominent target of criticism.[24] Tanzania's decision to accept IMF credits in 1986, along with required economic reforms, was forced upon the socialist state in part because of these failures in food performance.

EXAMINING THE EVIDENCE

Much of the argument that underlies the criticisms I have reviewed rests on detailed studies of institutions in particular countries, such as Mali or Tanzania, or on inferences from neoclassical economic principles applied to the aggregate statistics of declining food production, declining GNP per capita, and the rise of "unmanageably large" state bureaucracies.[25] If indeed the growth of an unproductive state apparatus has served to increase income inequality and has systematically been either a cause or consequence of food system failures, as both socialist and neoclassical analyses have proposed,[26] then this relationship should be observed in statistics. Similarly, if subsidies undercut food production incentives, evidence of that relationship and its likely importance should also be discoverable.

To test these assumptions, I set out to gather data relevant to these variables. The information sought included (1) the size and growth of government food bureaucracies in African states, principally national governments; (2) the annual size of fiscal subsidies of food; (3) the total annual value of subsidies, that is, both the government and producer costs, if any; (4) the annual caloric availabilities in a country and, where possible, the separate figures for the urban and rural populations' food consumption; (5) the proportion of each major commodity controlled by state marketing policy; (6) changes in food production; and (7) estimates of the effect of subsidies on the political expectations of populations. What I have discovered is that very little appropriate data exist. Moreover, the reliability of the data that do exist is debatable.

One of the most difficult measures on which to secure data was government size. The IMF reports data on government consumption expenditure and national expenditure, and this can be used to trace shifts in the relative size of the national government. Where a time series going back to the 1960s was available, the data were recorded. This is, however, a rather cruel and possibly misleading indicator. For example, IMF aggregate numbers suggest a rapid growth in Zambia's government role (likely) and a shrinking of the state in Zaire (not so likely). Efforts to develop cross-national indices have concluded that complicated and sophisticated measures are needed in order to capture the real growth of governments.[27] Moreover, evidence of growth in food-marketing parastatals is especially difficult to secure, even for one country, let alone in some comparable fashion to show relative impact on each national economy over time. This is because subsidies can be passed through ministries of agriculture; alternatively, profits from selling food aid can take the place of direct treasury subsidies. In some cases records of these parastatals are disorderly and untrustworthy.

In general, the criticisms of food policy suggest that growing government regulation and low food prices go together and that these in turn are correlated with and indeed cause poor performance in the food system. No tests of this hypothesis, however, have been done to my knowledge. Gross, aggregate statistical tests yield weak and insignificant results, as one might expect from such complexly generated measures examined across countries.

Why are the strong conclusions and policy recommendations of aid officials not based upon careful empirical studies? Partly because each country has its own pattern of food problems, with exogenous factors such as civil strife, as in Uganda and Mozambique, having overpowering effects. It also is possible that the conclusions about the performance of price policy and marketing organizations are based on implicit comparisons with a past that cannot be sustained or with features of industrial-country food systems rather than on the more realistic comparisons across African states. Whatever the reason, I was surprised to discover that the cross-national evidence did not reveal any meaningful pattern. It may be that better and more complete data would lend more support to the "conventional" criticisms and theories of Western analysts. The reports by the World Bank do not yet do this. Detailed studies are especially needed, given the absence of clear diachronic or cross-national evidence of the relationships between high fiscal costs borne by an overburdened state, the rise of urban food subsidies, and food system failures.

ASSESSMENT OF FOOD POLICY REFORMS

Many African states have altered their food policies in response to prodding from studies, policy discussions, and lending preferences of foreign assistance agencies. The most frequent action has been to raise producer prices and, concurrently, consumer prices. Some countries have reduced the range of state intervention, as Mali has in its grain restructuring and Tanzania has in its opening for intermediate marketing.[28] Are these changes wise? Will the desired effects be obtained?

The redesign of a state's role in food production and marketing is an important undertaking. Significant policy steps in this area are usually preceded by wide consultation and lengthy cabinet deliberation. The commitment of political leadership to changes entails a political risk and exposure to criticism. If there are subsequent failures in food availability, for whatever reason, or if the benefits promised from a lowered role for the state are not realized, often within a very limited time span, government opponents gain an issue to use in their maneuvering for power.

Food subsidies and marketing bureaucracies, once established, take on political significance. As I noted earlier, expectations of cheap food become incorporated into criteria for the legitimacy of a government.

They can represent a form of social contract between the government and the benefitted populace. This is especially important for urban workers who use a high proportion of their income on food purchases. In Egypt bread subsidies have been a major symbol of a continuing commitment of the government to protect the well-being of low-paid workers. Egypt's economic liberalization in the 1970s could probably not have occurred without turmoil if increasing food subsidies had not been a major guarantee.[29]

Political machines are also important in sustaining governments. Food parastatals create an important fraction of the jobs and resources that political organizations have to distribute to their clients. Without them the network of reciprocal obligations would be reduced, and with it loyalty to government structures controlled by the ruling cadre. Thus not only a general subsidy, but preferred access to it by civil servants, the military, or other key groups, such as unions, can help support the intangible predispositions toward acceptance of authority. Remove these and authority is weakened.

In African states where authority structures have remained weak since independence and the role of international resources and legitimation has helped sustain state structures,[30] recommendations to reduce or end subsidies are not mere economic proposals, but have significant political implications as well. The coalitions that have been maintained and the interests that have been served by the food policies that evolved after independence will not be indifferent to reform, nor are they likely to disappear as a force in a state's politics.[31] The result is that many states have resisted pressure from the IMF, World Bank, and bilateral donor agencies to make substantial changes in their food policies or to reduce the role of marketing boards. Kenya, for instance, was urged by donors from 1979 through 1985 to remove controls over marketing and to lower the mandate of the National Cereals Produce Board, but consistently sidestepped this pressure. Changes made in Kenya during 1980–85 were largely to consolidate the board's operations and to improve, not decrease, market management.

Should African political leaders feel confident that reducing subsidies and other government market intervention actions will improve the economy and not cause serious harm to the urban poor? The evidence reviewed in this chapter gives little basis for optimism. Marketing boards may be inefficient, but alternatives are politically costly. In addition, a significant prospect exists that elimination of subsidies will not improve the economies of African states. If this is the case, the wave of policy reforms of the 1980s may turn out similar to the policies of import-substitution industrialization adopted in the 1960s. Enthusiastic donor encouragement may be followed by blame for poor economic performance and increased dependence on imports of production goods such as seeds, pesticides, and farm equipment.

NOTES

1. Sara Berry, "The Food Crisis and Agrarian Change in Africa, *African Studies Review,* 27, no. 2, June 1984, 59–112; Carl Eicher, "Facing Up to Africa's Food Crisis," *Foreign Affairs,* 61, Fall 1982, 151–74; Carol Lancaster, "Africa's Economic Crisis," *Foreign Policy,* no. 52, Fall 1983, 49–66; FAO, *Food Crops and Shortages,* Rome, August 1985.

2. David Abernethy, "Bureaucratic Growth and Economic Stagnation in Sub-Saharan Africa," manuscript prepared for American Political Science Association Meeting, Washington, 1984; Richard W. Franke and Barbara H. Chasin, *Seeds of Famine,* Montclair, N.J., Allenheld Osmun, 1980, 21–39; Michael F. Lofchie and Stephen K. Commins, "Food Deficits and Agricultural Policies," *Journal of Modern African Studies,* 20, March 1982, 1–25; World Bank, *Accelerated Development in Sub-Saharan Africa: An Agenda for Action,* Washington, D.C., World Bank, 1981; U.S. Department of Agriculture, *Food Problems and Prospects in Sub-Saharan Africa,* Washington, D.C., 1981.

3. Henry S. Bienen and Mark Gersovitz, "Economic Stabilization, Conditionality, and Political Stability," *International Organization,* 39, Autumn 1985, 729–54: Joan Nelson, "The Political Economy of Stabilization: Commitment, Capacity, and Public Response," *World Development* 12, October 1984, 983–1006.

4. Deborah Bryceson Fahy, "Food and Urban Purchasing Power: The Case of Dar es Salaam, Tanzania," *African Affairs,* 84, October 1985, 499–522.

5. Shubh Kumar, "Design, Income Distribution, and Consumption Effects of Maize Pricing Policies in Zambia," Washington, D.C., International Food Policy Research Institute (IFPRI) typescript, May 1984.

6. Raymond F. Hopkins, "Food Aid: Solution, Palliative or Danger for Africa's Food Crisis," in Michael F. Lofchie, Stephen K. Commins, and Rhys Payne, eds., *Africa's Agrarian Crisis: The Roots of Famine,* Boulder, Colo., Lynne Reinner, 1986, 201.

7. Charles Tilly, ed., *The Formation of National States in Western Europe,* Princeton, Princeton University Press, 1975, chapter 5.

8. Tanzania Market Development Bureau, *Price Policy Recommendations for July 1982,* and *Price Policy Recommendations for July 1984,* Dar es Salaam, Government of Tanzania, 1982, 1984.

9. John Waterbury, *Senegal,* manuscript, Princeton University, 1985, 113.

10. Shlomo Reutlinger and Marcelo Selowsky, *Malnutrition and Poverty: Magnitude and Policy Options,* Baltimore, Johns Hopkins University Press, World Bank Staff Occasional Paper, no. 23, 1976.

11.   World Bank, *Toward Sustained Development in Sub-Saharan Africa,* Washington, D.C., World Bank, 1984, 84.

12.   D. Gale Johnson, "The World Food Situation," in D. Gale Johnson and G. Edward Schuh, eds., *The Role of Markets in the World Food Economy,* Boulder, Westview, 1983, 8–9; also Berry, "Food Crisis," 89–97.

13.   Leonardo Paulino, *Food in the Third World: Past Trends and Projections to 2000,* Washington, D.C., IFPRI, June 1986, 72.

14.   Robert H. Bates, *Markets and States in Tropical Africa,* Berkeley, University of California Press, 1981, 30–44; U.S. Department of Agriculture, *Food Problems and Prospects,* 1–26.

15.   Peter Timmer, Walter Falcon, and Scott Pearson, *Food Policy Analysis,* Baltimore, Johns Hopkins University Press, 1983, chapter 4.

16.   Bates, *Markets and States,* chapters 2 and 3.

17.   David B. Jones, "State Structures in New Nations: The Case of Primary Agricultural Marketing in Africa," *Journal of Modern African Studies* 20, no. 4, December 1982, 553–69.

18.   World Bank, *Accelerated Development,* 58.

19.   World Bank, *Toward Sustained Development,* 37.

20.   Kumar, "Design, Income Distribution and Consumption Effects," Tanzania Market Development Bureau, *Price Policy Recommendations for July 1984,* 12–28; U.S. Department of Agriculture, *Food Problems and Prospects,* 200.

21.   Harold Alderman, "Food Subsidies and State Policy in Egypt," International Fund for Agricultural Development (IFAD) Conference Paper, Cairo, September 1984, 3–5.

22.   Ibid., 18–25.

23.   Tanzania Market Development Bureau, *Price Policy Recommendations for 1984,* 39–45.

24.   Frank Ellis, "Agricultural Price Policy on Tanzania," *World Development,* 10, 1982, 263–83.

25.   World Bank, *Toward Sustained Development,* 41.

26.   René Dumont and Marie-France Mottin, "Self-Reliant Rural Development in Tanzania," Dar es Salaam, Prime Minister's Office, draft manuscript, 1981, 98–105; World Bank, *Accelerated Development,* 24–80.

27.   Charles Lewis Taylor, ed., *Why Governments Grow,* Beverly Hills, Calif., Sage, 1983, passim.

28.   Cheryl Christensen and Lawrence Witucki, "State Policies and Food Scarcity in Sub-Saharan Africa," in F. LaMond Tullis and W. Ladd Hollist, eds., *Food, the State, and International Political Economy,* Lincoln, University of Nebraska Press, 196, 63.

29.   Alderman, "Food Subsidies," 18–26; Raymond F. Hopkins, "Political Calculations in Subsidizing Food," in Per Pinstrup-Andersen, ed., *Consumer-Oriented Food Subsidies,* Baltimore, Johns Hopkins University Press, forthcoming, chapter 9.

30.   Robert H. Jackson and Carl G. Rosberg, "Why Africa's Weak States Persist," *World Politics* 35, October 1982, 1–24.

31.   Robert Bates and W. P. Rogerson, "Agriculture in Development: A Conditional Analysis," *Public Choice* 35, 1980, 513–28.

8
Institutionalizing Rural Development: Lessons from Evaluation

Ruth S. Morgenthau

FIGHTING HUNGER IN A WORLD FULL OF GRAIN

Confronted by pictures of wandering Ethiopians and starving children, most people reach into their pockets to give them a hand. The response to Live Aid concerts shows how many people are generous, with a strong inclination for solving the hunger problem. "This is a good time for hunger in Africa," said a USAID friend of mine. "We can give over a billion dollars worth of surplus grain." He was glad to be working on food assistance; at least he had something to contribute at a time when development aid is dwindling.

Food aid is at best a mixed blessing. Not long ago, at the request of some African colleagues working to increase national production by low-income farmers in spite of inadequate rainfall, I located five tons of potato seed temporarily unobtainable on the national market and was able to arrange delivery. Naturally, I asked my Sahelian colleagues: "Can you pick up the potato seed the day it arrives?" In West Africa's hot climate, potato seed would sprout if left to stand. Though they lined up transport,

Brown University's Hunger Program and Brandeis University supported my work on this chapter. I am grateful to Morris David Morris of Brown University's Center for Comparative Study of Development and Benjamin V. Peña-Olvera of the Colegio de Postgraduados, Chapingo, and Brandeis University, coordinator of CILCA's technical services, for their helpful and illuminating comments.

they could not guarantee a timely pickup. Why? "Ports stuffed with food aid," they telexed. There was no way to get the potato seed to the farmers, since air transport was too expensive. The potato seed, which would allow the waiting villagers to be self-reliant and help meet national needs, had no operational priority. Everyone, donor and recipient, gave the principle of self-reliance lip service, but when it came to results, forget it!

This brought home the contradictions of so-called development assistance and the way donors press African governments to dance to their tune. Food aid is the ultimate "top-down" assistance. All over the world, and particularly in Africa, development experts have come to recognize that the "top-down" approach to rural development simply does not yield the desired benefits. Apart from dealing with an emergency, food assistance is a help only if it is part of an integrated rural development plan, such as tiding farmers over after a drought when they start to plant again. In the past, food imports helped people in some countries, in India for example, to mitigate famine while they take the range of actions necessary to improve their agriculture. But today many governments of industrialized countries are making food aid an excuse to do less long-term development and are also giving an excuse to some officials in African and other poor Third World governments not to provide necessary support to their farming sectors.

No one likes to speak up against food assistance when there is clear evidence that many people, particularly in Africa, are starving. In crisis we must take the most direct course to prevent famine. But let us be very clear on the limits of emergency food. It is a stopgap, better suited to reducing surplus grain than solving the long-range development problems of the rural poor.

At the end of the 1980s the world grain surplus is growing and granaries are overflowing. Agriculture in the United States has become almost too successful, as in Canada, Europe, and Australia. Many other governments have also learned to help their farmers achieve enormous yields, using techniques of the "Green Revolution." But world surpluses will not solve the problems of producers in the early stages of development. To build their nations, preserve their communities, and maintain their culture and their families, they must make progress by themselves.

The progress already achieved by countries like India, Pakistan, Brazil, China, and Argentina, now largely self-sufficient, demonstrates that any famine today, as in Africa, is not inevitable. It is also not simply due to drought or other natural disasters. Remember the monsoons of

India? Who talks of the Indian monsoons, formerly an explanation of "inevitable" famine in India, now that its producers cover domestic need? There is hunger in India because many millions are landless and without jobs. Poverty and inequity, not scarcity, is the reason.

More than enough food is presently produced for every person now alive. Recent gains in world food production have kept ahead of world population growth. Scientists estimate that a further doubling of yield may be possible from the application of technology now in the pipeline. Furthermore, it is not automatically true that more food means more people. From Latin America, India, and China, for example, we learn that as people produce more food, become entitled to it, and progress in other ways, many no longer feel compelled to have many children, because they will now have a better chance of surviving. Though there are time lags, families on all continents — Buddhists, Catholics, Hindus, or Muslims — decide to limit the number of children as they become better able to nourish and educate them. The great debate among demographers of our generation is when, not whether, the "final doubling" of the world's population will come. They fully expect the world's population to stabilize in the twenty-first century.

Africa in the 1980s can be compared with Asia of two decades ago. Though population in Africa is presently growing twice as fast as food production, we know that the population growth is more symptom than cause of declining per capita agricultural output. Africa's food exports are declining by nearly 5%, while imports increase by more than 7% a year. The hunger in Africa is clearly not due to global scarcity. The scarcity is in the local and national food systems. Most African countries need to increase their production, not their imports. They have too many debts already.

Since Africa is a latecomer to development, much of the prevailing wisdom has little basis in African reality. Conditions of soil, rainfall, and social organization of production, marketing, and access to institutions vary greatly. Unlike Asia, Africa has mostly rain-fed agriculture; soil is more fragile and less fertile; population density is lower; transportation costs are higher (twice those of Asia); and the prospect of large-scale irrigation is dimmer than in Asia. So far, scientists know little about increasing the yields of millet, cassava, and sorghum, the African drought-resistant cereals. The Green Revolution has scarcely touched the villages of Ethiopia or Sahel, where low-income farming families have to survive under some of the harshest environmental conditions in the world.

African social organization of production is distinctive. Women do most of the farm work. The wife often sells produce to obtain vegetables, fish, chicken, and condiments and to buy cloth and other necessities. She takes care of her own fields, accomplishes certain set tasks in the men's fields, gathers firewood, carries water, cooks, cleans, and cares for children. On top of this unequal customary division of labor came further inequities after the introduction of cash crops. Rulers impose inflexible taxes that go up as the state needs money. Most villagers must pay what seems an endless round of national and regional taxes. Men often leave the village to look for paid work in town, leaving women and children to perform all the farming tasks. They work to the very limit of human energy.

There is no single explanation for a breakdown of the food system in specific African villages. Fluctuation in rainfall, a political upheaval, war, or changes in world commodity prices can produce wide swings in the local market that crush vulnerable subsistence farmers. Food prices escalate, even for local produce, sometimes just when chances for off-farm employment dwindle. An embattled farm family, unable to sell labor, eats seeds, sells animals, tools, even land on which next year's sustenance depends, and may in desperation migrate or die. Food aid rarely reaches such isolated rural families in time. It is therefore vital to find other ways to reduce their vulnerability. That means helping them increase their production of food for themselves and for the market.

There is urgent need, therefore, to find improved agricultural strategies, since the productivity of African farmers is declining, and many villagers are steadily becoming poorer. People have no money for costly inputs or tools. In Mali, for example, per capita income annually is $160.[1] Though population is growing, the percentage of labor in agriculture declined to 73% in 1980 as compared to 94% in 1960.[2] Yet labor-intensive strategies hold little promise of increased production in Africa, unlike Asia.

Improved rural strategies must rest on social as well as technical and economic analysis. For example, social and economic roles of women and men in different communities are related but distinct and must be considered if real incentives and realistic avenues to productivity are to be identified. Some crops in specific areas, like vegetables, are mostly women's crops, while other crops, like cereals, are mostly men's. There is a division of labor by sex in animal husbandry also. New policies that ignore these divisions may be counterproductive. For example, cash-crop production can go up while family nutrition and child health go down. Improved rural strategies also require some technical changes.

Many donor organizations from developed countries overemphasize the technical constraints on production and stress the need for costly research, training, and technology, sometimes, perhaps, to feather their own nest. I believe that a better match in method and technology for African villages may be derived from successful self-help village projects in other Third World countries.

I have seen the effectiveness in Tanzania and Zimbabwe of Mexican agronomists with experience in the "Plan Puebla" method of supporting traditional farming communities. I have also seen the effectiveness of experienced village workers from Sri Lanka's Sarvodaya Shramadana Movement working among African villagers. Both the Mexicans and the Sri Lankans have a track record; they use low-cost methods and know how to communicate with farmers and strengthen their rural institutions.

Many technical solutions to Africa's agricultural problems already exist, but they need to be adapted to social and environmental conditions in the villages. That means research in farmers' fields to discover the best ways to retain water, fertilize, and cultivate. It means emphasis on water management. Often drought can be a misnomer when it follows flood. Too much rain may come at the wrong time, run off soil and erode it rather than penetrate.

What institutions are best suited to help Africans adapt available technical solutions to African conditions? The institutions have to be national and begin at the village level. The development establishment in government agencies and educational and research organizations have paid too little attention to an essential fact about hunger in Africa: it is decentralized and requires decentralized remedies to reach into local village structures.

Centralized bureaucracies have great difficulty applying such remedies. For one thing, they are too costly. To maintain one UN expert costs at least $100,000 a year. But the poor are scattered across huge countries like Ethiopia or Mali, each of which has more than 10,000 villages. Fielding enough international experts would cost hundreds of millions of dollars in salaries alone.

Existing rural development practices rarely bridge the gap between officials in the town and the smaller farmers in the countryside. Donors and national officials are too busy with each other and absorb a disproportionate amount of development assistance. In 1981 340 foreign donor missions visited projects in Upper Volta.[3] In 1984, some 30 donors visited 600 projects in Kenya.[4] How can technicians find time to communicate with villagers when they must play host to so many visiting firemen? The problem of cost and technical outreach to the numerous and scattered African low-income villagers calls for different techniques and new approaches.

In search of useful lessons for Africa from experiences in other Third World countries, I have been involved with the creation of CILCA (International Liaison Committee for Food Corps Programs), a nongovernmental liaison group that represents a breakthrough in South-South cooperation. I have had the privilege of working with and learning from Asian, African, and Latin American nationalists who want to improve and strengthen their own national societies. CILCA as a liaison group strengthens the associated national projects, wholly "owned and managed" by national leaders. CILCA eschews the standard nongovernmental organization (NGO) approach of controlling its overseas projects. CILCA's Board of Directors has a Third World majority. The approach is rooted in the premise that the hungry, if given a chance, could do much to pull themselves out of poverty's grip into a life of rising prosperity. To help make these efforts succeed, national technicians have access to the expertise of seasoned scientists and development specialists, particularly from Asia and Latin America, and share insights with each other. CILCA seeks alternative rural development approaches that are low in cost, in harmony with existing national institutions, and targeted to needs of traditional farmers. The group has generated projects in villages in Africa, Latin America, and Asia with the goal of increasing food production and improving people's lives. At the same time, CILCA is engaged in an inductive search for development knowledge.

Early results have been promising from projects in Zimbabwe, Tanzania, and the Sahel; more are starting in the highlands of Peru and in Guinea. All are testing new methods appropriate to the conditions of the village poor. Because of CILCA's unique decentralized network structure, all this can be done at minimum cost. The approach requires working with governments as well as villagers and is no panacea, but it is a fresh example of what can be done to reduce the likelihood of rural hunger.

After five years of project start-up, CILCA took stock. In the thinking of the experienced rural development practitioners who attended the Evaluation and Training Workshop in Puebla, Mexico, in August 1985,[5] many prevailing practices are too costly and centralized, overly destructive of family and community, and likely to overlook the assets and interests of the rural poor. Criticism goes further: high-cost technical choices mortgage future generations, while top-down practices weaken local institutions and sacrifice people's power to decide for themselves.

These professionals agree on three additional points. Money has no automatic relation to project result. The same act of rural assistance — money or equipment, a well, food aid, a training course, technical assistance — will effect change only to the extent that it has impact on the recipients' institutions. Assistance can drain away or be consumed, leading to division and disappointments; or it can lead to lasting improvements. The organization of a project and its particular relationship to local, regional, and national institutions are crucial factors.

Second, increased yield has no automatic social benefit. The same production results, such as an increase in cereal or vegetable yields, can have dramatically different effects on people's livelihood and on the capacity of villagers to sustain positive results. Ironically, in some circumstances production increases can be accompanied by more malnutrition, even hunger and out-migration, while in other circumstances increased production encourages farmers to build effective institutions for their own and their nation's development.

Finally, policy changes bring no automatic operational benefits. The same national government policy, using identical language but different methods and institutions, can elicit quite disparate results in such areas as food availability and performances from technicians.

The founders of CILCA, who look at social realities in Third World countries, participated at the Puebla Workshop, which was cosponsored by the Colegio de Postgraduados of Chapingo and CILCA. Scientists, agronomers, technicians, social scientists, public servants, farmers, and educators attended. Those from Mexico and Sri Lanka have decades of practical experience in successful low-cost participatory development. They know how to break down some of the structural barriers that leave out the rural poor, devalue their achievements, and diminish their institutions.

The Africans in CILCA are particularly eager to revive village agriculture in their countries. They came of age after independence, when agricultural production declined on the continent. Most of their domestic national agricultural markets are stagnating, with hunger driving villagers to migrate to cities, across borders, and into refugee camps.

In CILCA, Third World practitioners engage in important dialogue about scarcity — not only of capital, but of trained people, inputs, spare parts, and means of communication. Their discussions acknowledge the burdens of uncertainty about water supply, currencies, prices, markets, government action, institutions, and human behavior. They ask, "Is it possible to transfer experience and methods to solve problems in vastly different rural environments and societies?"

CILCA associates are microdevelopers who ask questions about the larger context of rural development practices. They know that growth and distribution respond to a range of interrelated dynamics at local and national levels. CILCA works to raise the income levels of rural groups, because poverty can intensify when juxtaposed with growth, and balance in the distribution of wealth is more likely if equity precedes other changes.

CILCA associates do not look for single causes or quick fixes to political, scientific, and spiritual problems. They avoid grandiose theories and sweeping statements about the inevitability of hunger and poverty. Instead, CILCA is committed to finding better ways of putting appropriate technical knowledge in the hands of the rural poor. CILCA participants work at the village level. They believe that poor farmers have much to give and teach about their own development. Village skills and institutions are precious assets in production and can protect future generations against the destructive forces of hunger, poverty, and homelessness.

CILCA's founders drew up guiding principles in Bellagio in 1979:

— Work objectives out at the village level, in line with existing institutions and policies, in a defined region; demonstrate effectiveness there before adapting the methods to other regions.
— Work with the whole village community; pay special attention to the central role of women in food production and nutrition.
— Build an interdisciplinary technical team that works together at the village level.
— Encourage the community to work together — in a spirit of voluntary sharing of time and energy — to improve village infrastructure and food production.
— Use appropriate low-cost and no-cost technologies; take village farmers and knowledge into account.
— CILCA's initiatives are people's initiatives, integrated with village efforts to strengthen health, education, and welfare.

— CILCA's actions should be simple, understandable, and immediate, best organized by nationals, and involve people most respected in the village community, men and women, young and old.
— An important component is village youth, living in the village, trained to improve production and bring about a more equitable distribution of income.
— Non-nationals might be invited to help — but only temporarily, as an exception, not the rule.[6]

CILCA's approach relies heavily on learning from mistakes and successes.[7] CILCA's founders know that naming an activity "rural development" does not make it so. Well aware that "most rural development projects undertaken so far have failed in their basic objective of reducing poverty,"[8] CILCA organizers analyze specific initiatives and search for shortcuts to increased food production, higher village income, and more effective institutionalization.

The national projects focus on specific regions, on villages with distinct identities, where people who have names live and work. The Puebla Workshop evaluated the first practical and intellectual results of these efforts from new projects in Africa and Latin America and two successful older ones: The Sarvodaya Shramadana Movement of Sri Lanka and the Plan Puebla team sponsored by the Colegio de Postgraduados of Chapingo, Mexico.

The Sarvodaya Shramadana Movement, a national, nongovernmental village uplift movement for physical as well as spiritual development, started from one Sri Lankan village project several decades ago. Now Sarvodaya projects touch thousands of villages, and regional structures maintain complex activities. Shramadana means "gifts of labor." Sarvodaya — a term coined by Gandhi meaning "awakening of all" — has grown into a vast movement through which villagers gain control over their lives and meet their own basic needs. The movement uses many techniques to awaken a village. Once it has been "awakened" to its own potential, the village forms a council to address needs for preschool programs, nutritional help, and other efforts.

Sarvodaya projects frequently involve the use of appropriate technology. The movement trains farmers, elders, mothers, young men and women, children, preschool toddlers, and even Buddhist priests to become responsible for development activities in specific villages and regions. Unemployed school leavers are candidates for the movement's leaders; young women become preschool teachers, store managers, or paramedics; young men become knowledgeable in water management, sanitation, marketing, construction, and agriculture. Training fits these young people for community leadership.[9]

In Mexico, Plan Puebla also began as one project; in a generation it evolved into many and fostered strong farmer organizations at the local level.[10] At the national level the technical team built up a low-key "magnet center" for training, capable of project replication, troubleshooting, and political dialogue. Many concrete achievements contributed to institutional strength, including warehouses, irrigation schemes, insurance programs, and credit plans. Technical and institutional capacities reinforced each other, and farmers were able to obtain official recognition and to compete for scarce national resources. Strong farmer organizations came to exist where previously none had been; their leaders know what will work and what will not, in good times and bad, and can point to visible increases in production and other community improvements.

When we compare results of the first three years of selected CILCA-sponsored projects in Mali (Katibougou and Toko) and Zimbabwe (Wedza) with lessons from Sarvodaya and Puebla experiences, we can draw out general patterns to guide future research, animate future training, and foster transfer of experience. Most poor villagers are already working as hard as they can to survive, and they need support services and appropriate technology. Institutional as well as technical constraints stand in the way of increasing production and people's income. Once they learn to produce more effectively at the local level, the challenge is to link their energies to larger possibilities of twentieth-century science and commerce. The effort requires inspired leadership, technical research, and institutional innovation.

The projects described below are in communities practicing traditional rain-fed agriculture, where land tenure is not a major problem but soil quality is often poor. Improving nutrition and increasing food production and disposable household income are the general objectives. Water management is a challenge. Wedza has somewhat more rain than Katibougou, which has more than Toko: with 500 millimeters of rainfall annually, Toko has barely enough for agriculture.

Scientific knowledge for increasing production has limited applications in these regions. There are few, if any, improved seed varieties to increase yields of cereal staples for Sahelian smallholders, and there is rarely enough rain to justify use of inorganic fertilizers. Though

Wedza grows maize from improved seeds even in drought periods, farmers hardly find it in their interest to buy fertilizer.

Production options available to the projects are limited by the environment, demography, and institutions. Though birth rates are high, population density is low, and settlements are often scattered. Able-bodied men often migrate to look for jobs, leaving labor in very short supply. Roads are inadequate, and villages are remote from markets. These projects operate under some of the most difficult conditions in the world, where there are no blueprints for building a healthy village society.

Each project must start with a thorough diagnosis: environmental, economic, and social. National teams with international CILCA support prepare, monitor, and evaluate projects with the best information available under the prevailing circumstances. National technical and research institutions assist, as do international agencies. ICRISAT (the International Center for Research in the Semi-Arid Tropics) and ATI (Appropriate Technology International) are but two of the existing organizations whose technical support has been invaluable to CILCA projects.

These projects, operating scarcely three years, demonstrate that with outside resources people can product more. Technical solutions and production increases are only a first step, however. Sometimes more difficult than short-term production increases is the institutionalization that gives villagers control over input decisions and entitles them to increases. Where they form institutions that give them such control and allow them to enter into a dialogue with national authorities, the farmers take part in a national decision-making process. They become part of an institutional chain from the local to the national level that is central to the development of a modern agricultural sector and a lasting solution to rural poverty and hunger.

THE PROJECTS

Wedza, Zimbabwe

The Wedza project began in 1982 on communal lands in Mashonaland East, just after the Zimbabwean government came under the control of an African majority. It was a moment in history when many Wedza families, who included freedom fighters among their ranks, hoped for better lives. The white farmers of Zimbabwe had retained big commercial farms, the best land, education, and technology, and comfortable incomes from the sale of agricultural surplus. The new Zimbabwe government wanted to adapt the existing technical capacity, previously concentrated in the white sector, and improve productivity among black African smallholders.

Wedza is a dryish zone with mediocre soil. The CILCA-sponsored project called for better service to and communication with the Wedza farmers, many of whom are women, to raise production, diversify, and increase income. The strategy involved farmers' participation in planning and implementing activities and collecting knowledge through research trials in family fields. Farmers' specific goals were to develop small-scale irrigation schemes, improve domestic water supply, establish tree nurseries for woodlots, and increase yields.

At the local level the project set out to strengthen farmer organizations. At the regional level the project promoted coordination among existing, often competing national services — for training, credit, extension, savings, inputs, and storage — and promoted the use of these services by the farmers. To this end, the project led to the formation and training of a technical team that was interdisciplinary, interdepartmental, and designed to serve the farmers' interests. The project developed grass roots leadership. It increased the number of existing farmer groups and trained elected farmer extension promoters (FEPs) to help group members take advantage of available knowledge. Group savings schemes were strengthened and group credit opportunities multiplied.

At the technical level the Wedza project involved the formation and the operation of an eight-member Project Implementation Team (PIT), which now has strong farmer representation and is coordinated by the senior Agritex representative in the region. PIT is the Wedza project's technical-planning and decision-making nucleus. It meets monthly, collects data, plans, monitors implementation, and keeps records. The monitoring and evaluation functions are undertaken with national support from the Ministry of Agriculture.

The project also cultivated links among institutions at three levels: the farmers, with their groups and FEPs; the Wedza technicians and national institutions, both governmental and nongovernmental, such as Agritex in the Ministry of Agriculture (extension), Silveira House (a Catholic nongovernmental organization with long experience in the area), the Savings Development Movement (nongovernmental), the Agricultural Finance Corporation, and the Ministry of Women's Services and Community Development. Connections among these institutions, informal and formal, reduced bureaucratic rivalries, improved communication among the people involved in the project, and transmitted information about the project's development process.

By 1985 Wedza farmers working with PIT had achieved quite a few positive results, in spite of drought. Many farmers diversified production and had increases in yields of maize, vegetables, fruit, fodder, firewood, and domestic animals. Agronomic trials on farms tested responses to low levels of manure and inorganic fertilizer. Farmers learned to improve cultivation and weeding techniques, winter plowing, and water retention methods. Distribution of inputs was more efficient, with the farmers assisting in construction of an input distribution center. There were changes in marketing, including the construction of one produce depot (others are under consideration). A start was made in the construction of small irrigation schemes, and farmers hand-dug five wells for clean drinking water; twenty more are planned.

Under the farmer-training program the Wedza farmers elected twenty-nine local farmers, including five women, as FEPs. The FEPs were trained in monthly sessions and passed their knowledge along to their neighbors. Farmer contact with extension went up from 41% in 1982 to 71% in 1984. The project also established a small revolving credit fund.

Roughly 4,000 farmer households were organized into groups by 1985, compared to 1,600 in 1982, and each household averaged seven members. These groups helped members solve production problems. Yields went up: in maize, group households averaged a yield of 2,473 kilograms per hectare, as compared with 1,709 kilograms per hectare for nongroup farmers. Groups now make better use of available technical information and collective labor, manage credit better, are more likely to save, take advantage of fertilizer packages, and tend to improve their economic returns.

Technicians in Wedza are learning how to most effectively serve the farmers. Wedza farmers are learning about planning, operating, monitoring, and evaluating their own rural development program and about lobbying for better technical advice, for training, and for services. The Wedza farmer groups now meet regularly, administer resources, and are a source of pride and prestige in the communities. They give feedback to technicians and make demands upon themselves and their government.

Toko, Mali

Mali is one of the world's poorest countries, where average annual per capita income (according to 1985 World Bank figures) is $160, in contrast with Zimbabwe's per capita income (which includes whites) of $740. Mali's depth of poverty becomes evident by contrast with another poor country, Sri Lanka, where average annual per capita income is $330. But the quality of life in Sri Lanka is considerably higher, if we consider the rates of literacy, child mortality, and longevity.[11] More than 50% of Sri Lanka's adults are literate and expect to live to be sixty-nine; of every thousand infants born, 37 die before they are one year old, and 2 per thousand die between the ages of one and four. In Mali, adult literacy is 10% and life expectancy is forty-five; 148 infants per thousand die before the end of their first year, and 31 per thousand die between ages one and four. Sri Lankans receive 107% of daily minimum calorie needs, but Malians only 86%.[12]

Though Mali is the size of France and Germany combined, it holds fewer than ten million people, most of whom are farmers. Settlement is sparse because rainfall is unreliable and soil fertility is variable. The village of Toko lies on a dirt road 12 kilometers from the nearest town, Ségou, and some 240 kilometers from the capital, Bamako. The road can become impassable in the rainy season, leaving the villagers entirely cut off from markets, medicine, and modern communication. When the rains are good, cereals and other crops grow, but recent rainfall averaged a mere 500 millimeters annually. If the rains are late, irregular, or scant, Toko is in deep trouble.

In the changing political context of Mali, independent since 1960, many villagers find it increasingly difficult to protect themselves against the vagaries of the environment. Mali's government is poverty-stricken, and it levies a variety of taxes on poor villagers. Toko inhabitants are good citizens who try to pay their taxes, which average somewhere around 4,000 CFA francs ($10) a person. They also want to buy cloth, medicine, tools, sugar, and other small items.

In recent years participation in the money economy has offered more drawbacks than benefits. Production rate and prices of commodities sold by villagers have declined, while prices for what they buy have risen. Higher oil prices mean no kerosene for village lamps; the higher costs of valuable tools mean fewer are purchased and used. To avoid buying firewood, villagers cut down precious trees and denude the dry soil. With nonarable land, granaries become empty. Houses fall into disrepair, wells are unattended, household animals are sold or eaten. The people get caught in a vicious cycle, sacrificing long-term interests to satisfy immediate, urgent needs. The market makes them even poorer and more vulnerable if the rains are late or sparse.

Then the city beckons to young people. They leave Toko, hoping for money, a transistor radio, or a sewing machine for the family, and for better things generally. But prosperity is elusive: Bamako offers few jobs. Nevertheless, fewer able-bodied people remain in Toko to farm, and as a result, families cannot produce surplus during a good harvest to store as defense against lean years. This has been a tragic decade of such years. Much of the burden falls on the women, who grow around 80% of the food for the family and must also carry water long distances, cook, clean, nurse, and bear many children. Toko's families survive only through their extraordinary hard work and the strong support of the village's social institutions.

CILCA's Malian associates gathered data on Toko and sought a strategy to arrest this depressing record of economic and social decline. They were painfully aware of drought and the impact of global recession. Though foreign aid to the Sahel went up rapidly — from $754 million in 1974 to $1.5 billion in 1980, after a commitment of $705 million between 1975 and 1980 — the record, ironically, shows economic decline and less food produced. Little foreign aid reached the people of Toko, who were hungry and had no school, no store, no dispensary, no maternity clinic, no modern services of any kind. The people were ready for a different approach.

The Toko project was designed to test the effectiveness of the Sarvodaya Shramadana Movement's strategy for integrated village development under Malian conditions. It aims for improvements in the subsistence economy, relies on the strength of indigenous value systems, and is designed to help villagers help themselves. The project encourages villagers' capacity to work together to solve their problems and build a healthy society.[13]

Activities were started by Malians supported by a remarkable Sri Lankan couple who lived in the village. Volunteers with extensive experience of Sarvodaya's mobilization techniques, they were able to reach out to both women's and men's groups. In 1983–84 three Malians were trained in Sri Lanka to carry on, and they started work in three additional villages. In 1985 the Sri Lankans returned home, and the task of coordinating technical support for Toko's project was taken over by the Malian Project Support Unit (PSU). The unit manages another project and is part of the teaching staff of the Institut Polytechnique Rural (IPR) of Katibougou. This Malian educational institution is assuming the tasks of research, technical support, planning, decision making, and evaluation for both Toko and Katibougou projects.

The Toko project has given special attention to women farmers. In 1982 the project set up a preschool so that young children could learn and mothers would be free to perform other tasks. Women built wells for safe drinking water, planted trees, grew more vegetables, cared for domestic animals, improved health and nutrition, and became literate. Evaluation in 1985 showed positive results in Toko village and more modest success in three neighboring villages that had begun work in 1984: Kerefebougou, Siola, and N'Goye. Some 2,000 to 3,000 people are now involved.

Four preschools are currently operated by girls from the village who were trained by CILCA. Children bring contributions of food for the noonday meal and learn about song, dance, and numbers as well as health, nutrition, and sanitation. Throughout the region villagers helped construct six shallow wells that now provide water for drinking and for growing vegetables. The national water service rehabilitated three tanks to irrigate vegetable farms. Villagers planted hundreds of trees, and households, particularly in Toko, enjoy greenery, food, fodder, fuel, and shade. Rudimentary medical services are available in Toko — a maternity clinic and a dispensary staffed by villagers who received some paramedical training. Night literacy classes are available. A steer-fattening program has been launched to bring income to participating farmers. These tangible results show modest improvements in the quality of life and some productive increases from vegetables, animal husbandry, and tree planting.

The record demonstrates that direct community mobilization techniques can achieve rapid and useful results in the quality of life. Evaluations show that sustaining them and fostering self-reliance are difficult. There are still many problems: cereal production has not increased, income remains limited, and institutionalization of the project is incomplete.

Katibougou, Mali

The Katibougou project started in 1983 in six low-income villages located near Katibougou's Institut Polytechnique Rural (IPR) but little affected by the proximity. By 1985 the number of villages had grown to nine, and a total population of 3,000 to 4,000 was involved. The project was initiated by an interdisciplinary Malian technical team trained specifically for implementation in Puebla, Mexico, and in Mali itself.[14]

The team currently includes two women, one an agronomist and the other a specialist in animal husbandry, and six men: an animal scientist, an agronomist, a researcher, an extension agent, a hydrological engineer, and an evaluator. Its goal is to help Katibougou villagers improve nutrition and raise income through increased production of cereals, vegetable crops, and animals. There is special emphasis on the role of women as producers, on supplying clean drinking water, and on conducting research through field trials.

The challenge in Katibougou is to supply appropriate technical packages, information, and services to farmers in one of the world's most difficult farming environments. Rainfall is low and unreliable, while temperatures are so high that evaporation often exceeds precipitation. Soil is sandy, fertility low. The people farm millet, sorghum, and cassava; when the rains are good, maize is also cultivated.

The Katibougou technical team studied the environment and social and economic conditions and planned specific activities in collaboration with villagers. In the implementation process the villagers contributed their knowledge of local procedures, time, energy, and their scarce resources. The interdisciplinary technical team, which operates as the decision-making and operating nucleus of the project, is based at the IPR and reports directly to the IPR director. The team has IPR's support in coordinating national services in agriculture, education, forestry, and animal husbandry and offers the benefits of its knowledge and experience to IPR's regular training courses.

The technical team carried out thirty-two field trials on farmers' fields to determine the best farming techniques for millet, sorghum, maize, and cowpeas. They then established special plots in farmers' fields to demonstrate the proper preparation of the soil, treatment of seeds, the advantages of planting early and in line, fertilization, and weeding. Team members emphasized vegetable production and water management, helped obtain inputs, credit, and marketing, and helped villagers dig six wells for drinking water. The project now includes a steer-fattening program and an animal health program for cattle and smaller domestic animals; services specifically for women farmers; and continuous farmer-training, monitoring, and evaluation activities.

Many technical and economic problems remain in Katibougou, and though farmer participation is evident, institutionalization remains slow. Progress is visible: additional water, more vegetables and domestic animals, and higher income levels are becoming available to participating farmers. Through plans, training, research trials, monitoring, and evaluation, the technical team has learned to become effective in the difficult Sahelian environment, to generate and adapt knowledge, and to help villagers.

SOME TRANSFERS OF EXPERIENCE

There is a continuous — and healthy — debate about project methods, results, and institutional practices within CILCA, and an awareness that no single blueprint will fit all sites. Each national project must find the structures and methods that work in its unique context. Projects vary considerably in technical success and production results, in the level of farmer-organized action, and in their ability to obtain institutional support at the national level.

Toko, the poorest area, offers important lessons to those who would write off such Sahelian villages despite their rich culture and tradition. Toko project results, though modest, are encouraging: better drinking water, a preschool to teach youngsters and liberate women's time, tree planting, a small savings program, and pooled labor to build up community services. The Sarvodaya volunteers managed to communicate knowledge directly to Toko village groups and helped the villagers to reallocate their time and energy as well as to adapt simple, available technology for their families' use. The Ministry of Agriculture assigned agricultural extension agents to the Toko project, and regional personnel from other ministries cooperated. While the Toko villagers were too poor to form marketing groups, they organized themselves effectively for the benefit of the entire community.

In Katibougou, village production results are also modest by absolute standards, with rainfall, evaporation, and soil quality serious limitations. Mali's farmers work under very difficult circumstances and need the best technical help. The technicians also need support: in Mali, a centralized one-party state, many official services are overstaffed but without resources, and getting technicians to remote villages is a significant problem. Interservice coordination is the exception, not the rule.

A pillar of the Katibougou project is the Project Support Unit (PSU), the Mexico-trained technical team that cooperates to collect data, identify and solve operational problems, train farmers, and monitor results. The PSU's assumption of responsibility for Toko project links the two projects, widens the data base from which to analyze needs and goals, and promotes more efficient use of available technical services. The Katibougou team is planning to further transfer what it learned by training a Guinean team eager to start a regional village-level project.

The PSU of Katibougou is fortunate to have the backing of an established educational institution, IPR, in a position to offer assistance in research, to collect data, to do technical analysis training, and to perform evaluation. Katibougou IPR's wide alumni network includes most people in existing government technical services and has access to the top in the Ministries of Agriculture and Education. A determined IPR director helps cut red tape, removes bureaucratic barriers, and attracts services and training resources. In collaboration with an experienced PSU capable of operating projects and training farmers, the IPR may become a "magnet center" for multiplying regional rural development activities.

Wedza's farmers also struggle with poor soil and unreliable rains, but conditions are not as harsh as in Mali. Wedza's farmers cooperate for many purposes. Groups can overcome labor constraints and increase knowledge — not just literacy, but technical control over such operations as the proper use of seed and fertilizer. Groups also form to save, for access to credit, and for bulk buying of inputs. Recently some Wedza farmer groups have decided to market together and are pressing the PIT for help on this most complex task.

Not all considerations are technical. Individual Wedza farmers choose as associates people with whom they want to work, whom they know well and trust, and whose respect is important to them. Grouped in this way, Wedza farmers learn quickly, and it is a matter of pride to pay back loans — inputs, money, or labor — to keep up the good name and the goodwill of their chosen group.

Wedza farmers teach others. In June 1985 they conducted a practical training course for another CILCA-sponsored project, the Tanzanian M'Bozi project.[15] The Tanzanian PSU studied how the Wedza farmer groups formed voluntarily through self-selection rather than by assignment. They observed how savings groups and credit groups worked, also on a self-selected basis. Most important, they saw the results of institutionalization by Wedza farmer groups that exercised genuine control over resources and inputs.

Some Tanzanians questioned the inclusion of nongovernmental organizations in the Wedza PIT; they also posed hard questions about the practice of paying a nominal monthly stipend to the elected FEPs, for they feared that this would diminish replicability. They recommended inclusion of a trained researcher in the Wedza project, so that the farmers could have access to the best possible scientific knowledge, and advised more support for research and training.

The Wedza project is aware that research is a problem and is looking for solutions; the structural gap in the Zimbabwean Ministry of Lands, Agriculture, and Rural Resettlement between extension and research must be bridged from the top in the political system. The project stands without the support of any single national institution (like IPR) capable of research, training, and interdisciplinary coordination. The Katibougou project, on the other hand, is fairly advanced in research capacity. Responsibility for Toko's research, previously neglected, was assumed in September 1985 by the PSU of Katibougou.

The national projects vary in their ability to reach various ministries or the office of the president, where political decisions that affect project villages are made. There are times when access to the top is vital: to obtain a small input (like food aid to supplement the daily contribution by children to the preschools' meals and thereby sustain a nutrition program) or substantial resources (like the International Fund for Agricultural Development's funds in Mali to double village savings, encouraging additional savings and productive investment). Ministers or the president can make vital personnel decisions, like appointing a dynamic IPR director who understands the importance of the projects to the nation. Top-level support is often needed to prevent local "big men" from diverting benefits from villagers.

Project personnel might discuss taxation policy with the president to raise the problem of overtaxing hard-pressed villagers. If villagers were permitted to keep some of the resources resulting from their production efforts, savings, investment, and further effort could be encouraged. Community self-reliance in Toko would be greatly enhanced if 25% of various taxes were rolled back into a local fund for production investment or used to pay the volunteer preschool teachers, the matrons in the maternity, or the first-aid paramedics who are forced to neglect their own fields in order to serve.

All the projects need to have allies in the capital. It helps to have an institutional base from which to raise vital issues and to reveal to national officials, in an unthreatening way, the dynamics on which projects depend. Sarvodaya has built a national nongovernmental movement as a base.[16] The Plan Puebla group is based at an institution of higher learning and operates a special training facility.

The role of outside resources varies among the CILCA projects, for policymakers understand the importance of covering costs nationally as quickly as possible. Self-reliance is measured by such national support, and the possibility of project replication rests on it. From the start, CILCA-related projects are staffed by nationals, paid from national contributions, who are sometimes detached from their administrative services to join project teams. They are motivated to serve the specific project's rural communities and to promote widespread development.

Important objectives of every project are independence from outside injections of aid and liberation of scarce resources for other regions that require stimulation.

In a growing Mexico, Plan Puebla achieved the goal of self-reliance in its first decade and now takes pride in working with national resources and helping people from other poor countries. Although Sri Lanka is poorer and has no oil, Sarvodaya also operates largely with national resources and manages to help villagers in other Third World countries. Of the new projects, Wedza already covers more than half its costs nationally; Mali's projects depend on foreign aid for 50% of their costs, and Tanzania's M'Bozi project receives at least 80% of its resources nationally.

CHANGE INVOLVES CONFLICTS

Rural change, even for the better, does not come overnight and often involves conflicts. Recent history in Zacapoaxtla illustrates the need to understand the possibilities for progress even in the midst of violent confrontation.[17] In Zacapoaxtla changes in political and economic institutions had to be made so that the farmers could become entitled to the fruits of technical changes in production. The experience suggests why achieving material results, though often possible and always important, is not enough for a project to be of lasting help to villagers.

The technical team, trained at Puebla, began by realizing that increasing production for Zacapoaxtla farmers would not improve people's lives as long as local middlemen, known as *coyotes,* controlled transport along the one solitary road leading in or out of the region, located on a high plateau. Farmers and technicians therefore devised a strategy to end this monopoly, starting with bulk buying. This yielded an income from a modest markup on sugar brought from town and sold in a newly set up community store, at prices still below those of the *coyotes.* The farmers used this income to organize and staff their own cooperatives and tool up for what became a lengthy and bitter struggle, in which the women sometimes took the lead during street confrontations, saying, "They will not shoot at women!"

There was some shooting. The local struggle for economic power attracted the attention of the regional governor, who sided with the *coyotes,* blamed the technicians, and insisted that they withdraw from the region. The Colegio's Plan Puebla staff discreetly sought intervention at the national level from the president's office in Mexico City. They successfully negotiated a political deal that allowed the fledgling farmers' cooperative to receive official legal recognition and thus to obtain credit, borrow from banks, hold assets, buy its own trucks, and organize its own wholesale purchases and marketing. With legal recognition, the cooperative could make sure that the farmers received a fair price for their produce and bought at the lowest possible price. As part of the political deal, the Colegio recalled the members of the first technical team involved in the confrontation and replaced them with other personnel.

These institutional changes in Zacapoaxtla were necessary parts of a development process in which the farmers learned to make improvements in production from which they themselves could benefit. Research in farmers' fields identified the best production techniques for higher yields of food for consumption and of pepper for cash income. Other research explored new international marketing arrangements. With their own cooperative, the farmers gained power over inputs and marketing. As the farmers' income grew and the cooperative prospered, it was able to organize training, credit, insurance, and specialized women's services.

Political change followed. Zacapoaxtla region has a representative in the national Congress who traditionally belongs to the PRI, the party that has controlled Mexican politics for more than half a century. Since the incumbent deputy sided with the *coyotes,* the farmers made it known that they wanted their own person. In the late 1970s the farmers nominated a candidate, the PRI accepted him, and the husband of one of the women involved in the confrontation was elected.

Zacapoaxtla project demonstrates that local conflicts, even in a one-party system, can be used constructively to further the interests of poor farmers. The key is making appropriate linkages. A technical team devoted to the progress of a specific rural community needs to be sophisticated about all levels of national politics so as to create situations that foster farmer initiatives.

INSTITUTIONALIZING AT DIFFERENT LEVELS

CILCA's experience has demonstrated the need to emphasize the institutional aspects of rural development among small farmers. Divorced from the ways people actually get things done, technical prescriptions are likely to be wasted or ignored. Institutionalization must occur on at least three levels: the local communities; the regional technical team; and the national institutions. Interaction among these levels is also vital.

Institutions embody a capacity for purposeful action. They regulate people's relations and allocate resources to achieve predictable results. Michael Bratton, in his Puebla Workshop paper on evaluating institutionalization, cited the classic definition of an institution as a "valued, recurrent pattern of behavior."[18]

Some of the institutions inherited by African governments from their colonizers had, by independence, lost the capacity for purposeful action. This was particularly true at the local level. The new states were built on imported models, honed to the realities of Europe and unresponsive to the contexts of the African nations. National policy decisions were often ineffective, since they failed to refer to the way things are really accomplished in African society. Expanding central administrations, the strategy followed by many new African states, soaked up scarce resources but hardly remedied gaps in organization and communication.[19]

At local levels, subsistence economies and the market interact in a logic independent of the rules written in distant capital cities. When precolonial, postcolonial, and modern institutions compete for precedence and power, local conflicts proliferate. The challenge is to promote cooperation amid rural progress by understanding how village society is stratified, how production is organized, and how institutions work.

Existing village institutions, formal and informal, embody a capacity for purposeful action, rule making, production, and reproduction. Based on past agreements, past experience, and pre-existing patterns of solidarity, they are both stable and able to lend impetus to rural development. Through careful data collection, research, and analysis, village institutions may be adapted to development purposes.

Social as well as technical change specific to each region must be promoted. It is not enough to simply superimpose new activities on existing structures. Past cooperation — in age group, in prayer, in sport, in study — can be transferred to new tasks. Identifying pre-existing solidarity groups and designing projects to facilitate their cooperation can free energy, produce results, and foster great commitment to projects.[20]

Established solidarity groups can be integrated into development work at all levels. The Toko project demonstrated that unmarried girls within an age group could take responsibility for running a village preschool, freeing mothers of young children to plant and harvest more vegetables. Sri Lanka's Sarvodaya Shramadana Movement trained Buddhist priests to become development animators. Wedza farmer groups harnessed the cooperative spirit born in literacy classes, politics, even war. Sarvodaya's first team was composed of a dedicated teacher and his students. CILCA's national teams studied together abroad and at home, while CILCA's international network includes many who worked together earlier on unrelated issues.

How can we identify the solidarity groups that will work well together and match them to the right tasks? How can we be sure that all are included? It takes careful methodology and research. For example, the leaders of CILCA's African projects know that women work harder in subsistence farming but are disadvantaged in access to the market and to inputs. Their interests must be monitored so that they can become full-fledged project participants and recipients.[21] By building on pre-existing links among women, dynamic networks can be created. The Toko project reached women farmers because a woman and a man comprised the first Sarvodaya team to start a development dialogue in the village; Sarvodaya uses couples to good effect. Katibougou's first all-male team became aware from observation in Toko of its limited ability to reach women farmers. The members recruited and trained two women and elaborated a women's program with the villagers, beginning in 1985 with preschools.[22] The Wedza project also has more women in farmer groups than it has female leaders and recognizes a need to open leadership positions to women farmers.

The economics of the rural household has its own calculus, involving a division of labor, energy, and resources, and a particular schedule essential for survival and reproduction. With little margin for error, farmers must minimize risk in order to survive on their own land. A technical prescription for change may suit the purposes of development, but it is never sufficient as the only element in a program of change. Change must be congruent with daily lives and the personal priorities of the villagers. Even where national governments announce policies favorable to village agriculture or official prices in the capital offer incentives to rural producers, the villagers must be convinced of the benefits of such policies in order to respond. In the villages, national rules and services are put to the test under special conditions. Only local institutions, linked productively to regional and national ones, can free farming households to take advantage of resources and opportunities for progress.

CILCA is aware that the evaluation of institutions requires methods different from the evaluation of technical matters.[23] While some production results are evident in a season or two, institutionalization may take years of effort. It is hard to measure and complex in nature. Yet institutions can accomplish specific tasks systematically, on a regular basis, and can pass on to succeeding generations the benefits of technical experience. Once established, institutions have memory; they embody people's commitment to work with each other and to carry progress forward through bad years as well as good.

In CILCA projects a most useful institutional device has been the interdisciplinary technical team trained to be responsive to project villagers and then assigned to work among them.[24] Training is an integral part of each CILCA-related project — training for actual regional projects, not for degrees or diplomas. The fielding of regional teams composed of national technicians who have different specializations and yet cooperate in the interest of farmers is not yet common practice. They gain valuable operational experience and can in turn train others. Such teams need continuous support after training. They also need career recognition, not for obedience to superiors, but for their effectiveness in the villages where farmers, not bureaucrats, judge their work.

Sometimes special intervention is needed to draw attention to conflicts between the project and a ministry about the time and effort a valuable PSU staff devotes to the village project rather than to routine departmental work. Rewarding members of the technical teams for good work in the villages is made difficult when they belong to centralized bureaucratic services. Yet building on the experienced people who know how to operate a specific project successfully is one of the secrets of drawing existing institutions — research, training, credit, transport, marketing — into the service of rural producers.

CILCA projects involve farmers, technicians, and national institutions in the village development process; each phase raises new problems and requires fresh analysis. Such a process requires a quiet conspiracy within national institutions on behalf of each regional project. It takes inspired leadership to break bottlenecks and foster village programs. The best people must be attracted, motivated, and properly rewarded. Such people will make good use of available knowledge and resources and build bridges from village to nation across the present structural barriers and gaps in communication.

The national technical teams working on projects like Wedza and Toko have a vision of evolution from a single village project into a national program of renewal. The national teams are committed, involved, and capable of solving problems. As they face numerous technical and economic problems, they ask how to establish needed institutions, how to strengthen institutions that exist, and how to make more effective institutions that are flourishing. They know that farmer participation is won only with tangible results; that disadvantaged social groups like women or land-poor families need extra attention; and that building one project into many is not easy. An experienced technical team can become the nucleus of a national "magnet center," capable of sustaining and replicating village projects and of radiating services to poor farmers.

Institutionalization of international liaison has also taken innovative forms. The liaison structure, to keep costs down, has operated without a formal headquarters. There are regional offices where the projects are. Board members have guided project preparation, training, and evaluation. A Project Preparation Team of specialists fields missions to a country starting a project and recommends acceptance to the CILCA Board of Directors only if the requisite elements for a functioning CILCA project have actually been assembled, with evidence of national institutional support, community involvement, available resources, and a strategy that meets CILCA guidelines. Only then does the board recommend training of national project leaders who then proceed with project implementation. An international Technical Committee monitors progress and recommends ways to solve problems as they arise.

How are the projects actually chosen? Why is Uyole the base for the Tanzanian project, why Mbeya? Why Katibougou in Mali? No project is an island. A network of relationships leads to and from each project region. Site choices were made in concrete negotiations involving national leaders, CILCA board members, and international consultants. We come from many disciplines and have the special bonds that unite students and teachers in a pioneering search for both knowledge and meaningful results. As the projects unfold, the members of CILCA's international liaison committee feel like explorers in search of the appropriate network, the connections opening the path to progress in specific villages. Once the process starts, there is no holding the villagers. They will push ahead.

Meeting the challenges of CILCA's start-up years has been stimulating and has taught all involved a great deal about the realities of rural development. We are keenly aware of the many problems that lie ahead. National, international, and local concerns intersect. From where will come the right technical package to significantly increase Sahelian production? Will there be enough changes in Tanzania's national economy to make it possible to market the potentially large cereal crop of the M'Bozi project? Will it be possible not only to sustain the momentum of Wedza project, but also to meet the expectation of replication in another environmentally difficult area of Zimbabwe? Will the slim CILCA liaison mechanism be able to keep track effectively of the necessary resources to help national teams prepare, train, monitor, evaluate, and replicate to meet the challenges ahead?

CILCA has joined national leaders who are making an encouraging start. It has been built out of links among men and women from different societies, institutions, religions, disciplines, and levels of education. The effort could have turned into a Tower of Babel, but has instead produced some progress.

CILCA's experiences show the importance of institutions that put responsibility into national hands from the beginning and that simultaneously give farmers at a local level a substantial share of control over production decisions. CILCA has shown that the transfer of methods and knowledge is possible. Helping low-income farmers improve their quality of life requires more than technical assistance, additional resources, appropriate economic policies, or increased yields. Rural development must focus on building a better society with what is socially and politically possible, what can be made to work in each region, each village, each household.

EPILOGUE

In low-income countries a greater political voice for farmers can help turn the agricultural tide. But can this happen if Third World governments can ignore the interests of their own rural inhabitants while obtaining cheap grain for the cities from overseas? The fate of the CILCA projects is related to larger development issues.

Through national efforts supported by CILCA, increases in yield of corn achieved in village fields in Tanzania's Mbeya province can be high. But will this bring prosperity to the village community? That partly depends on the price they get, on whether the crop reaches the urban market. Perhaps the city will eat corn from Iowa! In Katibougou village project in Mali, cattle fattening has yielded a profit for the villagers. They send the fattened steers to city markets. Due to preferential trading treaties with Western Europe (under the Lomé agreement), European beef is arriving on the coast, fattened with grain produced by European state subsidies under the Common Agricultural Policy. For how long can Katibougou's steer fattening be profitable?

Though capital-intensive techniques of agriculture in developed countries are often not suited to Third World conditions, there is one aspect of U.S. farming experience that offers some useful insights. American agriculture started free from the competition of foreign imports and from the mixed blessings of food aid. Except for black sharecroppers in the South, most U.S. farmers historically had some political clout in their communities, in their states, and in the nation. Through this they gained access to land, transport, energy, water, education, research, and on-farm extension, to stable prices, storage, credit, insurance, and, more recently, land conservation. Farmers' organizations, from early on, taught government how to help farmers generate the surplus that became the basis of further national development.

A healthy agricultural sector provides a sound basis for national development. Most governments know that agriculture is distinctive for its ability to provide a safety net under changing international patterns of trade and production. Therefore most want institutional arrangements that allow domestic agriculture to flourish.

CILCA's experience shows that alternate forms of international development assistance can be fashioned. It is time that policymakers take this experience into account, so as to eliminate the contradiction of hunger that need not be in a world market full of grain. Both the glut and famine are part of a larger crisis of economic management, reflected in chronic deficits in national budgets and balance of payments. With reshaped policy and changes in practice, there are grounds for optimism about world food security. More reliable access to food is within reach. There is hope for Africa and for others endemically hungry. We can leave to our children a world free from hunger.

NOTES

1. *World Development Report, 1985,* New York, Oxford University Press, 1985, 174.

2. OECD Club du Sahel "Reflection of the Role of the Club du Sahel," typescript, April 1983, D(83), 196. See also Anne de Lattre and Arthur M. Fell, *The Club du Sahel,* Paris, OECD, 1984.

3. Nilgun Gogkur, "Taxation of the Rural Sector: The Case of the Upper Volta," typescript, April 8, 1983.

4. Speech by Wilfred Thalwitz of the World Bank at the Kennedy Institute, Harvard University, April 26, 1985.

5. The workshop was organized with the support of the Sarvodaya Shramadana Movement, the Mexican government, CIDA (Canadian Aid), the Rockefeller

Foundation, the Ford Foundation, and Brandeis University. For more details, see the forthcoming volume, coedited by Leobardo Jimenez-Sanchez and Ruth Schachter Morgenthau, *Fighting Hunger in a World Full of Grain.*

6.   Ruth Schachter Morgenthau and Ally Cissér, eds., *Report of the Second International Workshop on Food Corps,* held in Bellagio, Italy, Washington, D.C., Action, 1979; CILCA, *Learning from Experience,* Harare Workshop, Boston, CILCA, 1983.

7.   See my "Evaluation and Feedback in Rural Development," typescript, Puebla, 1985. See also the evaluation of CILCA by Jean Beaudoin, typescript, 1983; and the evaluation by George McCrobie and Jacqueline Kizerbo, typescript, 1982.

8.   Sartaj Aziz, "Rural Development — Some Essential Prerequisites," *International Labor Review* 123, no. 3, May–June 1984, 283.

9.   See Sathis de Mel and Harsha Navaratne, "Summary of the Evaluation of Hambantota Community Development Project," typescript, 1985. See also, Sarvodaya Project and Programme Division, Moratuwa, "An Evaluation of the Sarvodaya Community Development Programme — Weliwela and Mattala Clusters in the Hambantota District," typescript, April 30, 1985.

10.   Heliodoro Díaz Cisneros and Leobardo Jimenez-Sanchez are editing an evaluation of Plan Puebla, forthcoming. See also Díaz, "El Proceso de evaluación en el Plan Puebla," parts 1 and 2, typescript, 1985. Evaluation of the Sarvodaya Movement is the subject of a doctoral dissertation by Ton de Wilde, forthcoming. See also his "Sarvodaya Shramadana Movement in Sri Lanka — An Assessment," typescript for Puebla workshop, June 1985.

11.   Morris David Morris, *Measuring the Condition of the World's Poor,* London, Pergamon Press, 1979, 3, suggests starting with these indicators.

12.   *World Development Report, 1985,* 218–23.

13.   See Françoise Levesque, "Evaluation de Project Mali-CILCA Sarvodaya-Toko," typescript, 1985; Anula and Subasena de Silva, operation reports, 1982–84; and my "Fighting Hunger — A Village in Mali," *Boston Review,* February 1985.

14.   See Aly Cissé and Moctar Koné, "Rapport de Evaluation du Project Mali-CILCA-Katibougou," typescript with annexes, April 1985.

15.   Ministry of Agriculture and Livestock Planning, "Report of the Evaluation of CILCA Project in M'Bozi District of Tanzania," typescript, May 1985.

16.   See the *Collected Work of Dr. A. T. Ariyaratne,* Moratuwa, Sri Lanka, Sarvodaya Research Institute, Sarvodaya Press, 1980.

17.   See Benjamin Peña-Olvera, "El Plan Zacapoaxtla: una estrategia para promover el desarrollo rural en un área con topografía accidentada," from "Seminario Internacional Sobre Producción Agropecuaria y Forestal en Zonas de Ladera de America Tropical," Informe tecnico no. 11, Centro Agronomico Tropical de Investigación y Enseñanza, Turrialba, Costa Rica, 1981; and Heliodoro Díaz Cisneros, "Impresiones del viaje de estudios al Plan Zacapoaxtla," typescript, n.d.

18.   Michael Bratton, "Evaluating Institutional Development in Small-Farm Project," typescript, 1985.

19.   See David B. Abernethy, "European Colonialism and Postcolonial Crises in Africa," chapter 1 in this volume.

20.   See A. O. Hirschman, *Getting Ahead Collectively,* London, Pergamon Press, 1984.

21.   See *La Formation et l'animation des femmes rurales,* edited by Aly Cissé and Ruth Morgenthau, Bamako, CILCA, 1983. Lucy E. Creevey has edited *Women Farmers in Africa: Rural Developments in Mali and the Sahel,* a book based on this workshop, Syracuse University Press, 1986. See also the report of the workshop organized in 1983 by the Zimbabwe government and supported by CILCA of Zimbabwe women farmers, *Learning from Experience,* 1983.

22.   See Françoise Levesque's doctoral dissertation for the University of Montreal on working with women farmers in the Sahel, typescript, 1988.

23.   See Haven North, "Pitfalls and Promises of Development Evaluation"; D. T. Myren, "Evaluation and Monitoring of Agricultural Development"; and Thomas C. Corl, "The Uses of Evaluation in Appropriate Technology Projects," all 1985 typescripts.

24.   See Benjamin V. Peña-Olvera, "La Capacitación como función de enlace en los programas CILCA: Principales lecciones y nuevos horizontes"; J. Francisco Escobedo C. and M. C. Alvaro Ruiz B., "Analysis de la experiencia de capacitación al personal tecnico del Plan Puno en Perú"; and Sathis de Mel, "Training Experiences of the Sarvodaya Movement in CILCA Programmes," all 1985 typescripts.

9
Getting Women on the African Agricultural Development Agenda

Barbara Lewis

The feminist revival of the late 1960s and early 1970s brought a sharply different perspective to the analysis of African social structure, sex roles, the household, and public policy. During the same period the deepening economic crisis in Africa led to a broad critique of dominant development strategies and, soon afterwards, to a focus on Africa's failing agriculture, particularly domestic food production. Feminist revisionism and the basic human needs approach to development share a commitment not to sacrifice equity for growth.

The feminist critique of previous scholarship and policy in Africa sought to end the invisibility of women in the labor force — as farmers, food processors, and retailers.[1] The feminist policy critique has been fundamentally shaped by the "development imperative": accumulated data on African women's activities reveals, with no public assistance, their dominant role in food production.

Western feminist policy activists have sought to influence the most accessible and appropriate avenue of policy change: international development assistance organizations. The desire to have an impact has produced more than a decade of scholarship shaped by the aid organizations and their prevailing ideologies. When the earlier efforts of the mid-1970s to promote equity as a criterion of development did not succeed, feminist policy advocates accepted the renewed commitment to economic production and growth.

176

More recently the feminists have joined with farming systems analysts to argue for a new model of the farming family and farming decision making. They have developed a provocative argument: that innovation in agricultural systems requires the promotion of women's interests in production, that is, their right to control the fruits of their labor. This approach seeks to resolve the ongoing tension between women's interests and the general welfare by gaining women's full participation in economic production and curbing their domestic exploitation, thus increasing equity by empowering women.

FEMINIST REVISIONISM IN AFRICAN STUDIES

The revival of Western feminism in the late 1960s was part of a broader attack on existing privilege and a search for equality. Feminists rallied against discriminatory attitudes and practices limiting women's access to socially valued resources and statuses. They sought "liberation" from those legal and cultural aspects of marriage that left women economically dependent on spouses and confined to an unrewarding domesticity. Women sought the fullest measure of self-determination.

While the women's suffrage movement of the turn of the century stressed political participation, the second-wave feminists sought self-determination through economic participation. They argued that self-determination is best promoted by full labor force participation, by good wages, and by women fully controlling their earnings. Women's earnings are finally the best source of influence within a marriage. Economic self-sufficiency permits the choice not to marry or to divorce. Domesticity — and the associated wifely virtues rooted in the Victorian period — were rejected in favor of the status and power deriving from the public sphere of politics, and beyond that, the sense of self, status, and autonomy accruing from personal economic independence. These values influenced feminist revisionism, and particularly policy activism, in African studies.

Many African women work more hours than their spouses, even excluding cooking and childcare. They play a more important role in the rural labor force than women on any other continent and dominate food-crop production.[2] Yet despite African women's unquestionable centrality in economic survival, observers agree that social organization and agricultural, educational, and administrative policy marginalize women in a number of ways.

Women's subordination is not solely the result of public policy. Women are often excluded from the public arenas in which village decisions are made, while religious and cultural norms segregate them from male areas of ritual and symbolic action. The colonial economy forced or drew men into cash cropping for export and wage labor in mining and in urban and agricultural enterprises. Due to this allocation of men's labor, women in many regions have come to dominate food production for domestic consumption. Because men rarely earn enough to support their families after taxes, women's food farms often make family survival possible. Nonetheless, women have faced increasingly difficult conditions in their efforts to feed their families. As more of their children attend school, women lose an important labor resource. As population grows and the expansion of cash cropping causes increasing land scarcity, the land allocated to women is often of poor quality or far from their homes. Declining yields in some areas reflect overcropping. Where men grow cash crops, their wives are often obliged to assist them. Women are sometimes rewarded with gifts when the produce is sold, but the gifts neither equal the labor market value of a hired substitute nor compensate for the labor withdrawn from their own crops. Where men migrate for work, women must provide for their families without husbands' help in clearing or plowing land.

Land shortages and the emergence of land as a commodity touch women farmers in numerous ways. In patrilineal areas, divorce means that a woman must give up the land she has been working and return to her family. Land scarcities mean that the divorcee will have difficulty "begging land" from her brothers or other kin.[3] The traditional advantages of women in matrilineal societies are declining as land and labor acquire new meaning. Women may inherit use rights to some land. Matrilineal women have had considerable leverage vis-à-vis their brothers, from whom their children have inherited. But this link between maternal uncle and children has diminished in the face of Western property law and the introduction of perennial crops such as cocoa and coffee. When fathers and sons invest their labor in this long-term commercial investment, the son's incentive to work is linked to his inheritance of the plantation. The decline of matrilineal inheritance has reduced the leverage of matrilineal women.[4]

Women have not been everywhere relegated solely to subsistence farming. Women traders, prominent in certain West African societies, have long impressed observers with their shrewdness and, in some cases, considerable economic power. In a few ethnic groups the gender division of labor that emerged during colonialism is reversed, with husbands only farming, and women farming and selling the produce of both spouses. Urbanization and the increasing demand for foodstuffs have had a much broader impact on the marketability of local foodstuffs and the gender division of labor in farm households. As food prices have risen, many of Africa's subsistence food-farming women have increased their saleable surpluses. Their cash earnings are limited by their access to markets and land and labor constraints on production beyond household needs. Their earnings are often slight, but even then they often span months in which men selling exports have no income. In some areas income from women's crops is considerable, approaching half of the income generated by men's crops.[5]

These changes have challenged the short-lived relegation of women to subsistence farming and have potentially increased women's value and influence in the household. But women's rights regarding such profits are variable. In many areas a husband may forbid his wife to engage in petty trade, claiming that such free movement in towns is improper or that she is needed at home. A husband may demand that his wife give him the money she has earned, claiming that she is not using it to benefit him and their children or that she manages it badly. A husband who forbids his wife to trade must weigh the resulting loss of household income against his own reasons for curtailing her trading activities. But his socially recognized right over his wife's trading revenues means that whatever economic independence she gains from trading is conditional on his approval. She must therefore monitor her own behavior accordingly. Nonetheless, her spouse may demand her savings without reference to her conduct to use as he wishes, including brideprice payment for an additional wife.[6] Women trading or selling surplus food crops do appear to have more leverage than women who only farm, but cultural and political values limit that leverage.

Women's considerable labor in farming often results in low production due to unimproved farming methods. The unquestionable official concern with export crops has, since colonization, left a legacy of serious agronomic research and agricultural extension, while such work on food crops has, until recently, been slight. Current research has generally not achieved results ready for dissemination to family farmers. The Green Revolution has decidedly not yet reached Africa, with corn a partial exception in some African regions.

If women's "invisibility" to agricultural extensionists is in the first instance because of the crops they farm, in those cases where extension workers do have relevant technical advice and inputs, gender emerges as a second-order barrier to improving women's farming productivity. In Kenya, where extension workers assist farmers with food crops, the extensionists tend to speak to husbands, even when women are the actual cultivators. Extensionists also fail to serve widows as well as women who are, due to their husbands' migration for work, de facto heads of household. One cause cited is the proscription against male strangers working with women; one solution, female extensionists, remains unproven.[7]

Another policy area in which women farmers fare badly is availability of agricultural credit for inputs such as high-yield varieties of seeds and farming equipment such as fertilizers, tools, and insecticides. Loans require collateral, which, for a peasant, can only be land. Because women rarely have rights in land, they are excluded from such credit programs.

Unequal access to education also hurts women farmers. The paucity of female extension workers is cited as one barrier. Unequal access to education means that peasant women are far less likely to speak the national language, while extension agents often do not speak the local language.

In the 1970s international attention to declining agriculture and resultant famine in Africa have brought African national policies affecting food production under scrutiny. This convergence of international feminism and international concern with Africa's growing food deficits provides feminist activists with a significant tactical opportunity. If gender equity is highly unlikely to alter priorities of international donors and host governments, the need to improve women's agricultural productivity is more likely to gain recognition.

But policies attentive to women's labor contribution may increase women's productivity without enhancing their earning power or empowering them in their households and communities. While women's heavy involvement in food production provides the potential for leverage, it also provides the potential for exploitation. Innovations that increase women's productivity may lower their benefits.

Nevertheless, policy activists, unable to get gender equity ranked with growth or development as a policy criterion, have sought to promote women's self-determination through more circuitous means. Given women's primacy in African food production, a primary effort has been to promote women farmers as policy targets on productivity grounds. Feminists' politics of advocacy have been necessarily shaped by the mandates and ideologies of the organizations in which they are active. The resulting strategic arguments reflect their adaptation to their "parent" organizations — their great concern with implementation and goal attainment and their effort to persuade decision makers that agricultural projects that ignore women's interests will fail.

POLICY ACTIVISTS AND THEIR ORGANIZATIONAL CONTEXT: USAID

Feminist activists have sought to improve women's status and women's rights in Africa through the media, private voluntary organizations, and multilateral and bilateral aid organizations. We focus here on the U.S. Agency for International Development (USAID), targeted by American feminist activists and scholars. The Women in Development (WID) office in USAID was formed in 1973 largely in response to feminist activists.[8] In addition to attempting to influence USAID policies and projects, the WID office has assisted the Department of State in its support of feminist views at two conferences on the status of women (Copenhagen, 1980, and Nairobi, 1985) and in the UN's specialized agency meetings, such as the FAO World Conference on Agrarian Reform and Rural Development in Rome in 1979.[9] In the thirteen years since its creation, WID has adapted its position and fostered extensive analytic and empirical writing on the place of women and on sexism in development. Much of our understanding of African women's situation is the creature of feminist policy activists' response to these organizations' internal priorities.

At the time of its foundation, WID sought to get a mandate from USAID that would fully support the feminist activists' view of women's interests. In 1973 USAID launched its New Directions policy, which mandates equitable development strategies, defining "development" as more than growth and productivity. For many, this mandated a shift from the modern sector and capital-intensive development to the informal sector, appropriate technology, and equity.

This "opening to the left" was a response to the stark fact that the U.S. Congress had not authorized the foreign aid bill in 1971. It marked a victory for a reformist coalition where the feminists appeared to find allies. The Percy amendment to the 1973 foreign aid bill put women on the USAID agenda. It defined the terms by which the WID activists could pursue their agenda within USAID and enunciated the principles upon which the feminist activists could claim USAID resources for Third

World women. The Percy amendment, section 113, "Integrating Women into National Economies," states:

> Sections 103–107 of this Act shall be administered so as to give particular attention to those programs, projects and activities which tend to integrate women into the national economies of foreign countries, thus improving their status and assisting total development.[10]

The language of the enabling legislation did not directly mandate or compel the adoption of policies promoting gender equity, but the call for integration mandates the inclusion of women in development projects and planning. The designation of "national economies" was consistent with the economic status activists sought. To improve women's status implies limiting exploitation of women's labor. The association of women's status and societal development did not make women's interests the goal of policy or programs. Instead it carefully posited a link between women's interests and the general welfare. (Some feminists chafe under this constraint. They would prefer that equity be a directly mandated goal so that women's interests need not be "bootlegged" under the guise of the general welfare.)

The language of the Percy amendment is conciliatory, avoiding any feminist threat to conjugal peace. It avoids a formulation in which women's interests conflict with men's or with the "general welfare." This courts the favor of those with little sympathy for feminism within donor agencies as well as in recipient governments, where one-party governments will not legitimate conflict. Given the emphasis on basic human needs in the New Directions policy statement, women's advocates could argue that producing food for in-country consumption was well served by making women beneficiaries of USAID.

After the Percy amendment took effect, the WID office became a base from which feminist activists could seek to educate, persuade, and pressure decision makers responsible for designing and authorizing projects initiated by country teams. By making women's interests a criterion of project acceptability, the WID advocates sought to move planners toward their position.

Finding the USAID bureaucracy recalcitrant, the WID office reached out to feminist scholars working on development to build their case. This literature not only documented the extent to which women had been overlooked in past policies and projects, but also sought to build the positive case: that the inclusion of women in development projects furthered, or was even imperative for, the achievement of USAID's development goals. WID documents often stressed that USAID's declared goals (more food production, better nutrition, population control) are enhanced if women are given productive resources. This strategic adaptation to the organizational environment runs through the main arguments about agricultural policy:

1. Women's specialization in food production in many areas of Africa makes women the appropriate population to be targeted by research into cropping methods and use of new high-yield varieties as well as in the training of agricultural extension workers.

2. A recurrent bottleneck to changing cropping systems is the constraints on women's labor. Women who spend hours each day trekking for water and firewood could devote additional labor to farming if they were given wells or more efficient stoves or alternative energy sources. Similarly, several hours a day spent processing grains or tubers for both consumption and sale could be allocated to expanded food cultivation if women had access to labor-saving mills and grinders. Other means of increasing women's labor efficiency — such as childcare centers — also promote food production.

3. Development assistance is often directed to men when it would be more effectively utilized by women. When extension workers do address food cultivation, they gather information from men and give instruction to men. These men are often far less expert or concerned than the women who actually cultivate the crop. Female extension workers should be trained and hired because they would be more interested and effective in helping the women actually growing the food crops in question.

In addition to the theme that policy should target women in male-headed households, WID activists have striven to get women heads of household on the policy agenda. Here the feminist activists' rhetorical task is different and perhaps easier: these women should get production assistance because they are in the same structural role as male heads of household, with numerous dependents. But these women do not get that aid, probably because women's productivity has been largely invisible to the official bureaucracy. For public purposes unmarried or divorced women fall under the authority of a brother or a father. Women whose husbands are migrant laborers are only de facto female heads of household. While they have an undeniable practical need for assistance in farming, such women usually do not have the legal right to make a binding commitment without their husband's consent. As legal minors, they cannot enter into credit cooperative agreements on their own. A very large number of African rural households are headed by women, the proportion rising to over 60% in southern Africa.[11] As these tend to be the very poorest, the need to get productive resources directly to these women is evident.

In responding to ways in which state institutions marginalize women, women's policy advocates have placed great emphasis on getting resources directly to women. The WID office struggled to get a meaningful "impact on women" statement required in all USAID project proposals. This requirement has elicited a predictable bureaucratic response: proposal writers have expanded the "boilerplate" (general and thus reusable paragraphs that tout the benefits of projects) to include what the women's advocates call the "women walk on roads" syndrome. Any developmental outcome could satisfy the Percy amendment and the WID mandate: a project that builds a new road impacts positively on women because everyone, including women, walks on roads.

The aspiration to improve women's economic status within the household and thus to increase women's leverage and independence is not readily embraced by international donors or host governments. Charges of social engineering, of divisive meddling within the family, and of attributing or encouraging individualism when the good of the family and society should be the goal make this avenue nearly impassable. The feminist activists in USAID pursued a more prudent strategy: they argued for increasing women's productivity and for protecting women's acquired rights to dispose of what they produce and to make their own economic decisions.

This defensive stance of defending women's acquired rights implied a significant task for the WID activists. Agricultural projects often depend on labor intensiveness. They are thus likely to require more labor from women in the crops selected. Innovations also may require more cash investments in the form of purchased inputs for which the legal head of household is responsible; this is likely to undermine the control women have enjoyed over certain crops. Planners tend to assume that the farm family is a labor pool managed by the head of household and that the head of household allocates family labor in keeping with the family's collective interest. This assumption ignores and undercuts islands of autonomy for women. Policy advocates seek to avert exploitation of women by increasing women's productivity and their control over their production. Responsive to their organization's rules of legitimacy, the policy advocates stress that such innovations undercut the collective good promoted by women's work. The principal steps of the argument are as follows:

1. Projects that increase a cash crop often require a greater output of labor. Weeding, widely seen as women's work, expands when plows are introduced and more land is cultivated; fertilizers also increase weeds. If the improved crop is a "men's crop," this work will limit the time women can spend on their "own-account" farms. Women may oppose this change because it undermines their own surplus sales and the leverage these sales afford them.

2. New crops that compete with regular women's crops are not only likely to absorb women's labor, but also to absorb land otherwise used for food crops. Where schemes undercut food cropping, they often undercut not only women's surplus marketing but also their ability to feed their children. Here the woman's ability to fulfill her obligations and her children's nutritional well-being are compromised.

Recurrent themes are the ways innovations may undercut women's interests and undermine the community welfare. The bureaucratic reader, if unswayed by the intimations of exploitation of women's labor, will presumably respond to the well-being of the community. Some activists find this rhetorical compromise irritating, but others see this effort to avoid isolating women's interests as prudent politics, given the official USAID priorities.

WOMEN'S COMPONENT PROJECTS VERSUS "WOMEN-ONLY" PROJECTS

Feminist activists had to overcome several obstacles in order to influence USAID policy. WID had a mandate with dull teeth and a small staff with which to try to move the large, established USAID bureaucracy. Efforts to ensure that agricultural projects did not cause a deterioration of women's status met with considerable frustration. Even those projects that did promise to surpass the "women walk on roads" syndrome and to benefit women directly were often disappointing.

By the end of the 1970s the experience of women's advocates in USAID suggested that the real choice was between "women-only" projects, which would promote some income-generating activity for women, and "women's components" in a larger rural development project. Integrated rural development projects that purported to address the activities of all community members were an ideal case in the typology. But USAID planners rarely included women as beneficiaries from the outset of project design. The result was a complex project with a "women's component" as an add-on that was rarely implemented due to poor management, inadequate funding, or simple omission. As an add-on, a women's component was expendable when funds were short. Project beneficiaries, who often shape projects during implementation, did not defend the women's component because women were not involved in these discussions with project implementers.

In contrast, "women-only" projects have the advantage of relative simplicity: they target one group, while integrated rural development projects attempt to deliver benefits to several target groups in a community. There would be no competing project constituencies to divert the resources of "women-only" projects. Because benefits to women constitute the sole criterion of success, project overseers and evaluators would be more likely to take women's benefits seriously. "Women-only" projects would be more likely to be administered by women who, less hindered by unsympathetic colleagues and superiors, would be maximally effective. The rationale for "women-only" projects is rooted in organizational behavior and the politics of implementation.[12] By enhancing women's separate economic sphere and women's autonomous activities, such projects were presumed to avoid economic exploitation.

"Women-only" projects have not fulfilled their promise. A recent critique of women's development projects finds these projects to be dependent on volunteers as managers and implementers, which deprives the project of the expertise and dedication needed.[13] "Women-only" projects are typically administered by the host country's Women's Bureau or Women's Ministry. Since these agencies are polyvalent in nature and low in funding, they rarely have the specialized personnel needed for project planning and implementation.

The African women's agencies that handled the "women-only" projects were created largely in the 1970s. One interpretation is that African governments responded to the UN Decade for Women by making ministries like the Ministry of Social Work into "the Women's Ministry." In addition to "good works" with the disabled, orphaned, and so on, this ministry was to undertake modest efforts to launch or to improve women's income-generating activities. It might, for example, tackle food-crop production in order to improve family nutrition and promote food surplus sales in order to increase women's incomes.[14]

These are laudable goals and far preferable to the home economics projects initially offered to women. But the women's agency has no trained agricultural extension personnel to instruct these women and ensure that they get needed seed, insecticides, and so on. The agency may assign its existing personnel, who are slightly trained social workers, to implement the project. It may seek the assistance of agricultural extensionists, almost certainly men, assigned by the Agricultural Ministry to assist these projects. The bureaucratic resistance to interministerial exchange, always considerable, is enhanced by the low political clout of the Women's Ministry. In addition, the Agricultural Ministry's male extensionists are often untrained regarding crops that women grow.

Other problems of the women's projects fielded by women's ministries include poor economic planning and confusion among participants regarding objectives and members' benefits. In Francophone Africa, both party and government frequently designate "community fields" as the way poor rural women can raise cash and thus be able to invest in some clear social good. But organizers and participants put forth the slogan "l'union fait la force" (power from unity) without specifying how individual participants will benefit. Village women are rallied to work one day per week in a community field to grow a crop to be sold at harvest, but there is often no consensus about how profits will benefit members. Local leaders envision a growing treasury for some significant collective purchase, while participants tend to prefer to have their share immediately and individually. Whether levels of absenteeism on work days will be reflected in how rewards are distributed is also ambiguous, increasing the incentive to be a "free rider."

Many production or sales cooperatives for women are launched without adequate studies of marketing alternatives and costs. If that increased production cannot be sold or profits are small, participants are left with debts for inputs they have bought. One international consultant argues that one of the great weaknesses of women's projects is that no serious economic feasibility study has been made. This may be because donors do not deem these "pin money" projects to be worth the expense of careful planning and analysis. When studies are done, they do not adequately account for the opportunity costs of women's labor, as they place little value on what women do with their time or overlook the value women attach to what they have been doing. Some international agencies feel constrained to "do something for the women," but not to explore rigorously what they will do.

ADAPTIVE STRATEGIES: INTEGRATED RURAL DEVELOPMENT AND ANALYSIS OF GENDER AND FARMING SYSTEMS

The vision of small pilot projects designed to be highly responsive to a female constituency has given way to a disappointing reality of projects that are underfunded and undervalued. USAID has been slow to fund these women's projects. Decision makers may have found them inconsequential. "Women-only" projects are small, in keeping with the limited capacity of the women's agencies implementing them and the funding allocated. For a large bureaucracy like USAID, small projects are costly in terms of organizational overhead. They require extensive administrative time and resources, but make only a small dent in the budget. Bureaucrats seek to allocate large chunks of their budget — yet another incentive to avoid small "women-only" projects. In the 1970s WID administered a number of "women's projects" partly by default. But the WID office, with its small staff and uneven linkages within the agency, had difficulty effectively overseeing the implementation of these projects.

These factors have contributed to the gradual phasing out of "women-only" projects in USAID. Had gender equity gained recognition as a development goal, "women-only" projects might have commanded significant attention and budget. Low funding, absence of specialized personnel assigned to women's projects, and declining prospects for the basic human needs coalition undermined "women-only" projects in USAID.

WID advocates now look to big agricultural and integrated rural development projects that command substantial funds as the best avenue by which to get resources to women farmers. The challenge is to make these resources work for women as well as for the community. Women's crucial labor contribution to agriculture — now widely substantiated by a decade's research — perhaps has made planners more inclined to include women in project design. But the old tension between women's interests and community well-being is not resolved. Women's advocates attempt to ensure that women farmers, now visible, can be more productive and less exploited. Women's advocates have turned to farming systems analysis and classical liberal economic theory to launch this new approach.

Farming systems analysis is an approach to the study of farmer decision making and behavior recently in favor at USAID. WID activists have found practitioners of farming systems analysis predisposed to include women's roles in research and project design. The approach's theoretical touchstone, the rational interest-maximizing individual, is compatible with feminists' understanding of women's self-interest.

A USAID/WID evaluation of USAID projects form 1972 to 1985 illustrates this shift in WID strategy and the new strategy's affinity to the farming systems approach. One of the reports in this evaluation states its author's view (and not an official agency view) that USAID has moved away from a "women-only" approach to an integrated approach "which stress[es] incorporating women into mainstream development activities."[15] Although this gives an exaggerated impression of previous funding for "women-only" projects, it confirms USAID's current disinterest in such projects. The stress on equity has receded, as has the feminist hope that simply promoting women's interests would suffice to obtain development funds. The remaining argument for funding women is that they must be included if projects are to succeed.

To be efficient, the new argument runs, agricultural and rural development project design must take into account the gender division of labor and gender-linked differences in access to and control of resources. The 1986 WID evaluation contrasts prior emphasis on equity and equal benefits for women with the current recognition of the need for "an adequate gender analysis" based on a decade's work to make women's work visible. The guidelines offered stress the interconnectedness of family activities and the need to serve both men's and women's interests:

— Both men's and women's roles should be analyzed.
— Analysis of the division of labor in project-related activities is not enough; it needs to be complemented by analysis of how project activities intersect with the other activities of men and women throughout the day or over the calendar year.
— To predict whether either sex will be willing to innovate, the differential stakes and incentives — with and without the project — must be estimated.[16]

In fact, USAID never mandated gender equity or required that projects equalize benefits to men and women. ("Women-only" projects might have fared better if USAID had.) Nonetheless, women's advocates had argued for both the improvement of women's status and societal development. Women's advocates have now narrowed the argument: the sex division of labor and women's interests are requisites of project success and thus of agency goal attainment. USAID's Blueprint for Development of 1985 outlines these goals: it stresses five sectors (agriculture, employment, education, energy, and water supply/ sanitation) as the means to achieve growth of national income and income of the poor, to reduce hunger and malnutrition, to improve health, and to reduce population pressure.

The relevance of women to USAID's current goals is clear. The empirical link between education for women and population control is direct. The case for making women beneficiaries of agricultural aid in order to reduce malnutrition and hunger is straightforward. That women should be in the targeted population in project design is evident. But to define the conditions of project success so that the project promotes women's control over their own production and thus empowers women is much more difficult.

Farming systems analysis offers the means for linking women's self-determination to success in agricultural projects. It thus encompasses the sector in which most African women are employed and a sector in which USAID spends a major portion of its budget. Farming systems analysis directs attention, as "system" suggests, to the entire range of farming activities of all members of the family or farming group. By carefully analyzing work calendars, the approach theoretically can predict labor bottlenecks caused by innovations at various points in crop cycles. Farming systems analysts will have gone beyond the relatively mechanical analysis of the allocation of labor and other resources and the identification of labor bottlenecks. They explore the differential utilities of different crops that often affect project success. For example, they note which crops provide a subsistence floor because of drought resistance and which crops provide greater income. Like any systems analysis, farming systems analysis prods the analyst to see the interconnectedness of farming activities in order to understand the trade-offs of a particular proposed innovation. Its promise is to predict when and why an innovation believed to be developmental will be rejected by those, or some of those, it is designed to help.

Farming systems analysis frames feminist activists' explanation of why certain projects fail when planners ignore women's share in productive work. For example, when Tanzanian farmers received plows and thus tripled their farm size, women could not or would not weed the large planted area. Production losses resulted, and the innovation's results fell far short of planners' expectations.[17]

This case illustrates why some explanations draw attention to women's labor contributions without promoting women's interests. If constraints on women's time explain project failure, the solution does not require empowering women. If planners had established an accurate calendar of crop cycles, labor requirements, and task allocation by gender, they would have seen that women could not weed the added acreage planted after the plows were introduced. This explanation indicates only that gender-related tasks and physical constraints on time must be taken into account, but does not infer that women have a veto power over projects that ill serve them. It is a very different matter to argue that women will not complete a task (such as the additional weeding) because the innovation does not serve their interests. This explanation compels the planner to promote women's interests to ensure that the project's production goals are reached.

The farming systems critique levelled at the standard conceptualization of the farm family as a firm provided the argument needed. In the classical approach, the head of the farm household is assumed to be the (authoritative) manager of the family enterprise, allocating family labor and other resources to maximize firm output. In this model, the head of household makes decisions in accordance with household utility functions.

The critique, while clearly normative in its implications, derives from the rationality models currently ascendant in the social sciences, and it claims predictive power. According to the critique, the classical model of the family firm misrepresents how the family members operate: rather than bowing mindlessly to the head of household's will, family members have their own interests and goals that they seek to maximize in the context of the family enterprise. Exploring the far more complex system of household members' diverse utilities and the trade-offs that an innovation presents for each actor is a more accurate predictive tool than the fiction of the head of household allocating labor.

The premise behind this model of household decision making is that every productive member of the household has leverage on how the system runs and how and whether it changes. Compared to the farm-as-firm approach, this view of the farming system is at once conservative and democratic. It is conservative (resistant to change) in that the tactical difficulty of protecting or improving the lot of each household member makes acceptable innovation elusive. Like pluralist interest group democracy, the process does not maximize community progress, but rather marks the common denominator of diverse individual interests.

The presumption of veto power wielded by women in this view of household decision making would leave many feminist scholars incredulous. The model suggests that apparently subordinate family members, like wives or younger brothers in an apparent patriarchy, can determine outcomes by working or withholding their labor. Is this then a denial that women are subordinate and relatively powerless vis-à-vis their husbands? What is the extent of women's veto power?

The extent of women's leverage and thus the effectiveness of their resistance to unwanted changes in the division of labor is unclear. The possibilities are complex, with coercion, trade-offs, and a variety of bargains and coalitions imaginable. This model of the farming family opens up a range of theoretical and empirical questions — questions of little utility to the women's policy advocate.

Women's interests in agricultural project design are best served by the assumption that women's leverage is sufficient to undermine projects and thus constitute a veto of a donor's engineered social change. This need not rest on the naive assumption that family labor is never coerced, but rather on the liberal precept that everyone is most productive if his or her interests are being served. Free labor works better than unfree labor; positive incentives are more efficient for mobilizing labor than negative incentives. Based on these assumptions, planning will be more successful if household members' interests are all promoted. Thus the elaboration of farming systems analysis appears to provide the grounds for both including women in agricultural projects and for promoting women's economic interests — defined as increased production plus decision power over disposal of that production.

Farming systems analysis has provided women's advocates faced with the USAID structure of goals and budget criteria the rhetorical leverage they sought to help women farmers. Failing the elevation of gender equity to a USAID policy objective, women's advocates have sought to build a case that recognizing women's activities and interests is a condition of project success when project success is independently defined. But the feminist's enduring purpose — to stop the exploitation of women's labor and promote women's self-determination through control over their own labor — seems attainable through the liberal perspective on labor: the ability of women to withdraw their labor and hence to veto projects.

The rhetorical shift from arguing that planners promote the general welfare by assisting women to arguing that women's veto power obliges them to do so was presaged in earlier writings. Discussions of failed village development projects have offered a variety of plausible explanations. The case of increased acreage and the case of the introduction of plows are prototypical. The interpretation of women's refusal to weed as their veto of unwelcome changes advances feminist goals. But a competing interpretation, that the project foundered on absolute constraints on women's labor, has considerable face validity. It is supported by evidence that agricultural tasks are often highly gender specific. In addition, students of Tanzanian development can think of other problems that undermined *Ujamaa* village development schemes. Poor external management (including inadequate or late supplies), arbitrary or authoritarian officials, and peasant resentment of imposed terms of trade are credible explanations for poor project performance. Proving the crucial strategic role of women's veto power in lowering project success is a persistent difficulty.

THE EVIDENCE: LINKING WOMEN'S INTERESTS AND PROJECT SUCCESS

Research is underway on the hypothesis that recognition of the differential stakes and incentives of men and women will increase project success. The current USAID evaluation of some eighty USAID projects from 1972 to 1985 in which both women and men are targeted is an impressive contribution. The principal finding is that gender-sensitive project design is positively correlated with the dependent variable, project success.[18] But causality is not clear, because the independent variable, "gender-sensitive planning," is also interrelated with planning sensitive to local farming systems and to farming groups in general. In short, good microplanning, presumably including sensitivity to numerous aspects of local conditions, makes for good results. The effort to justify inclusion of women in project design shows promise, but evidence is not conclusive. It is not clear whether gender sensitivity is operationalized to mean (1) isolating gender-specific tasks from gender-specific interests, that is, planning to avoid labor bottlenecks; (2) providing incentives for women in response to bottlenecks; or (3) providing incentives for women in response to their stakes in the project.

In addition, projects are rarely constructed like scientific experiments, so intervening variables and multiple causes muddy analysis. The USAID evaluation presents one exceptional, controlled comparison: in a Central American project, cooperatives employed village men and women. One village co-op paid wives and husbands separately, while another paid the salary of both spouses to the husband. The children in the village where wives were paid directly were significantly better nourished than in the village where husbands received both salaries. This case clearly supports the theory that women's control over their earnings promotes a larger public interest. But the other cases in the analysis do not prove the link between project success and empowering women.

While the USAID evaluation is cautious, other studies by women's advocates, like those of many advocates in policy research, have advanced the tactically desirable explanation over other plausible ones. A study of female heads of household illustrates this causal ambiguity. Given the feminist commitment to improve women's economic self-sufficiency, why wives of migrant workers have not adopted improved varieties of corn in southern Africa is troublesome.

One interpretation is that women are not confident that they will be free to dispose of their corn as they wish, because corn is seen as a man's crop; thus they prefer to allocate their labor to other crops of which ownership is unambiguously theirs. [19] In this view, stake and incentives explain women's behavior, and the women's implicit goal is self-determination. Another explanation is that these women do not have the money for inputs, that is, for hiring a man with a plow, so they elect crops with lower overhead costs. Thus women's lack of capital to invest in what ought to be a more profitable enterprise explains their "marginalizing" behavior. A third explanation is that the cost of renting plow and plowman and their uncertainty of getting the plowman's services when needed make it more cost effective for women to grow other crops with lower overhead costs and lower risk.

The absence of clear evidence for one explanation over the other is all the more perplexing because divergent explanations suggest different remedies. In the case above, the assumption that the wives' overriding concern is that the spouse (or his kin) will take her produce away focuses exclusively on conjugal competition. Women's need for credit and reliable timely access to a plow at acceptable cost are other possible explanations.

Other findings regarding women's stakes and incentives are suggestive. In an irrigated rice scheme, widows outproduced wives in rice: widows chose the great profitability of rice, while wives worked more on sorghum, which is wholly theirs, than on their rice plots, of which husbands claim a share.[20] The planners of one Zambian agricultural project finally decided to provide inputs to two crops, although one alone might have been more profitable.[21] Because women controlled one crop and men the other, planners assumed that the two-crop strategy, with greater production incentives to both men and women, would produce higher yields.

The evaluation of eighty projects also tests other familiar propositions regarding the impact of including women. When agricultural extension workers instruct husbands about wives' crops or tasks, the wives rarely receive the information accurately. It also confirms that extension workers tend not to visit female heads of households.

In addition, the study rebuts some well-worn feminist arguments. For example, promoting women as extensionists has been seen to advance two feminist goals: providing salaried employment for women and increasing the access of women heads of household to improved technology. But the evidence is that women extensionists do not appear to serve female heads of household better than male extensionists. The women heads of household are among those numerous small farmers whose low political status and highly constrained production make them, in the extensionists' eyes, unresponsive clients. Reportedly, "sisterhood" does not prevail over women extensionists' occupational interest. In a similar vein, building wells and thus saving hours of women's labor may not lead women to devote their new free time to other "productive" field labor. Such findings gainsay the link between assistance for women and promotion of other growth/development objectives that feminists have sought to parlay into budgetary resources. These apparently pessimistic findings support the rationalist theory that exploring payoffs to farming women will explain why they opt for particular work. The new liberal emphasis is on women's rational pursuit of self-interest. In this revisionist view the greater good is served when the changes introduced are consistent with women's interests, as well as with the interests of other household members. Sahelian women will use the free time gained from wells to work if that work pays off.

More research on gender-specific stakes and incentives is being conducted and will provide more insight into the impact of gender on farming groups' responses to innovation. To date, the evidence relating bottlenecks in women's work calendars to project success is as credible as the evidence that women's stake in personal empowerment determines their incentive to do work that will promote project success.

OVERVIEW AND CONCLUSIONS

If the empirical evidence is inconclusive, the change in advocacy style has been considerable. The language of individual stakes and incentives establishes substantial common ground between policy economists and the new women's policy advocates. This dialogue may be more fruitful than the WID activists' failed campaign for gender equity. The premise that interests that they pursue rationally marks progress over an assumption of stifling altruism or unreflective traditionalism.

This rhetorical and conceptual shift has not greatly changed the feminists' central purpose or the strategic imperative imposed by the policy environment. The emphasis on economic avenues to gains for women and the concern that women's increased productivity translate into leverage for self-determination are unchanged. So is the conflation of women's interests and the community welfare. Agricultural development has, in the face of Africa's agrarian crisis and women's preeminent place in food production, provided the obvious vehicle for feminist policy activists. But planners' commitment to protect women's interests in projects to increase agricultural productivity remains tenuous. This is likely to persist as long as growth and societal progress, and not fairness to women or gender equity, are the legitimating standards.

Necessarily, the preoccupation of policy activists has been to legitimate women's interests and ensure resources to promote them. Proving that women's interests "count" and getting them into project design are persistent hurdles. The practical obstacles to implementing projects remain an issue beyond the task of getting women included in projects. The arguments marshalled in favor of "women-only" projects remain valid and apply to the gender-sensitive farming systems approach that women policy advocates currently favor.

The practical pitfalls of this approach are several. The extensive analysis of farming systems, including study of gender stake and incentives, required in project design is intellectually challenging and attractive. Such analysis is also demanding and, despite the guidelines for planners that feminists have provided, difficult to routinize.[22] The incentive balancing crucial to the promotion of women implies considerable feats of social engineering. In addition, integrated projects involve multiple services to be delivered to multiple constituents in a carefully scheduled sequence. Such projects are prone to breakdown due to their logistical complexity. These projects' success is also dependent on the state of agronomic research, which lags in Africa, particularly in food crops. Despite the tactical and theoretical appeal of gender-sensitive farming systems projects, the effectiveness of this current strategy remains unclear. The resources actually supplied to women farmers since 1975 have been consistently slight; recognition of women's agricultural importance through effective assistance to women is yet to be achieved in international development efforts.

The project-centered and production-centered focus of agencies like USAID inevitably omits many gender-related development issues. Diplomatic necessity and faith in the ameliorative effects of economic growth lead international donors to concentrate on certain economic processes, while they steer away from other thorny policy questions. Some governments outlaw or harass political and parapolitical associations, including women's associations that could give inestimable vitality to local development efforts.[23] The impact of legal codes regarding marital property and divorce is not a policy question that USAID hastens to address. Land fragmentation is already a hot issue: promoting inheritance rights for wives and daughters raises a specter of accelerated miniaturization of holdings. Given the poor repayment record of many smallholder credit programs, administrative officials resist credit programs for wives and women heads of household, who have neither the legal status nor the collateral of male borrowers. Physical intimidation of women is not easily addressed by an international donor, but it doubtless figures in the negotiations among members of domestic groups. Thus the concepts and models women's advocates advance in the hope of gaining resources for women are shaped and limited by their organizational context. The economistic approach that such organizations may themselves be constrained to adopt provides a partial view and partial explanation of social processes.

Exigencies of policy activism in a particular organizational context invite a "marriage of reason." Feminist advocates have beat a tactically informed retreat from questions of social and political inequality and from explicitly promoting economic equity. They have sought to retrieve self-determination for women by establishing the leverage and veto power of women as family workers. Paradoxically, while in fact women may not have such veto power in a village, projects designed as if they do should empower women. Thus if women's acceptance of innovation is believed to depend on credit for wives, separate payment from a cooperative, or specified exchange of services for weeding time, and the project gives women these incentives, the project may well increase women's leverage and even independence in the domestic farming group. Yet this model of gender relations seems an incomplete guide to complex strategies and negotiations likely in a farm family, particularly in the absence of a project as *deus ex machina*. The model may promote a desirable outcome, but it still rests on incomplete theory.

How and why women's status changes and how family roles shift with social change are expanding, fertile fields of inquiry. Social historians of Africa, Europe, and elsewhere are pursuing numerous avenues ranging from mortality and fertility trends to cultural components of power, the cause and impact of legal change, and the link between changes in economic activity and individual autonomy. Game theorists explore bargaining between unequals and conditional spheres of independent action that appear to better approximate African women's situation than the assumption of bargaining among equals common to economic discourse. Africanists explore variations in gender roles across different social structures and situations. These investigations yield theoretically and empirically rich resources for policy advocates' dual tasks of persuasion and explanation.

The link between policy advocacy and empirical and theoretical research, like the link between all normative concerns and efforts at explanation, is not always smooth and direct. The object here has not been to fault policy activists for incomplete evidence or partial theory, but rather to explore the pressures that have shaped policy advocates' arguments.

The gains in building the case for policies promoting women have been considerable. In the last decade policy advocates have established women's place in African agriculture and made a powerful case for putting what women do on the development research agenda. Economic rationalism has replaced the obscurity of women's presumed altruism or "traditional attitudes" with a view that women have interests that they promote. In addition to its policy relevance, this perspective is critical to understanding gender relations and social change. Its promise surpasses the limitations of the model evolved in response to the politics of donor agency agenda setting. That promise is best realized by clear acknowledgment of overarching equity concerns.

NOTES

1.   Jean O'Barr, "Making the Invisible Visible: African Women in Politics and Policy," *African Studies Review* 18, 1975, 19–28, is to my knowledge the first to stress the official oversight of women's contribution. The World Bank echoes the invisibility theme in *Recognizing the "Invisible" Women in Development: The World Bank's Experience*, Washington, D.C., 1978, and I used it in the USAID publication I edited: *Invisible Farmers: Women and the Crisis in Agriculture*, Washington, D.C., 1980.

2.   Jane Guyer, "Women's Role in Economic Development," in Robert J. Berg and Jennifer Seymour Whitaker, eds., *Strategies for African Development*, Berkeley, University of California Press, 1986, 394. Guyer discusses the different measures of women's economic contribution, noting that while official figures of labor force participation put African women at slightly less than half of the rural labor force in Africa, detailed local studies in societies as diverse as those of Burkina Faso and Liberia find that women's contribution in hours far exceeds men's. See Ruth Dixon, "Women in Agriculture: Counting the Labor Force in Developing Countries," *Population and Development Review* 8, no. 3, 1982, 539–66, and Brenda Gael McSweeney, "Collection and Analysis of Data on Rural Women's Time Use," *Studies in Family Planning* 10, no. 11/12, 1979, 378–82.

3.   My research in Central Providence, Cameroon, suggests that in overpopulated areas a brother would not refuse his sister home and land, but her sister-in-law would not welcome sharing scarce land with her.

4.   See, for example, Mary Douglas, "Is Matriliny Doomed in Africa?" in Mary Douglas and Phyllis M. Kaberry, eds., *Man in Africa*, Garden City, N.Y., Anchor Books, 1971, 123–38; Poly Hill, *The Migrant Cocoa Farmers of Southern Ghana*, Cambridge, Cambridge University Press, 1963. There is debate both about whether matrilineal descent is incompatible with modernization and about the causes of the decline of matriliny.

5.   Jane Guyer, *Family and Farm in Southern Cameroon*, Boston University African Research Series, no. 15, Boston, African Studies Program, 1984.

6.   The example, from my work on the Beti in Cameroon, should not be assumed to represent the conditions under which all African women trade. Both a woman's control over her production and her leverage seem to me to be stronger in other groups.

7.   Jacqueline Ashby, "New Models for Agricultural Research and Extension: The Need to Integrate Women," in Barbara Lewis, ed., *Invisible Farmers*. Ashby stresses the greater legitimacy women extensionists will have with rural women, given the segregation and social distance between men and women.

8.   Kathleen Staudt, *Women, Foreign Assistance, and Advocacy Administration*, New York, Praeger, 1985, 32–35. Staudt provides an excellent summary of how the rise of American feminist activists extended to USAID and the creation of WID. Beyond attention to U.S. policy issues such as equal opportunity, the scheduling of the International Women's Year Conference for 1975 in Mexico increased concern with whether foreign aid helped women. Irene Tinker, presiding officer of the Federation of Organizations for Professional Women, was active in creating a women's caucus in the Society for International Development. The highest-ranking women in the Department

of State called for a conference on women in development for NGO in preparation for the Mexico City conference. Arvonne Fraser, president of the Women's Equity Action League, worked to establish support on the House Foreign Aid Committee, and her husband, chair of the International Organizations and Movements Subcommittee, held hearings on the status of women in October 1973. Senator Charles Percy finally introduced the amendment to the foreign aid bill that led to the creation of WID in USAID.

9.   Some radicals have complained that the State Department has used the gender equity question as a foil to anti-Israeli and anti–South African coalitions, inevitably anti-American as well, in the United Nations.

10.   Stuadt, *Women*, 34.

11.   Jane Guyer, "Women in the Rural Economy: Contemporary Variations," in Margaret Hay and Sharon Stichter, eds., *African Women South of the Sahara*, London, Longman, 1984, 19–32.

12.   Ruth Dixon, "Assessing the Impact of Development Projects of Women," USAID/WID Project Evaluation Paper, 1980.

13.   Mayra Buvinic, "Projects for Women in the Third World: Explaining Their Misbehavior," Washington, D.C., International Center for Research on Women, 1984.

14.   Barbara Lewis, "Creating a Women's Ministry: Cameroon," manuscript, 1986. Conversations with USAID, EEC, and CIDA officials suggest that this example is not an exception.

15.   Constantine Saffilios-Rothchild, Population Council, personal communication, 1985.

16.   Alice Steward Carloni, "Lessons Learned 1972–1985: The Importance of Gender for AID Projects," draft, USAID, 1986, 27.

17.   Louise Fortmann, "Women's Work in a Communal Setting: The Tanzanian Policy of Ujamaa," in Edna Bay, ed., *Women and Work in Africa*, Boulder, Colo., Westview, 1982, 191–205.

18.   Carloni, "Lessons Learned." Project success is defined as immediate goal attainment as well as long-range impact on production, employment, income, and quality of life.

19.   Ingrid Palmer, *The Impact of Male Out-Migration on Women in Farming: Cases for Planners*, Hartford, Conn., Kumarian Press, 1985, 40.

20.   Christine Jones, "The Mobilization of Women's Labor for Cash Crop Production: A Game Theoretic Approach," *American Journal of Agricultural Economics* 65, no. 5, December 1983, 1049–54.

21.   Personal communication, Conference on Gender Issues in Farming Systems Research and Extension, Gainesville, University of Florida, February 26–March 1, 1986.

22.   Catherine Overholt, Mary Anderson, Cathleen Cloud, and James Austin, eds., *Gender Roles in Development Projects: A Case Book*, Hartford, Conn., Kumarian Press, 1985.

23.   Guyer, "Women's Role in Economic Development," 402.

10
Development and Deviance: A Situational Perspective on African Governmental Corruption

Robert Washington

Governmental corruption is widely perceived as one of the most formidable obstacles to the development of African societies. Though no one knows if there is more governmental corruption in Africa than in other regions of the Third World, it is generally assumed that Africa's dismal economic performance is in part a by-product of governmental corruption. In short, if the reports and testimony of knowledgeable observers are to be believed, governmental corruption is not just crippling African societies; it is bleeding their development potential.[1] Shorn of moralism and racist arguments alleging an innate incapacity of Africans to manage efficient and effective government institutions, this conclusion is the basis for my assumption that the economic crimes of African governmental officials are one of the major causes behind Africa's development crisis.

Corruption, according to one frequently cited definition, is "behavior which deviates from the formal duties of a public office because of private-regarding (personal, family or private clique) wealth or status gains: or violates rules against the exercise of private-regarding gains: or violates rules against the exercise of private-regarding influence."[2] The aspect of corruption of primary concern in this chapter is that which

The author gratefully acknowledges the assistance of Karen Booth in the research for this chapter.

results in financial gain, though much of the discussion will be relevant to status gains as well.

Examples of corruption among African government officials are too numerous to recount; however, perhaps a few of the more flagrant instances of abuse of public office for financial gain are worth citing to provide points of reference:

I.   Reported by the German former director of the Zairian Central Bank, Erwin Blumenthal, under President Mobutu:
   1. Soldiers arrived at the bank one evening about 7 P.M., long after the bank had closed, to demand the equivalent of $30,000 for the general who was Mobutu's father-in-law.[3]
   2. Approximately $4 million was drawn from the bank in payment to a Belgian professor for a study of poverty. This study turned out to be bogus. The Belgian was the guardian of Mobutu's son.
   3. Two million dollars was drawn from the bank, allegedly to pay Mobutu's architect.
   4. Approximately $14.5 million was drawn from the bank by Mobutu for his special accounts. The money was apparently used by Mobutu to pay his secret police and military.

II.   Reported by a former Zairian prime minister:
   1. Secret sales of cobalt were made to South Africa, and the payments were made to Mobutu's secret Swiss bank account.
   2. Mobutu's personal fortune is estimated at $4 billion.

III. Reported in a special judicial hearing to investigate the alleged crimes of a former Kenyan attorney general, Charles Njonjo:[4]
   1. Njonjo siphoned off charitable contributions intended for the poor and handicapped into his personal checking account.
   2. Fifteen thousand dollars was paid to Njonjo by the former chairman of the National Bank of Kenya, who was under suspicion for fraud.

IV.   Reported by an American General Motors manager in a private conversation:[5]
   1. Njonjo received thousands of dollars yearly from Mercedes-Benz company to prevent domestic assembly of General motors automobiles in Kenya.

V. Reported in Ghana in a governmental investigation following the overthrow of the Nkrumah government:[6]
    1. Collection officers of the Cocoa Marketing Board had taken 10% of farmers' crops as illegal commissions for fulfilling their duty to buy the crop.

VI. Reported in Nigeria by an official government investigation after military overthrow of the civilian government:[7]
    1. Government officials had embezzled billions of dollars from the sale of Nigerian oil during the 1970s.

A number of books and articles have been written proposing a variety of explanations of governmental corruption in African societies. Among those explanations, the most frequently cited are the following:

1. Conflict between traditional and modern cultures[8]
2. Inadequacy of legal traditions derived from European cultures of their former colonial rulers, and the colonial legacy of arbitrary governmental powers[9]
3. The African love of pleasure and ostentation[10]
4. Corruption as an expression of both domestic and foreign social class exploitation[11]
5. Weak public morality or civic consciousness in African societies, reflected in tribalism and other forms of particularism[12]
6. The low moral character of the men who emerged from the struggle for power in postcolonial African nations[13]

The objective of this chapter on African governmental corruption is to provide a conceptual reorientation. It departs from previous analytical perspectives not because they are irrelevant (some of the factors emphasized in the literature will be incorporated into the present discussion), but because they are too narrow in scope. Focusing on only African governmental corruption, most have lost sight of corruption as part of a larger social process of deviance in developing societies. Moreover, following from this tendency, they have failed to explore comparatively the implications of structural arrangements and developmental disjunctions for the social psychological meanings of deviance prevailing within these societies.

The present discussion, in contrast, is informed by a phenomenological perspective on deviance — that is, a perspective focused on the interaction between institutional change and the emergent discrepancy between laws and operative norms of social control as the basis of phenomenological categories of deviance in developing societies. These operative norms of social control, it is argued, determine the actual spheres of tolerated versus proscribed behavior — the definition of situations — that facilitate governmental corruption. That is because in developing societies undergoing institutional change the operative norms of social control — not the laws — shape the existential patterns of social organization and their phenomenological meaning.

The thesis of this chapter is that explanation of African governmental corruption must incorporate several previously neglected concerns: an implicit comparative perspective that locates the cultural and structural frameworks of African societies within the larger universe of developing societies experiencing similar processes of institutional transformation; a phenomenological perspective that focuses on the implications of those cultural and structural frameworks of African societies — and particularly their operative norms of social control — for the subjective meanings of corrupt acts to the government officials involved; and a comparative typology that differentiates African governmental structures in terms of their degree of vulnerability to corruption.

Focus on the phenomenological level of analysis, it should be noted, comprises the pivotal issue of the analytical perspective presented. As such, it points toward a new direction of theoretical emphasis. This chapter is only a beginning application of that perspective to the problem of African governmental corruption. It suggests the need for more careful empirical observations of the operative norms of social control to establish the actual boundaries of permitted and proscribed actions underlying the phenomenological categories of deviance within African governments.

Thus, as an explanation of African governmental corruption, this chapter aims to provide an integrated focus on the following issues:

1. The social processes of development and deviance
2. The limitations of the structuralist and sociological conception of deviance
3. The problematic relationship between laws and norms in developing societies
4. The governmental apparatus of social control and the phenomenological meaning of illegal behavior for the officials involved

5. The potential positive functions of corruption for certain types of African political structures
6. The comparative implications of this analytical perspective for explaining different levels of corruption within African governments

The primary focus of this chapter will be on capitalistically oriented African societies; however, its implications should have relevance to socialistically oriented African societies as well, insofar as they show cultural and structural characteristics identified as conducive to phenomenological definitions of private financial gain as a prerogative of public office.

THE SOCIAL PROCESS OF DEVELOPMENT

As a sociological phenomenon, development entails the establishment of new normative boundaries, new guidelines of behavior, which serve as the foundation for the emergence and expansion of more efficient and productive social organizations. In short, development fosters normative and organizational transformation. This may be the result of largely unconscious social evolution, as it was in much of the Western world, or deliberate ideological design, as it has been in the Soviet Union and China and has become with limited degrees of success during the latter part of the twentieth century throughout the Third World.

DEVELOPMENT AND DEVIANCE

Though seldom perceived as such, development — that process of normative and organizational transformation — inevitably entails problems of social deviance. In fact, from the standpoint of traditional social structure, the process of development itself may be viewed as deviant, as shown by the often-hostile reaction of traditional groups to modernization. The fundamentalist Islamic revolution in Iran is a recent dramatic manifestation of this tendency. If development is to succeed, it must weaken the prevailing traditional mechanisms of social control. Here is the paradox. It must typically weaken the latter before it has established alternative normative controls that are compatible with the efficient functioning of modern social institutions. Thus all developing societies experience this transitional phase, varying in duration, when they are highly susceptible to pressures toward rapid acceleration of new forms of deviance, as evidenced in their increased rates of robbery, bribery, embezzlement, larceny, fraud, and the like. In other words, all demonstrate an increasing incidence of behaviors that deviate from the normative rules of the modern social institutions they are seeking to establish. This is not to say that social deviance is peculiar to developing societies; such a statement would be absurd. But developing societies do encounter special problems of deviance — among which flagrant corruption certainly must be included — because often neither the masses of the population nor those charged with administering the new social order have sufficiently internalized its formal legal guidelines for behavior.

To illustrate the pertinence of the sociological concept of deviance for understanding the problem of normative transformation in African capitalist societies, it is perhaps best to begin our discussion with the social structural perspective exemplified in Robert Merton's famous theory of anomie and social structure.[14] This approach conceives of deviance as the product of contradictions between societally prescribed cultural goals (the rewards of success deemed worthy of pursuit) and societally prescribed means (the normatively sanctioned channels for attaining those rewards). Based on the individual's commitment (present/absent) to these societally prescribed ends and his access (open/closed) to institutionally prescribed means for their attainment, the Mertonian theoretical model postulates five patterns of action in any society (Table 10.1).

Conformity characterizes the behavior of individuals having both commitment to societally prescribed rewards and access to institutionally prescribed channels for attaining the latter. This is the sphere of conventional social life. Ritualism, in contrast, typifies the behavior of individuals who have access to institutionally prescribed means but lack commitment to societally prescribed rewards in their everyday conduct. Alienated from prevailing cultural inducements to action, ritualists enact hollow gestures of conformity reflected in aimless adherence to conventional behavior. Retreatism and rebellion constitute sharp departures from the above two patterns. They typify individuals who lack both commitment to societally prescribed rewards and access to the institutionalized channels for attaining those rewards. Retreatists merely withdraw from conventional society — a response characteristic of vagrants, skid row alcoholics, drug addicts, and, in the extreme, suicides. Rebels, however, taking an opposite direction, attempt to

TABLE 10.1
Patterns of Social Action Relating Goals and Opportunity Structures

		(Cultural Goals) Societally Prescribed Ends	(Opportunity Structure) Societally Prescribed Means
1.	Conformity	+	+
2.	Ritualism	–	+
3.	Deviance	+	–
4.	Retreatism	–	–
5.	Rebellion	+/–	+/–

establish a new set of cultural goals and institutionalized rules for their attainment. This is the sphere of radical political action.

Last, and for our purposes most important, is the action pattern of innovative deviance. Here the prevailing societal goals are embraced, but the institutionally prescribed means for attaining them are inaccessible. This is the sphere of economic crimes. Such a situation, Merton argues, usually results from a disjunction between cultural emphasis on rewards, which are held out to all, and the opportunities for their attainment, which are unavailable to many.

This structural perspective, presented here in a brief and simplified form, has been extensively applied to the phenomenon of deviance in developed capitalist societies. The objective in presenting it here is to gain a sharper focus on corruption from a structural perspective, which views deviance as a response to contradictions in the social system. Though helpful in clarifying the societally induced motivations to deviance, this structural perspective has several serious limitations. It takes into account neither the actual prevalence of deviance nor its effects for the pattern of a society's social organization. In short, it says nothing about the consequences of innovative deviance. Yet consideration of the latter is crucial for explanation of governmental corruption and other forms of economic deviance as *commonplace* features of a society's social organization, for the concern here is with the organizational arrangements that facilitate high levels of tolerance for innovative deviance.

From a structural perspective this would seem a contradiction in terms. If the behavior in question is highly prevalent, it would in effect be normative: an established feature of the society's social organization. The structural perspective operates on the assumption that a society's norms and laws tend to coincide — an assumption that seems relevant only to certain types of social orders, those characterized by highly institutionalized legal norms, which is only another way of saying social orders in which the laws are viewed by the population as legitimate. An example of this would be a developed capitalist democracy such as the United States where there is continuous interaction between public opinion and legislative processes through the mechanisms of mass media and elections.

Such a situation of relatively high congruence between laws and prevailing social norms is rarely evident in developing societies, which is one reason why these societies seldom sustain political democracies. More often the objective of laws is not to reflect the norms of public opinion but to shape and control its expression. Typically, in these societies a wide gap yawns between many of the laws and social norms. In contrast to developed democratic societies, where laws tend to operate as institutionalized (public sanctioned) norms, in developing societies many laws tend to operate as directive precepts or ideal norms.[15]

In such a situation, but for reasons different from those adduced by the structuralist perspective, there will be strong motivational pressures toward deviance, pressures to violate laws that conflict with prevailing social norms — that is, situations of asymmetry between the legal and normative order. In these asymmetrical legal and normative orders the relevant analytical problem for understanding deviance is that of determining the state of the governmental apparatus of social control, that is, the latter's capacity to achieve compliance. This can be achieved through either ideological socialization that creates normative identification with the laws or through coercive actions — in short, vigilant law enforcement. Developing societies such as China, Singapore, Taiwan, and South Korea have all apparently achieved high levels of compliance by relying, to a varying degree, on both indoctrination and coercion. To state the matter somewhat differently, these societies effectively manage the asymmetry between social norms and laws. Of particular importance, they achieve high levels of compliance with the laws governing their economic systems, a fact directly related to the apparent success of their development efforts.

But this is not true of all developing societies. In some the gap between the laws and prevailing social norms is accompanied by a weak governmental apparatus of social control and high levels of economic crime. This is the situation of most capitalistically oriented African societies.

A PHENOMENOLOGICAL PERSPECTIVE

To understand deviance in social situations of weak or arbitrary social controls, where some types of deviance are a commonplace feature of social organization, demands a conception of deviance that delineates its phenomenological forms — specifically, how the acts are perceived by participants in actual social life.[16] This conception of deviance requires an analytical perspective on social organization based on the following assumptions:

1. Not all violators are apprehended, even though their offenses may be known officially.
2. Of those who are apprehended, not all are punished; and of those who are, not all are punished in the same way.
3. Finally, not all legal behavior publicizing acts of deviance is officially tolerated.

In short, this perspective suggests that some illegal acts may be prevalent and functional features of social organization. But first, before analyzing the fostering conditions and the governmental structures that facilitate innovative deviance, it is necessary to delineate these major situational forms of deviance and their different implications for social organization (Figure 10.1).

The category of legitimized normative behavior refers to those social actions that are both approved by the formal legal system and tolerated by the operative governmental norms of social control. This is the domain of conventional behavior.

In contrast, the category of soft deviance refers to illegal acts that are tolerated by the operative governmental norms. This category includes both violators and illegal acts that have a low probability of punishment. Behavior falling within the category of soft deviance is significant

Operative Norms of Social Control

	Tolerated Behavior	Punished Behavior
Approved Behavior	category of legitimized normative behavior	category of residual deviance
Proscribed Behavior	category of soft deviance	category of hard deviance

Legal Norms

Figure 10.1
Situational Domains of Behavior in African Government Organizations

because it is indicative of areas of weak institutionalization. Wherever soft deviance exists, there is a blurring of the boundaries between permitted and proscribed conduct. Soft deviance is hardly unique to African societies, as is evidenced by the tolerance of prostitution, gambling, and certain types of white-collar crimes in the United States. What is, however, apparently unique to capitalistically oriented African societies is the broad range of this category of soft deviance, encompassing many illegal economic acts, within the governments themselves. Bribery, embezzlement, extortion, and misappropriation of governmental property, to cite only the most commonplace types of governmental corruption, tend to occupy the normative status of soft deviance. This has been detrimental to the economic growth of these societies because a weak or arbitrary government apparatus of social control has debilitating effects on the functioning of a capitalist economic system, not only because of ineffective enforcement of laws regulating the economic system but also because of the large role of governments in the economies of capitalistically oriented African societies.[17] In such situations tolerance of economic crimes inevitably results in a severely crippled and inefficient economic performance.

Soft deviance is the outcome of legal-normative conflicts in social organization and, as such, has the function of preserving the latter's continuity. Typically it involves the straddling behavior (part-time deviance) of strategically situated participants on whom the social organization depends to maintain its stability. In short, it is organizationally accommodated deviance. Prostitution in the United States, for example, tends to exist as soft deviance — a pattern of illegal behavior that is tolerated because by providing an outlet for the sexual proclivities of otherwise conventional males and avoiding entangling emotional commitments, it preserves the institution of monogamous marriage.[18]

In a similar fashion the soft deviance of corruption in the governments of African capitalist societies has the function of preserving the stability of certain types of governmental structures. Indeed, as I will later suggest, the greater the threats to the stability of these governments, the more extensive the range of economic crimes falling within the category of soft deviance (that is, toleration of corrupt acts committed by officials).

Hard deviance, in contrast, refers to the category of both violators and illegal acts that have a high probability of punishment. As such, it is indicative of areas of strong institutionalization. Typically, in African capitalist societies robbery, homicide, physical assaults, and possession of firearms, violations most evident among lower-class groups, tend to be treated as hard deviance. In Kenya, for example, robbery accompanied by violence, a crime that is usually committed by members of the lower class against members of the upper strata, is a capital offense punishable by hanging. Also, in these societies the illegal acts of lower-level officials are more likely than are the illegal acts of upper-level officials to fall under the category of hard deviance. The important point is this. In the case of hard deviance the boundaries between permitted and proscribed behavior are sharply delineated. In short, the broader the range of illegal acts or violators encompassed by the category of hard as opposed to soft deviance in a society, the stronger is the institutionalization of its social organization.

Finally, there are behaviors falling under the category of residual deviance. This represents a radically different type of deviance, for unlike soft and hard deviance, it consists not of violations of law but of extralegal norms of state security. It is behavior operating within the law but subject to punishment because it is perceived as a threat to the power structure. This typically applies to negative comments or criticisms of government through the exercise of free expression. Public speech, newspapers, books, plays, and the like fall into this category.

An example of this can be briefly illustrated from a conversation I had with a young reporter working for a newspaper in an African country I visited that is reputed to be stable. A recent graduate of a journalism school in the United States, this young man returned home committed to the professional norms of American journalism. After several weeks of investigation, he wrote a feature article on instances of corruption by government officials in the capital city. The next day, he said, he was "picked up" by the police. They held him approximately one week, during which time he was subjected to long hours of interrogation about his contacts in the United States and the source of his financial support while attending journalism school. They accused him of having been paid by the American CIA to write the corruption article and warned him that he would be jailed if he persisted in attacking the government. "I got the message," the young reporter told me, noting that he now avoided writing about sensitive issues.

What is referred to as "whistle-blowing" within government organizations often falls under the category of residual deviance. Public allegations of malfeasance by one government employee directed against another government employee are often subject to negative sanctions, even when the allegations turn out to be valid. These informal norms against organizational disloyalty are hardly unique to African capitalist societies. They are frequently in evidence in the United States among policemen, medical doctors, and government bureaucrats, who are apt to use a variety of negative sanctions against an insider who "rats" on his colleagues.

There are many interesting implications of this category of residual deviance that cannot be explored here. For our purposes what is most important in African capitalist societies is the tendency for behavior falling under soft deviance within government organization to correspond to a broad category of behavior falling under residual deviance both within and outside government organization. In short, a reciprocal relationship exists between the categories of soft deviance and residual deviance. To thrive, governmental corruption demands suppression of public information about its activities. Every area of soft deviance has a corresponding area of residual deviance. Thus it is possible to differentiate three hypothetical patterns of opportunity or risk associated with corruption based on this correspondence between categories of soft and residual deviance (Figure 10.2).

Corresponding to the first pattern, which facilitates a high level of corruption, there will be a tendency toward repression of all public discussion or criticism of alleged corruption committed by government officials. In contrast, corresponding to the second pattern, which facilitates a moderate level of corruption, there will be a tendency toward repression of public discussion in reference only to some alleged types of violators or corruption among government officials. Others will not be insulated from public allegations. Finally, corresponding to the third pattern, which conduces to a low level of corruption, there will be tolerance of public discussion of all alleged types of violators and illegal acts among government officials. In short, under this pattern all acts of corruption by government officials are subsumed under the category of hard deviance.

I will return to this model in reference to the facilitating conditions that dispose specific types of African governmental structures to each of the above patterns. But a point of qualification concerning the limitations of this analytical approach should be noted. No government is entirely free of corruption. This analytical approach refers to situations where corruption is a commonplace feature of government organization. The relevant questions are these: What happens when corruption among government officials is suspected? Can it be publicly discussed or

Category of
Soft Deviance

Category of
Residual Deviance

Level of Vulnerability
to Corruption

1. Broad ----------------------> Broad -------------------> High

2. Limited ----------------> Limited -------------> Moderate

3. Non-existent ------------> Non-existent ------------> Low

Figure 10.2
Reciprocal Relationship between the Categories of Soft Deviance and Residual Deviance and the
Level of Vulnerability to Corruption in Governmental Organization

alleged? Are the officials subject to arrest and conviction? The focus here is on a government organization's vulnerability to corruption rather than on its actual amount of corruption. Actual prevalence — like most primary deviance, because its manifestations are usually hidden — cannot be precisely determined. Nevertheless, it is the assumption of this analytical approach to corruption as deviance that the level of a government organization's vulnerability to corruption can be determined by noting the range of illegal acts and types of government officials insulated from public allegations. Moreover, it is assumed that there exists a relatively high correlation between the degree of a government organization's vulnerability to corruption and its actual level of corruption.

FOSTERING CONDITIONS

Now we can turn to consideration of the fostering conditions that lie behind high levels of governmental corruption in African capitalist societies. First, there is the disjunction between a postindustrial capitalist consumption ideology and a coexisting protocapitalist economic system. Unlike the early phase of Western capitalism, which emerged within a strong cultural framework that imposed disciplined restraint,[19] the early phase of African capitalist development exists within a weak cultural framework. In Western societies there was considerable balance between the ideological-motivational restraints on materialistic aspirations and the structural growth of capitalism, so that the capitalist consumption ideology assumed dominance only during the latter postindustrial phase of its structural development. By contrast, in African societies the capitalist consumption ideology assumed dominance before their industrialization. The subsequent motivational pressures toward economic deviance in such situations can perhaps best be termed the African capitalist dilemma: the worse the system works, the more people violate its rules; the more people violate its rules, the worse the system works.

Where the ideological outlook that conditions personal expectations is severely misaligned with the capacity of the economic system to yield even moderate satisfaction, a strong proclivity to violate laws governing economic conduct is virtually inevitable. This explains the prevalence of strong motivational pressures to commit economic crimes among both lower- and upper-status groups in African capitalist societies.

But why are similar effects not observed in other capitalistically oriented developing societies such as South Korea and Singapore? These societies possess what I term "tight cultures" — strong overarching religious-ethical traditions that restrain ideological-motivational orientation. Tight cultures are characterized by continuity and adaptation of their religious-ethical traditions in the process of development. This does not mean that tight cultures evidence no economic crimes, nor that all tight cultures are necessarily disposed to capitalist enterprise, but only that they more effectively restrain the growth of materialistic consumption ideology.

African states, by contrast, are characterized by "loose cultures," by the absence of overarching and unifying religious-ethical traditions. Because African societies are comprised of plural and often conflicting ethnic groups with different traditional heritages, development has entailed emphasis on universalism and secularism devoid of a unifying religious-ethical framework. Hence they have lacked effective restraints on the growth of materialist consumption ideology. As a consequence, African capitalist societies have been more susceptible to contemporary Western cultural influences — via movies, music, magazines, and so on — that inevitably transmit and reinforce the consumption ideology of postindustrial capitalist societies. This ideology has not been simply inappropriate; it has been destructive of African capitalist development through its generation of motivational pressures for material consumption that cannot legitimately be fulfilled by protocapitalist economic systems.

The second fostering condition for high levels of African governmental corruption was the feeble development of the private sector of African societies at the time of independence. This resulted not only in a major role of the state in the economy but also, given the previously noted consumption orientation, in the manifestation of the ideological-structural contradictions of African capitalism in the state apparatus itself. There were few alternative means to acquire wealth. Thus the chief effect of the postindustrial capitalist consumption ideology was to channel motivations for affluence into public office, which offered much opportunity for the illegal acquisition of wealth.

The third fostering condition, unlike the first two, which are predispositional, focuses on facilitative factors that actually pave the way for high levels of governmental corruption in African capitalist societies. These concern the effects of the government's level of political legitimacy on the form of its administrative structure and hence its degree of tolerance or intolerance of corruption.

STRUCTURAL PATTERNS OF AFRICAN CAPITALIST GOVERNMENTS AND THEIR VULNERABILITY TO CORRUPTION

A basic pattern of African capitalist governmental organization is the authoritarian patrimonial administrative structure.[20] This is the pattern of those African capitalist states characterized by weak legitimacy and the absence of a disciplined party. In these societies the state is seldom separated from the person of the ruler. Frequently camouflaged in rhetoric emphasizing the importance of stability, the primary objective of the administrative apparatus is to maintain the prevailing system of personal domination. Its secondary objective may be economic development. In short, the administrative apparatus is the chief support network underlying a system of authoritarian personal rule. As a consequence, there exists a conflict between the priorities of personal political allegiance and administrative efficiency. In other words, punishment of corruption and adherence to norms of administrative efficiency based on impersonal universalistic rules are incompatible with the maintenance of a system of personal domination.

That is not because such an administrative structure openly promotes corruption but rather because the conditions of its survival necessitate a different conception of organizational rationality. To survive, it must rely on a pyramid of patron-client bonds governed beyond all else by obligations of personal loyalty. But this does not explain its vulnerability to corruption. To explain the latter, we must note the ruler's dependency. Given the weak legitimacy of his power, he can survive only if the administrative apparatus — including the police and military — are personally loyal, committed to a personal-political rather than an impersonal-bureaucratic conception of organizational ratonality.

Thus a patrimonially rationalized administrative apparatus, while permitting little political detachment, necessitates a wide range of administrative discretion. Officeholders must be responsive to personal political considerations that cannot be officially codified. This essential elasticity of administrative practices permits not only the infusion of subterranean personal political considerations in the actions of government officials, but also widespread corruption.

In short, vulnerability to pervasive governmental corruption is a functional consequence of weak political legitimacy underlying personal systems of political rule. A symbiotic relationship of reciprocal dependency prevails between the ruler and his administrative staff. Even if evidence of corruption among his administrative staff displeases the ruler, which is hardly certain, repressive actions against them is likely to jeopardize his political survival. Negative sanctions against corruption, by depriving his subordinates of extralegal rewards of office, may destroy the incentives behind their commitment to his rule. By subjecting them to punishment, he is apt to erode the most important base of his political power.

This patrimonial administrative structure may assume one of two forms: a predatory form, as in Zaire, or an attenuated form, as in Kenya. The former, where the government possesses virtually no legitimacy, has high levels of vulnerability to corruption. The latter, where the government possesses weak legitimacy, has moderate levels of vulnerability to corruption. Another pattern of governmental organization is the rational-legal administrative structure, characteristic of such governments as that of Zimbabwe, which possesses relatively strong legitimacy and has low levels of vulnerability to corruption. The characteristics of each of these administrative structures are the following:

I.   Predatory patrimonial administrative structure
   1. Government possesses virtually no political legitimacy.
   2. High level of vulnerability to corruption.
   3. Little outward appearance of rational-legal bureaucracy.
   4. Corrupt practices are often open and flagrant.
   5. Corruption exists as soft deviance if committed by all or most government officials.
   6. Tendency toward repression of public discussion or criticism of all alleged illegal acts and violators among government officials.

II.   Attenuated patrimonial administrative structure
   1. Government possesses weak political legitimacy.
   2. Moderate level of vulnerability to corruption.
   3. Outward appearance of rational-legal bureaucracy.
   4. Corrupt practices tend to be hidden and discreet.
   5. Corruption exists as soft deviance if committed by ruling clique and upper-status officials.
   6. Tendency toward repression of public discussion or criticism of only some alleged illegal acts and violators among government officials.

III. Rational-legal administrative structure
1. Government possesses relatively strong legitimacy.
2. Low level of vulnerability to corruption.
3. Corrupt practices very carefully hidden.
4. Corruption exists as hard deviance.
5. Tolerance of public discussions and criticisms of all alleged illegal acts or violators among government officials.

It should be noted that these conceptual characterizations are intended as ideal types consisting of the logically interdependent attributes of administrative structures that make them more or less conducive to institutionalized corruption. Specific African governments are likely only to approximate one or another of these abstracted administrative structures. However, the objective in presenting these ideal types is to provide a basis for classifying different African governments in terms of their vulnerability to corruption.

Zaire, under the unrelenting personal domination of Mobutu Sese Seko, is one of the African governments that closely approximates the predatory-type patrimonial structure. Described by one author as "an extreme version of the Sun-King," Mobutu has the distinction of presiding over one of the most corrupt governments in Africa.

> In the orbits closest to him circle the dozen or so members of the presidential clique. These are his trusted kinsmen, the men who occupy the most sensitive and lucrative government positions. The presidential brotherhood is somewhat further from the sun. Theirs are the top political and administrative posts and their relationship with the President is symbiotic. He demands their absolute personal allegiance and, in return, grants them access to power and illegal opportunities to accumulate wealth. His displeasure guarantees personal ruin and even imprisonment. The most distant satellites are the thousands of middle-level officials, army officers, and university personnel. While their opportunities for aggrandizement are more limited, they can still become well off. And they aspire to join the brotherhood. Meanwhile, the mass of the population is excluded from the spoils and subject to repression.[21]

Uganda under the chaotic tyrannical rule of Idi Amin represents another example of an African government that closely approximated the predatory-type patrimonial structure.[22]

Because their political survival depends on force and intimidation rather than on popular support, these governments manifest the least sensitivity to outward appearances of official conduct. The following excerpt from a Mobutu speech illustrates this point:

> In a word, everything is for sale, anything can be bought in our country. And in this flow, he who holds the slightest cover of public authority uses it illegally to acquire money, goods, prestige or to avoid obligations. The right to be recognized by a public servant, to have one's children enrolled in school, to obtain medical care, a diploma, etc. . . . are all subject to his tax which, though invisible, is known and expected by all.[23]

Having no legitimacy to preserve, these governments demonstrate the most blatant and pervasive practices of corruption. Public welfare and economic development are apt to be of little if any concern. As has been noted in reference to Zaire:

> The Zairian political aristocracy manifests a weak sense of public purpose and collective or societal good. It has demonstrated a notably feeble commitment to increasing the standard of living of the masses over whom it rules. . . . As a result, "development" programs usually get only what is left over after the political aristocracy has achieved its class project, resulting in a general pauperization of the bulk of the state's subjects.[24]

Plunder is institutionalized. Given the operative norms of the governmental apparatus of social control, private financial gain through the performance of official duties is perceived not as theft but as an entitlement of office. Needless to say, the prospect of significantly reducing corruption under this type of administrative structure is bleak.

In contrast, a government approximating the attenuated patrimonial structure will tend to exhibit some constraints on official corruption because of a desire to prevent further erosion of its weak legitimacy. Among the many possible reasons for the ruler's desire to preserve or enhance the government's limited legitimacy, interests in maintaining a favorable image in the eyes of foreign donors and capital markets or concern with avoiding a military coup are likely to be paramount. The resulting constraints on official corruption will tend to be manifested in two ways: more frequent prosecution (than in predatory-type governments) of lower-level officials and controls on the outward appearance of conduct by upper-level officials. The latter's corrupt practices are likely to be discreet. In other words, this type of administrative structure conduces to the tolerance of private financial gain by upper-level government officials so long as it is not flagrant — that is, does not detract from the government's outward appearance of rational-legal administration. In situations where an upper-level official has been involved in flagrant corruption that has aroused public discontent, the leader may choose to "sacrifice him," to terminate his service because he has become too great a liability. Also, occasional criminal prosecutions of upper-level officials may be used as a device for punishing those who have fallen from grace for other reasons.[25]

Another constraint imposed on this type of administrative structure is that of public welfare. Given the ruler's desire to preserve the government's limited legitimacy and avoid exacerbating public discontent, there is likely to be genuine — albeit secondary — concern about public welfare and economic development. This will impose some limits on the amount of public funds that can be expropriated because of the need to maintain basic public services.

Kenya, Zambia, and the Ivory Coast are examples of governments that approximate this attenuated patrimonial structure, which is most vulnerable to corruption among the ruler and upper-level officials. The Ivory Coast provides an interesting illustration of this pattern of institutionalized elite corruption. In 1983

> Houphouet-Boigny had come under strong attack for his own and his family's financial interests. He responded with a long detailed statement, felt by many observers to be disastrously frank, in which he commented that "I have billions abroad in Switzerland, but I also have billions in the Ivory Coast, which proves that I have confidence in my country."[26]

Such a public confession is the exception rather than the rule for leaders of attenuated patrimonial structures. But the point about constraints on corruption in this type of structure is illustrated in the Ivory Coast. Despite the prevalence of elite corruption, Houphouet-Boigny's government has maintained sufficient administrative rationality to avoid degeneration into a predatory patrimonial administrative structure.

> The Ivorian civil service is an effective institution and this is because Houphouet-Boigny has shielded it from the corrosive effects of personal rule. True, the President and his lieutenants distribute patronage to maintain political loyalties. . . . Some resources have, therefore, been wasted. And official corruption is not unheard of in the Ivory Coast, though this is an occasional, not a universal phenomenon.
>
> The President continues to insist that (nonpatronage) employees must prove their competence before they can be promoted. The bureaucracy has been insulated to some extent from the game of factional manoeuvre.[27]

In general, while the administrative structure of attenuated patrimonialism is more efficiently managed, its institutionalized elite corruption still imposes debilitating burdens on the economy.

Last, unlike the two forms of patrimonial administrative structure, the rational-legal administrative type shows low vulnerability to corruption. This is not to say that corruption does not occur but rather that it risks negative sanctions. In other words, it is treated as hard deviance. This type of administrative structure conduces to the normative perception of corruption as criminal activity. Thus the corruption that does occur is obliged to be carefully hiden. Moreover, and perhaps most important, corruption is not a by-product of the conditions for the government's political survival. Governments approximating this type of administrative structure operate within a constitutional framework and possess relatively strong legitimacy or a disciplined dominant party. Critically important to the low vulnerability to corruption of this type of administrative structure are a highly professionalized police investigative unit and an autonomous judiciary. These conditions militate against the formation of ruler-centered patrimonialism.

Unfortunately there have been no studies of corruption in African governments approximating this type of rational-legal administrative structure. Thus the present designation of African governments with low vulnerablity to corruption must be speculative. Both Botswana and Zimbabwe appear to approximate rational-legal administrative structures. As has been noted by the authors of a recent study of Botswana, one of the few countries in Africa to have democratic multiparty elections:

> Our judgment is that both Sereste Khama and Quett Masire are personally deeply committed to the concept of multi-party democracy. . . . Perhaps the best evidence for this is the extraordinary respect for the constitutional rule of law which the country's leaders have always shown. . . . The few minor changes to the constitution which have been made have been approached with considerable reluctance and caution, while the constitution has been rarely flouted.[28]

This, of course, is only indirect evidence. But the absence of any reference to corruption in the authors' discussion of Botswana's politics suggests, in contrast to discussions of politics in most other African countries, where it is frequently mentioned, that corruption is not an institutionalized pattern in Botswana's political life. Zimbabwe presents a different and more complex case. Having achieved democracy based on universal franchise, Zimbabwe's government appears to approximate the rational-legal administrative structure. Evidence suggests governmental intolerance of corruption.[29] But this may soon change if the current leaderhsip succeeds in transforming Zimbabwe into a one-party state. The rights of political opposition will end. The government will then run the risk of declining legitimacy and degeneration into attenuated patrimonialism to sustain its political survival. Already there are signs of this eventuality in increased government control over the press.

> The United States Department of State's human rights report for 1981 stated that the editorial policy of the daily press was uniformly progovernment. Although some parliamentary and other criticisms of the government had been reported, there were numerous allegations that many events reflecting poorly on the current leadership had been suppressed.[30]

If Zimbabwe does shift to a one-party state, the only condition that is likely to militate against its political degeneration into patrimonialism and increased vulnerability to institutionalized corruption is the existence of a disciplined dominant party.

Of course, the breakdown of the rational-legal type of administrative structure need not result in stable patrimonialism. The postindependence civilian governments of Nigeria and Ghana, both plagued by corruption, are examples of repeated unsuccessful efforts to establish rational-legal administrative structures that devolved not into stable patrimonialism but into a series of military coups.

AFRICAN SOCIALIST GOVERNMENTS AND CORRUPTION

The present discussion has been focused on corruption in African capitalist governments, but this is not intended to imply that African socialist governments are immune to corruption. A government's vulnerability to corruption is determined by its operative norms of social control, not by the type of economic system it embraces. Given the much greater role of African socialist governments in the economies of their societies, the opportunities for corruption would be far greater. However, there are several factors that might militate against pervasive corruption in African socialist societies. First, these societies tend to place less cultural emphasis on individual material consumption, so that the motivational pressures to commit economic crimes are likely to be less intense than they are in African capitalist societies whose stratification hierarchy is based on wealth. Second, because the standard of living of upper-level officials in African socialist governments tends to be lower than that of their counterparts in African capitalist governments, officials who expropriate large amounts of public funds could not use these to support an affluent lifestyle. Luxury consumption would be conspicuous and arouse suspicions in a way it would not be likely to do in African capitalist societies, where it is common for government officials to own businesses, real estate, and other sources of private income. In short, there are likely to be severe constraints on the use government officials can make of large amounts of illegally acquired wealth.

This is not to say that corruption among government officials in African socialist states is therefore obviated. Small amounts of illegally acquired wealth can be used for less conspicuous consumption, or larger amounts can be deposited in foreign banks. But these limits on consumption will decrease the incentive for corruption in African socialist states. Finally, though the African governments adhering to socialism constitute a bewildering variety of forms, in general they may be more likely to possess a dominant and ideologically disciplined party than are African capitalist governments. Insofar as this is the case, the party will tend to operate as a functional alternative to patrimonialism and the tolerated corruption that accompanies it as a means of maintaining governmental stability in the absence of strong legitimacy.

The African socialist governments that appear to conform to this pattern of a dominant and ideologically disciplined party are Congo-Brazzaville, Mozambique, Angola, and Ethiopia. We would expect these governments to evidence low vulnerability to corruption. Given the paucity of information about their internal operations, this conclusion is at best speculative. It should be emphasized that there is nothing about an African government's commitment to socialism per se that makes it invulnerable to corruption. In fact, with the characteristic tendency of African socialist states to suppress political opposition and free expression, those lacking a dominant and ideologically disciplined party are likely to prove quite vulnerable to patrimonialism and corruption. As previously noted, however, the consumption incentives typically associated with African capitalist governments will tend to be lower.

The above designations of specific African governments in terms of their administrative structures and vulnerability to corruption are tentative. They are intended primarily to illustrate the analytical model based on the phenomenological conception of deviance developed in this chapter. Further research is needed before a more definite classification of African governments in terms of this model can be established.

CONCLUSION

This chapter suggests the need for the study of phenomenological categories of deviance in African governments. Because of the sensitive nature of the subject, the difficulties of gathering direct empirical data on African governmental corruption are formidable. But this need not preclude comparative studies of the problem of African government corruption.[31]

Since the object of this type of phenomenological inquiry is to determine the levels of vulnerability to corruption rather than the actual amount of corruption, indirect empirical data (preferably based on observations and informal interviews gathered in the country in question) that allow one to make inferences about the operative norms of social control are likely to prove quite useful. From these data inferences can be made about which types of economic crimes and what level of officials committing such acts are likely to fall under the categories of soft or hard deviance. Similarly, inferences based on indirect empirical data can be made about which types of activity publicizing corruption are likely to fall under the category of residual deviance. Such inquiries, because their aim is to delineate normative organization, follow the procedures of ethnographic research, which is a methodology much more suited to studying corruption and other forms of deviance than is that of survey research.

As regards policy recommendations, external governments and agencies concerned with the problems of African governmental corruption are obviously limited in what they can do. Nevertheless, within those limitations there are measures they might stipulate as conditions for their development assistance that could reduce significantly a government's vulnerability to corruption. External governments and agencies might promote respect for autonomy of the judiciary and protection of the rights of free expression, particularly in reference to matters pertaining to the honesty of public officials, as well as legislation in Western nations that would oblige Western banks to open their records on bank accounts held by African politicians. Currently, Western banks that refuse to divulge information about the accounts of African government officials actually benefit from African governmental corruption. Providing open access to these secret sanctuaries would remove the primary means used by African government officials to hide large amounts of illegally acquired funds. Finally, there is the need for an Amnesty International–type organization to investigate and collect information on corruption with the objective of creating unfavorable international opinion toward those governments where institutionalized corruption prevails. This would provide an alternative to local African media, which are typically subject to governmental controls.

Future research focused on levels of vulnerability to corruption of specific African governments will yield further insights into this most debilitating by-product of weak African governmental institutions. It seems hardly an exaggeration to say that many African governments are preserving their stability at destructive costs to their economies.

NOTES

1.   Gideon S. Were, *Leadership and Underdevelopment in Africa*, Nairobi, Gideon Were, P. O. Box 10622, 1983, 8, 9.

2.   J. S. Nye, "Corruption and Political Development: A Cost-Benefit Analysis," in Arnold J. Heidenhiemer, ed., *Political Corruption*, New York, Holt, Rinehart and Winston, 1970, 566–67.

3.   This and other reports about corruption in Zaire were taken from Were, *Leadership and Underdevelopment*, 29–32.

4.   *Weekly Review* (Nairobi), August 24, 1984, 5–11.

5.   Private conversation with a plant manager at the General Motors Division in Nairobi in July 1980.

6.   R. B. Seidman, "Why Do People Obey the Law? The Case of Corruption in Developing Countries," *British Journal of Law and Society* 5, no. 7, Summer 1978, 49.

7.   Larry Diamond, "Nigeria: The Coup and the Future," *Africa Report* 29, no. 1, March–April 1984, 9–15.

8.   Stanislav Andreski, *The African Predicament*, New York, Atherton Press, 1968, Chapter 7; Ken Kotecha with Robert W. Adams, *African Politics: The Corruption of Power*, Washington, D.C., University Press of America, 1981, chapter 3.

9.   Seidman, "Why Do People Obey the Law?" 45–68; R. B. Seidman, "Law, Development, and Legislative Drafting in English-Speaking Africa," *Journal of Modern African Studies* 19, no. 1, 1981, 133–61.

10.   John Iliffe, *The Emergence of African Capitalism*, Minneapolis, University of Minnesota Press, 1983, 20–22.

11.   David J. Gould, "Local Administration in Zaire and Underdevelopment," *Journal of Modern African Studies* 15, no. 3, 1977, 349–78; Femi Odekunle, "Capitalist Economy and the Crime Problem in Nigeria," *Contemporary Crises* 2, 1978, 83–96.

12.   Varda Eker, "On the Origins of Corruption: Irregular Incentives in Nigeria," *Journal of Modern African Studies* 19, no. 1, 1981, 173–82; Colin Leys, "What is the Problem about Corruption?" *Journal of Modern African Studies* 3, no. 2, 1965, 215–30; Ronald Wraith and Edgar Simpkins, *Corruption in Developing Countries*, London, Allen and Unwin, 1963, chapter 5.

13.   Were, *Leadership and Underdevelopment,* 5–14.

14.   Robert Merton, ed., *Social Theory and Social Structures,* Glencoe, Ill., Free Press, 1957, 121–94.

15.   It should be noted that there are some laws in developed democratic societies that also operate as ideal norms. The law prohibiting drinking (the Volstead Act) in the United States was an example. The distinction here between developed democratic and developing societies is relative: many more laws operate as ideal norms in developing societies than in developed democratic societies.

16.   This approach derives from the phenomenological and symbolic interactionist traditions of the sociology of deviance. See Jerome G. Manis and Bernard N. Meltzer, *Symbolic Interaction: A Reader in Social Psychology,* Boston, Allyn and Bacon, 2nd ed., 1978, 11–92.

17.   Richard Sandbrook with Judith Barker, *The Politics of Africa's Economic Stagnation,* London, Cambridge University Press, 1985, 14–41.

18.   For a functional analysis of prostitution that fits this conception of soft deviance, see Kingsley Davis, "The Sociology of Prostitution," *American Sociological Review* 2, 1937, 744–55.

19.   Max Weber, *The Protestant Ethic and the Spirit of Capitalism,* New York, Charles Scribner's Sons, 1958, 47–78 155–83.

20.   Max Weber, *The Theory of Social and Economic Organization,* Glencoe, Ill., Free Press, 1947, 346–58; and Thomas M. Callaghy, *The State-Society Struggle: Zaire in Comparative Perspective,* New York, Columbia University Press, 1984, 185–92, 252–53, 273, 274.

21.   Sandbrook, *Economic Stagnation,* 91.

22.   David Martin, *General Amin,* London, Faber and Faber, 1974, 154–57.

23.   Quoted in Sandbrook, *Economic Stagnation,* 95.

24.   Callaghy, *State-Society Struggle,* 188.

25.   The recent public hearings investigating the conduct of former Kenyan Attorney General Charles Njonjo were an example of this technique. Though Njonjo was not criminally prosecuted because President Moi apparently wanted to avoid offending his Kikuyu political base, the public hearings served the objective of publicly discrediting Njonjo and hence removing from power a potentially dangerous political rival. See *Weekly Review* (Nairobi), August 24, 1984, 5–11.

26.   *African Guide,* Essex, England, World of Information Publishers, 1984, 159.

27.   Sandbrook, *Economic Stagnation,* 120–21.

28.   Christopher Colclough and Stephen McCarthy, *The Political Economy of Botswana,* London, Oxford University Press, 1980, 46.

29.   The conclusion is based on informal conversations I had with academics and others during my visit to Zimbabwe in January 1986. There was a general view that the government was intolerant of corruption.

30.   Harold D. Nelson, ed., *Zimbabwe, A Country Study,* Area Handbook Series, Washington, D.C., U.S. Department of the Army, 1983, 202.

31.   The role of foreign corporations and governments who pay bribes to promote their economic and political interests in African societies needs mentioning. Sandbrook observes, "The fact is that foreign corporations, salesmen, and investors are frequently quite willing to offer secret inducements to obtain plush contracts or access

to natural resources or protected markets in Africa. And these corporations normally receive a high return on the ten per cent 'commissions' paid to public officials or agents. Bribery, these foreigners say, is a necessary business practice. However, their willing collusion spreads the malady they so loftily condemn in public" (*Economic Stagnation*, 96). These payments are especially menacing, not only because they provide illegal financial gains that cannot be detected from audits of government budgets, but also because they typically entail subversions of public interests to foreign interests — resulting in privileges and exemptions — that are often injurious to the economic performance of African societies.

11

Accepting the Challenge of the Crisis of Development in Africa: Conclusions and Implications

Harvey Glickman

It might be legislated by an assembly of social scientists that anyone who believes he has discovered a new obstacle to development is under an obligation to look for ways in which this obstacle can be overcome or can possibly be lived with or can, in certain circumstances, be transformed into a blessing in disguise.

. . . actions and decisions are often taken because they are earnestly and fully expected to have certain effects that then wholly fail to materialize.[1]

A crisis is "an unstable condition in political, international, or economic affairs in which an abrupt or decisive change is impending."[2] This volume represents an exploration of ways to define the crisis of development in Africa and of approaches to paths for coping with that crisis.

DIVERSITY IN ANALYSIS

Each of the chapters in this volume illustrates the major theme that diversity in analysis of the crisis in Africa can contribute to insights into ways of coping. Part one of this volume explores explanations for the poor performance of Africa's governments and economies. It is important to place Africa's problems in their historical context without blaming all difficulties on colonialism. David Abernethy notes the incongruence of the structure of colonial rule in relation to the structures of legitimacy in

229

African societies. The African independent state inherited a colonial administration suspended above but not integrated into African society. Government meant bureaucracy whose numbers, salaries, perquisites, and functions related to Europe, not to Africa. Elite self-interest and national development ideology came to support a continuation of bureaucratic administration and supervision rather than political and economic reconstruction.

The contradiction exposed by Abernethy and the task of political and economic reconstruction mislead if reform moves unilaterally in the direction of attacking the state. Harvey Glickman and Sayre Schatz each attempt to restore a more balanced view. Glickman observes that a severely reduced state in Africa cramps the authority necessary to impose the reform conditions required by the World Bank and the International Monetary Fund. Austerity undermines authority in circumstances where legitimacy in great part depends on distributive capabilities. A reduction in the overhead authority of the state, especially in the midst of the attempt to introduce austerity reforms, opens up new opportunities for ethnic and class conflict. Suppression of conflict, in turn, risks reliance on force alone.

Schatz demonstrates that external factors explain a great deal about the decline of African economic performance, contrary to what has become mainstream economic analysis of the African crisis. The type of economy operated by African states, what Schatz labels "low-powered capitalism" dominated by world trade and open to foreign market swings, renders them vulnerable to global trends. External shocks, often seen as aberrational, are really normal for Africa. A set of reforms tied to laissez-faire economics alone may worsen rather than correct present trends. By implication, an effective lead from the public sector is necessary for Africa's development.

Vremudia Diejomaoh also focuses on external factors, confining his analysis to foreign investment, but confirming the importance of political decisions and a strong public sector. He calls for expanded public as well as private foreign investment. Recognizing that foreigners as well as Africans agree on the necessity of heightened self-reliance for African economies, he renews the appeal for regionally integrated economies in Africa as the only long-term solution for reducing dependency and building complementarity into Africa's relationship to the world economy.

Ravi Gulhati and Satya Yalamanchili reflect sensitivity to the concerns of Africans like Diejomaoh and the changing views among economists at the World Bank. They recognize that the political costs and needs of African governments must be attended to. While their contribution offers a number of useful indicators of excessive statism in the African economies, they observe that recovery policy is not a scientific enterprise and that economic instruments, such as pricing policy, are often less flexible than initially perceived (a direct connection to Raymond Hopkins' chapter on food subsidies). They emphasize what uninformed critics of the World Bank often forget, that the success of structural adjustment and policy reform programs requires the administrative cooperation and strong financial contribution of foreign donors. These factors are critical to Africa's own efforts toward economic recovery.

The short contribution by Princeton Lyman reflects the perspective of an American government official with long experience in dealing with African affairs. He attempts to deflect the doctrinaire criticism that the United States is deserting African development. In fact, the United States has become a major factor in providing foreign assistance to Africa, but Lyman indicates the necessity of cooperative efforts.

Part two focuses on three matters that have attracted much comment in the African development debate. Two matters — the involvement of women in economic activity and subsidies in food pricing policy — relate to the overriding necessity for increased agricultural production to serve as the engine of economic recovery and future development. The third issue, corruption in government, bridges popular and scholarly comment on African development. Each case study illustrates the significance of adopting a mixture and a variety of strategies rather than a single one. These contributions clearly do not exhaust discussion, but they suggest new perspectives.

Regarding corruption, Robert Washington confines his discussion to African capitalist countries, but he broadens the perspective to include the way matters appear to participants, that is, the meanings of events. He introduces the concept of an organizational rationality that deals with what makes sense to ordinary people. The implication is that governments vulnerable to corruption may need outside pressure, applied parallel to efforts at foreign assistance, in order to alter behavior that is counterproductive. Further implications would tend to support, from a cultural perspective, the notion of management conditionality in return for financial assistance.

Washington's foray into the theory of corruption raises the question of what appears situationally rational to African citizens in ambiguous circumstances. By implication, Raymond Hopkins' contribution on the specific question of food subsidies leads to the suggestion that the perceived political reasons that undergird such subsidies (a form of "social contract") also undermine the shaky logic of linkages between big government, price supports, and food shortages. Hopkins' findings question the conventional wisdom. They indicate that the evidence thus far does not support the conclusion that food subsidies on their own cause food shortages.

Another conclusion to draw from Hopkins' research is caution in designing new policies that undermine existing institutions. Similarly, Ruth Morgenthau's contribution leads to the conclusion that considerably more can be expected from grass roots organization in increasing peasant production. Much can be learned by international agencies from village-oriented assistance. Weak and vulnerable governments in Africa would be strengthened by efforts directed at local-level participation that enlist local solidarity groups.

Finally, Barbara Lewis' case study of getting the concerns and needs of women on the agenda of U.S. foreign assistance to Africa illustrates the utility of a multifaceted approach. She demonstrates that aid money can be directed to help women specifically by emphasis in analysis on both the arguments of economic rationalism and the special role of women in the African family. In other words, both feminist and productivity concerns can coincide in eliciting money for improving the position of African women. At least in this case, analytical alternatives can serve to complement one another in a policy context.

THE DEVELOPMENT DEBATE:
A PREMATURE CONSENSUS?

This book as a whole can be seen as an entry in the African development debate of the 1980s. By design, there has been no attempt to impose agreement on the analyses or the policy views in this volume. Analyses and views here, however, interact with major positions and issues ventilated in the past decade.

The key questions in the debate are these: What has gone wrong with Africa's development? What should be done about it? The debate originates with the Lagos Plan of Action of the Organization of African Unity in 1979, which dwelled on the need for more outside aid to African states. Ignition was supplied by the World Bank's "Berg Report," a supposed extension of the Lagos plan, which actually reformulated the whole analysis in 1981 toward the policy failures of African governments.[3] After several years of debate in a variety of forums, and after the adoption of policy "reforms" inside many African states, a consensus has emerged on what went wrong with Africa's development and on what to do about it.[4] The thrust of the advice has been to expand the role and influence of markets, domestic and international, in finance and in production, parallel to calls for increases in donor assistance. Nevertheless, several authors in this volume can be read to question the analytical basis on which consensus comes to rest. An interesting implication is that what passes for consensus at present may be less the result of analytical persuasion than the pragmatic belief in "no alternative" or a reflection of the ability of the World Bank and the IMF to impose conditionality on African governments. The policy significance of the consensus is that it essentially rests on a view of development that projects for Africa a path that is workable only by integrating African economies in their present circumstances more firmly into the world economy. That may be helpful now, but it should be clear that embarking on such a course has the effect of foreclosing basic political choices for Africa's peoples.

A major conclusion drawn from a review of the chapters in this volume is that the imperative of attention and aid to Africa ought not prematurely to close the debate. The record of success for policy reforms remains mixed. Financial austerity has increased the threat to political stability. Expanded production for export faces shrinking world markets for many of Africa's commodities. Sufficient increases in donor assistance or in debt relief have not been forthcoming. There remains a need for continuing consideration and toleration of mixed, multiple, or even alternative strategies for economic recovery and long-term development. The need remains also for reckoning with the political ability to make economic changes and for cushioning the political consequences of those changes.

GLOBAL IMPLICATIONS

The African crisis is not Africa's alone. It is also an institutional crisis of global proportions. African governments, foreign governments, and international institutions share in the responsibility for Africa's difficulties. While African governments made serious policy mistakes, as summarized in the "Berg Report," many foreign donors, including the World Bank in an earlier policy phase, encouraged African governments along the way. ("Redistribution with Growth" was a policy theme of the

1970s.) The authors in this volume are positioned along a spectrum of views. They avoid the polarization of postures stimulated by the initial juxtaposition of the Berg and Lagos reports of the early 1980s. A number of chapters support views critical of the policies of African governments. Others lean toward questioning those criticisms. The close reader will recognize what successive follow-up reports of the World Bank also came to see: neither internal factors nor external ones alone fully account for Africa's problems of the 1980s.[5]

CHALLENGING THE CONSENSUS

What new light have we shed on the key categories of discussion in the development debate? Regarding "what went wrong" with the political economy of Africa, both external economic shocks and poor economic management policies of governments have been cited. In assessing what went wrong for Africa, Diejomaoh and Schatz emphasize the severity of the external economic shocks to which African states were subjected from the onset of the oil-price rise in the mid-1970s. Diejomaoh notes the shortfall of expected private foreign investment. Schatz observes that the policies of economic management of the African states were not worse in outcomes than were those of other countries elsewhere with comparable per capita incomes.

A second set of factors in explaining what went wrong in Africa deals with political instability. The weakness of regimes — in authority and in administrative capacity — has often been cited. Political instability is also related to state intervention in the economies, but a straight causal line is challenged in this volume. State intervention distorts markets and results in inefficient production and distribution. Economic costs yield political discontent and hence contribute to instability. Schatz, Glickman, and Hopkins wonder whether the amount of state involvement in the economy can be singled out as a cause of so many problems.

Ethnicity — Africa's notorious tribalism — is a third major factor, although clearly it is connected to undisciplined pluralism and therefore to political instability. As a cause of development failure, ethnicity undercuts economic rationality when it underlies patronage. Washington raises the question of what is perceived as socially rational when many forms of deviance, not just departures from economic decisions, are regarded as normal.

Finally, the changing and conflicting aims of assisting foreign governments and international agencies are familiar as contributing to Africa's development difficulties. This volume does not quarrel with that view. Lyman, Lewis, and Morgenthau emphatically agree. Lewis and Morgenthau suggest alternative bases for donor contributions to African efforts. Diejomaoh urges encouragement by donors of efforts toward economic integration of African states.

On the question of what is to be done, the consensus viewpoint on policy reform attracts varying degrees of support from the authors in this volume. In summary, the present reform view is that agriculture is central to African economies; encouraging agricultural exports and food production is a primary requirement. Expanding production also requires reduction of excessive state controls on the economy, reduction in government expenditure on services, reduction in government subsidies — especially to food prices — and adjustment of exchange rates to realistic levels in order to expand exports and squeeze out luxury imports. Earning of foreign exchange to pay off previous debts and pay for necessary imports is emphasized. When such conditions of comparative austerity are in place and combined with targeted program aid by cooperating donors, then it is concluded that African governments will be on the road to more self-reliant policies. The present consensus on reform favors private enterprise as against the previous predilection of African governments for centralized state control over economies. In addition, there is a distinct downgrading of direct donor interest in social engineering projects.

POLITICAL ECONOMY QUESTIONS

This book raises questions about the political economy elements in the policy reform consensus. There is still considerable controversy about the appropriateness or the consequences of private enterprise capitalism in Africa's conditions.[6] Even those favoring private enterprise join in the view that Africa's recovery requires enormous amounts of public or publicly guaranteed financial assistance. The reduction in government controls may be overdone. In many cases in Africa, fostering a healthier private sector contributes to a more robust economy. Arguably, it also contributes to undercutting purely ethnic divisions and therefore leads to a healthier political pluralism. Yet while "statism" is a grave problem, getting the state out of the African economies — creating free enterprise capitalism — is not a realistic aim. Worse still, it can create a mask for expanding foreign privileges.

In league with other analyses of Africa's problems of development, this book suggests that the economic crisis is at bottom a political crisis.[7] Economic development requires political power. It requires not just less government, but a particular kind of state. The experience of the "newly industrializing countries" of Latin America or Asia is probably not applicable to Africa. At present it does not seem politically possible. It may not be desirable. Development in the NIC states requires the insulation of the state from society, a build-up of the ability of the state to suppress welfare demands, to resist patrimonial penetration, and, at critical moments, to rule by force alone.

An expanded private sector, if it consists largely of foreign companies, requires a strong and determined host government to maximize its investment effectiveness for national development. In addition, generating spillover effects and backward linkages requires an emerging entrepreneurial class, itself dependent on legal and administrative guarantees. Schatz and Abernethy cast doubt on the viability of an African bourgeoisie. Diejomaoh is more disposed to seek foreign private investment and to attempt national controls over it. The implication is that we need a clearer view of precisely who will be strengthened if the private sector grows stronger. In some countries a stronger local bourgeoisie means an enlarged role for non-African minorities, a possibility that creates or resurrects racial tensions. Many Africans already suspect that the call for increased private enterprise is a cover for non-African domination.

A reduced public sector risks weakening central governments with national support already stretched thin. On the other hand, a constrained central government may represent an opening toward constitutionalism in African politics. Much depends on the strength of groups whose status is not dependent on government position. A benign perspective on foreign investment can see contributions to the beginnings of democratic pluralism. Either way, economic reform cannot escape political choices — choices that require a comprehensive airing.

LEVELS OF ANALYSIS AND ACTION

The probings of our contributors range over three levels of action: international, national, and local. The results suggest that effective analysis and policy must operate at all three levels and that both public and private sectors must be involved. Policy departures inside African governments, while important, will be insufficient to make basic differences. Institutional changes are required. The mechanisms of cooperation that at one time harnessed private and public capital and national and international agencies for project aid in Africa now need to be reconstructed around economic management and development programs. In this perspective the directive to reduce government is clearly insufficient. It must be supplemented by a multifaceted strategy to prune and strengthen government management of the economy. The task requires not only leaner government in African countries but also more effective government. A start can be made at the local government level. Deconcentrating power and decentralization of administration are important, but on their own they can become a disguise for patronage. New resources must be organized. Rural women remain a largely untapped resource, as noted by Lewis. Private, grass roots–oriented international agencies can play a constructive role, as noted by Morgenthau. Village-level associations, enlisting the participation of women in deciding and implementing production and service programs, need more emphasis. The turn to renewed roles for the institutions generated by and dependent on Africans at the grass roots can inject new meaning into the aspiration for democratic development.

FURTHER INQUIRY

This volume will achieve its primary goal if it succeeds in raising questions about the conventional wisdom, about what may be a premature policy consensus, or about the consequences of contemporary policy moves. A fuller understanding of what contributes to effective and durable development in Africa implies even broader inquiries than those already suggested.

Perhaps most important, we need to know more about making the private sector work where it is appropriate today in Africa. The economic management of African governments has received much deserved criticism. A recent issue of *Jeune Afrique* announced "Goodbye to Marxism" in describing changes in the direction of free enterprise in the People's Republic of Benin.[8] Of forty-five countries in sub-Saharan Africa, twenty-eight have begun the process of structural reform, making them eligible for special loans from the World Bank, by adopting exchange rates in line with world trading levels, raising prices for farm products, reducing public bureaucracies, and privatizing unprofitable public enterprises. But several years of experience of policy reform and adjustments in a number of African states have yet to demonstrate a pattern of policy successes. It is clear that African states cannot shrink too much. Public-sector management, parastatal corporations, and government subsidies will not disappear in the face of a newly robust private sector. We need to know more about workable state intervention in African economies in order to compare practices in different countries and to compare economic sectors inside countries. Africa's relative "success stories" — Ivory Coast, Cameroon, Kenya — are not countries of unbridled capitalist private enterprise. Rather, they are examples of effective state management of the economy, with substantial state sectors, yet countries that welcome foreign and domestic private enterprise.

We need to learn more of developmental possibilities below the level of the national state as well. Long-term economic development for Africa may require "capturing" Africa's hard-pressed peasants in the discipline of the market; intermediate-term economic development may require price incentives to reverse their "withdrawal."[9] But governments today need to be energized and helped to provide adequate extension services and appropriate technological inputs — none of which can be bought by peasants alone.

A second important area for further inquiry is the role of donors and donor coordination. Despite the agreement at the UN Conference on African Development in 1986, which seemed to commit Western countries to raise their levels of assistance to African countries in return for stepping up progress toward more open economies in Africa, the combined totals of aid have remained at about $9 billion. Bilateral economic assistance to sub-Saharan Africa from the United States fell from $972 million in 1986 to $772 million in 1987.[10] In the light of Africa's continuing debt commitments and the drop in Africa's main export commodities, foreign relief seems essential. Putting aside the morally unassailable argument of fighting starvation anywhere, the national interests of foreign donors — public and private — compel some responsibility for Africa's predicament. If foreign aid can be sold to domestic constituencies as serving the interests of domestic groups — farmers in the United States would be one prominent example — those interests extend to the use to which aid can be put. Markets for foreign products and foreign capital shrivel in declining economies. Loans made require prosperity to be paid back. Lenders, donors, and foreign aiders need to recall that protectionism at home is self-defeating. Developed countries need to assess how long they can endure living with an African slum in their common world.

Finally, there is the continuing question of the uniqueness of Africa relative to other parts of the Third World. The patrimonial-bureaucratic state, the relative brevity and uneven impact of colonial rule, the peculiarities of African rural life and ecology, and the differential response capabilities of Africa's "balkanized" continent suggest that future comparative studies will yield further particularities rather than assured generalizations for the whole of Africa.

NOTES

1.   Albert O. Hirschman, "The Search for Paradigms as a Hindrance to Understanding," in Norman T. Uphoff and Warren F. Ilchman, eds., *The Political Economy of Development*, Berkeley, University of California Press, 1972, 70; Albert O. Hirschman, *The Passions and the Interests: Political Arguments for Capitalism before its Triumph*, Princeton, Princeton University Press, 1977, 131.

2.   *The American Heritage Dictionary of the English Language*, Boston, Houghton Mifflin, 1973, 314.

3.   World Bank, *Accelerated Development in Sub-Saharan Africa: An Agenda for Action*, Washington, D.C., World Bank, 1981; Organization of African Unity, *Lagos Plan of Action for the Economic Development of Africa, 1980–2000*, Geneva, International Institute for Labour Studies, 1981.

4.   See the valuable summary by Jennifer Seymour Whitaker, "The Policy Setting: Crisis and Consensus," in Robert J. Berg and Jennifer Seymour Whitaker, eds., *Strategies for African Development*, Berkeley, University of California Press, 1986, 1–22.

5.   World Bank, *Sub-Saharan Africa: Progress Report on Development Prospects and Programs*, Washington, D.C., World Bank, 1983; *Toward Sustained Development in Sub-Saharan Africa: A Joint Program of Action*, Washington, D.C., World Bank, 1984; *Financing Adjustment with Growth in Sub-Saharan Africa, 1986–90*, Washington, D.C., World Bank, 1986.

6.   John Iliffe, *The Emergence of African Capitalism*, Minneapolis, University of Minnesota Press, 1983; Nicola Swainson, *The Development of Corporate Capitalism in Kenya, 1918–77*, Berkeley, University of California Press, 1980; Sayre P. Schatz, *Nigerian Capitalism*, Berkeley, University of California Press, 1977.

7.   John Ravenhill, "Africa's Continuing Crisis: The Elusiveness of Development," in John Ravenhill, ed., *Africa in Economic Crisis*, New York, Columbia University Press, 1986, 1–43.

8.   James Brooke, "A New Economic Order Comes to Africa," *New York Times*, July 19, 1987, 12F.

9.   For these views, see Goran Hyden, *No Shortcuts to Progress, African Development Management in Perspective*, Berkeley, University of California Press, 1983, 191–200; Robert H. Bates, *Markets and States in Tropical Africa*, Berkeley, University of California Press, 1981, 119–32.

10.   Brooke, "New Economic Order," 12F.

Selected Bibliography

Acharya, Shankar N. "Perspectives and Problems of Development in Sub-Saharan Africa." *World Development* 9, 1981, 109–47.

Adedeji, Adebayo. *The African Development Problematique*. Addis Ababa, Economic Commission for Africa, March 1985.

Adedeji, Adebayo, and Shaw, Timothy M., eds. *Economic Crisis in Africa*. Boulder, Colo., Lynne Rienner, 1985.

African Development Bank and Economic Commission for Africa. *Economic Report on Africa, 1984*. Abidjan, 1984.

Amin, Samir. "Underdevelopment and Dependence in Black Africa — Origins and Contemporary Forms." *Journal of Modern African Studies* 10, December 1972, 503–25.

Andreski, Stanislav. *The African Predicament*. New York, Atherton Press, 1968.

Bates, Robert H. *Markets and States in Tropical Africa*. Berkeley, University of California Press, 1981.

Bay, Edna, ed. *Women and Work in Africa*. Boulder, Colo., Westview, 1982.

Berg, Robert J., and Whitaker, Jennifer S., eds. *Strategies for African Development*. Berkeley, University of California Press, 1986.

Berry, Sara. "The Food Crisis and Agrarian Change in Africa." *African Studies Review* 27, June 1984, 59–112.

Bienen, Henry S., and Diejomaoh, V. P., eds. *The Political Economy of Income Distribution in Nigeria.* New York, Holmes and Meier, 1981.

Bienen, Henry S., and Gersovitz, Mark. "Economic Stabilization, Conditionality, and Political Stability." *International Organization* 39, Autumn 1985, 729–54.

Brietzke, Paul, guest ed. "The World Bank's Accelerated Development in Sub-Saharan Africa: A Symposium." *African Studies Review* 27, no. 4, December 1984, 1–60.

Browne, Robert S., and Cummings, Robert J. *The Lagos Plan of Action vs. the Berg Report: Contemporary Issues in African Development.* Washington, D.C., Howard University Press, 1984.

Callaghy, Thomas M. "Africa's Debt Crisis." *Journal of International Affairs* 38, no. 1, Summer 1984, 61–80.

Carlsson, Jerker, ed. *Recession in Africa.* Uppsala, Scandinavian Institute of African Studies, 1983.

Cooper, Frederick. "Africa and the World Economy." *African Studies Review* 29, no. 2/3, June/September 1981, 1–86.

Eicher, Carl. "Facing Up to Africa's Food Crisis." *Foreign Affairs* 61, Fall 1982, 151–76.

Ekeh, Peter. "Colonialism and the Two Publics in Africa: A Theoretical Statement." *Comparative Studies in Society and History* 17, no. 1, January 1975, 91–112.

Ergas, Zaki, ed. *The African State in Transition.* London, Macmillan, 1987.

Franke, Richard W., and Chasin, Barbara H. *Seeds of Famine.* Montclair, N.J., Allenheld Osmun, 1980.

Green, Reginald H., guest ed. "Sub-Saharan Africa: Toward Oblivion or Reconstruction?" *Journal of Development Planning,* no. 15, 1985.

Helleiner, Gerald K. "The IMF and Africa in the 1980s." *Canadian Journal of African Studies* 17, no. 1, 1983, 17–33.

Hopkins, A. G. *An Economic History of West Africa.* New York, Columbia University Press, 1973.

Hyden, Goran. *Beyond Ujamaa in Tanzania: Underdevelopment and an Uncaptured Peasantry.* Berkeley, University of California Press, 1980.

Hyden, Goran. *No Shortcuts to Progress: African Development Management in Perspective.* Berkeley, University of California Press, 1983.

Iliffe, John. *The Emergence of African Capitalism.* Minneapolis, University of Minnesota Press, 1983.

Institute for Development Studies (Sussex). "Accelerated Development in Sub-Saharan Africa: What Agenda for Action?" *IDS Bulletin* 14, no. 1, January 1983, whole issue.

Jones, David B. "State Structures in New Nations: The Case of Primary Agricultural Marketing in Africa." *Journal of Modern African Studies* 20, no. 4, December 1982, 553–69.

Kasfir, Nelson. *The Shrinking Political Arena: Participation and Ethnicity in African Politics.* Berkeley, University of California Press, 1976.

Kirkpatrick, C., and Nixson, F. "Transnational Corporations and Economic Development." *Journal of Modern African Studies* 14, no. 3, 1981, 367–99.

Lancaster, Carol. "Africa's Economic Crisis." *Foreign Policy* no. 52, Fall 1983, 49–66.

Lancaster, Carol, and Williamson, John, eds. *African Debt and Financing.* Special Reports, 5. Washington, D.C., Institute for International Economics, May 1986.

Langdon, Steven, and Mytelka, Lynn K. "Africa in the Changing World Economy." In Legum, Colin, et al. *Africa in the 1980s.* New York, McGraw-Hill, 1979, 123–211.

Leys, Colin. "African Economic Development in Theory and Practice." *Daedalus* 3, no. 2, Spring 1982, 99–124.

Lofchie, Michael F., and Commins, Stephen K. "Food Deficits and Agricultural Policies." *Journal of Modern African Studies* 20, March 1982, 1–25.

Lofchie, Michael F., Commins, Stephen K., and Payne, Rhys, eds. *Africa's Agrarian Crisis: The Roots of Famine.* Boulder, Colo., Lynne Rienner, 1986.

Masini, Jean, et al. *Multinationals and Development in Black Africa: A Case Study in the Ivory Coast.* West Mead, N.J., Saxon House, 1979.

McNamara, Robert S. *The Challenge for Sub-Saharan Africa.* Sir John Crawford Memorial Lecture, November 1, 1985. Washington, D.C., World Bank, 1985.

Mowoe, Isaac J., ed. *The Performance of Soldiers as Governors: African Politics and the African Military.* Washington, D.C., University Press of America, 1980.

Munroe, J. Forbes. *Africa and the International Economy, 1800–1960.* Totowa, N.J., Rowman and Littlefield, 1976.

Nelson, Joan. "The Political Economy of Stabilization: Commitment, Capacity, and Public Response." *World Development* 12, October 1984, 983–1006.

O'Barr, Jean. "Making the Invisible Visible: African Women in Politics and Policy." *African Studies Review* 18, 1975, 19–28.

Organization of African Unity. *Lagos Plan of Action for the Economic Development of Africa, 1980–2000.* Geneva, International Institute for Labour Studies, 1981.

Organization of African Unity. *What Kind of Africa by the Year 2000?* Addis Ababa, OAU, May 1979.

Ravenhill, John, ed. *Africa in Economic Crisis.* New York, Columbia University Press, 1986.

Robinson, Pearl, and Skinner, Elliott, eds. *Transformation and Resiliency in Africa.* Washington, D.C., Howard University Press, 1983.

Rose, Tore, ed. *Crisis and Recovery in Sub-Saharan Africa.* Paris, OECD, 1985.

Rothchild, Donald, and Olorunsola, Victor, eds. *State versus Ethnic Claims: African Policy Dilemmas.* Boulder, Colo., Westview, 1983.

Sandbrook, Richard, with Barker, Judith. *The Politics of Africa's Economic Stagnation.* London, Cambridge University Press, 1985.

Sandbrook, Richard. *The Politics of Basic Needs: Urban Aspects of Assaulting Poverty in Africa.* Toronto, University of Toronto Press, 1982.

Schatz, Sayre P. "Pirate Capitalism and the Inert Economy of Nigeria." *Journal of Modern African Studies* 22, no. 1, March 1984, 45–58.

Schatz, Sayre P. *Nigerian Capitalism.* Berkeley, University of California Press, 1977.

Schiavo-Campo, Salvatore, et al. *The Tortoise Walk: Public Policy and Private Activity in the Economic Development of Cameroon.* A.I.D. Evaluation Special Study no. 10. Washington, D.C., USAID, 1983.

Shaw, Timothy M., ed. *Alternative Futures for Africa.* Boulder, Colo., Westview, 1982.

Shaw, Timothy M., and Aluko, Olajide, eds. *Africa Projected: From Recession to Renaissance by the Year 2000?* London, Macmillan, 1985.

Sklar, Richard. "The Nature of Class Domination in Africa." *Journal of Modern African Studies* 17, no. 4, 1979, 531–52.

Swainson, Nicola. *The Development of Corporate Capitalism in Kenya, 1918–77.* Berkeley, University of California Press, 1980.

United Nations Economic Mission for Africa. *ECA and Africa's Development, 1983–2008: A Preliminary Perspective Study.* Addis Ababa, ECA, April 1983.

United States Department of Agriculture. *Food Problems and Prospects in Sub-Saharan Africa.* Washington, D.C., 1981.

Were, Gideon S. *Leadership and Underdevelopment in Africa.* Nairobi, Gideon Were, P.O. Box 10622, 1983.

Wheeler, Douglas. "Sources of Stagnation in Sub-Saharan Africa." *World Development* 12, no. 1, 1984, 1–28.

Wolgin, Jerome, et al. *The Private Sector and the Economic Development of Malawi.* A.I.D. Evaluation Special Study no. 11. Washington, D.C., USAID, 1983.

World Bank. *Accelerated Development in Sub-Saharan Africa: An Agenda for Action.* Washington, D.C., World Bank, 1981.

World Bank. *Financing Adjustment with Growth in Sub-Saharan Africa, 1986–90.* Washington, D.C., World Bank, 1986.

World Bank. *Sub-Saharan Africa: Progress Report on Development Prospects and Programs.* Washington, D.C., World Bank, 1983.

World Bank. *Toward Sustained Development in Sub-Saharan Africa: A Joint Program of Action.* Washington, D.C., World Bank, 1984.

Wortman, Sterling, and Cummings, Ralph W., Jr. *To Feed This World: The Challenge and the Strategy.* Baltimore, Johns Hopkins University Press, 1978.

Young, Crawford. *Ideology and Development in Africa.* New Haven, Conn., Yale University Press, 1982.

Zartman, I. William, ed. *The Political Economy of Nigeria.* New York, Praeger, 1983.

Index

African Development Bank, 44
African State, 24–43; and capital
  formation, 55–56; as a cause of food-
  system failures, 140–42; and control
  of food supply, 134–37; derivations
  from political sociology and economy, 33–35; distortions of economic
  policy, 96–101; economic decline of,
  26–28, 101; emergence in Africa,
  64–65; food production and marketing policy, 142; global explanations
  of decay, 30–32; impact of overextension, 34, 41; institutional
  reform, 41; major explanations of
  decay, 25–26; middle-range theories,
  32–33; and patrimonial-administrative state, 35–36; period of economic
  growth, 27; policy on exchange
  rates, 101; and policy reform, 37–40;
  political instability, 234; popular
  images of, 117–18; and the soft
  state, 30; and statism, 235; role of,
  4–5; state-centric policies, 28–30;
  urban-biased development coalition
  model, 36
Agriculture: annual growth rates, 45;
  breakdown of food system, 149; and

capital formation, 52, 54; development strategies, 34; division of labor
  by sex, 149; failure of domestic food
  pricing, 79–80; farming systems
  analysis, 188–93, 197–98; food
  production, cause of crisis in, 129;
  food production, growth rates in
  eastern and southern Africa, 87–88;
  food production, per capita rates,
  131–32; food production, primacy of
  women in, 177, 180; food production, social organization of, 149;
  gender-sensitive planning, 193–96;
  government intervention in pricing,
  97, 98, 100; increased productivity of
  women in, 177, 180; and laissez-faire
  pricing strategy, 76–77; negative
  environmental factors, 92; policy
  indicators, 100; policy reform, 235;
  technical solutions to problems, 150;
  and women's role in development
  agenda, 176–200; world food surplus,
  148. *See also* CILCA; Development
  crisis; Food production; Food
  subsidies; Policy reform; Rural
  development
Algeria, 4, 8, 49

247

Contributors

DAVID B. ABERNETHY is Professor of Political Science and co-chair of the Program in International Relations at Stanford University. He has been a visiting lecturer at University College, Dar es Salaam, Tanzania. He is the author of *The Political Dilemma of Popular Education: An African Case* (1969) and of articles on teachers in Nigerian politics, U.S. policy toward South Africa, and political and bureaucratic aspects of Africa's economic crisis.

VREMUDIA P. DIEJOMAOH is currently the Chief of the Jobs and Skills Program for Africa (JASPA) of the International Labor Organization in Addis Ababa, Ethiopia. Educated at Princeton and Harvard, he has served as Professor, Head of the Department of Economics, and Dean of the Faculty of Social Sciences at the University of Lagos, Nigeria, and as Director-General of the Nigerian Institute of Social and Economic Research. He has published extensively on Nigerian and African development problems, including *The Political Economy of Income Distribution in Nigeria* (1981), with Henry Bienen.

HARVEY GLICKMAN is Professor of Political Science at Haverford College, Pennsylvania. He has been a research fellow at University College, Dar es Salaam, Tanzania, a visiting lecturer at Cape Town University, South Africa, and a visiting professor of African studies at Hebrew University, Jerusalem, Israel. He has published articles on political parties and political ideology in Africa in a number of journals and edited collections. He has also served as consultant on African problems to U.S. government and international agencies. Formerly book editor of *Africa Report,* he is now editor of *Issue — A Journal of Opinion,* a publication of the African Studies Association.

RAVI GULHATI is Senior Adviser in the Economic Development Institute of the World Bank. He has served as Chief Economist in the World Bank's Eastern and Southern Africa Region and as Director of its Economic Development Department. He is the author of books and many articles on external debt issues and on economic policy in sub-Saharan Africa.

RAYMOND F. HOPKINS is Professor of Political Science at Swarthmore College, Pennsylvania, and Director of the Food Systems and Food Policy Program. He has written books on Tanzania, international politics, and international problems of food and hunger, as well as many articles. His work on food problems has been supported by major foundations, and he has served as consultant to U.S. government and international agencies.

BARBARA LEWIS teaches comparative politics at Rutgers University. She has written a number of articles in journals and edited collections on aspects of women and development in Africa and on food production and distribution in several West African settings. For USAID, she edited *Invisible Farmers: Women and the Crisis in Agriculture* (1980). She is currently writing *Côte d'Ivoire: A Profile.*

PRINCETON LYMAN is United States Ambassador to Nigeria. He has served in the U.S. Department of State as Deputy Assistant Secretary for African Affairs, with primary responsibility for economic matters and policy planning, and in the U.S. Agency for International Development as Director of the USAID Mission in Ethiopia. He has taught at the Johns Hopkins School of Advanced International Studies. He is the coauthor with David Cole of *Korean Development: The Interplay of Politics and Economics* (1971) and the author of numerous articles on political and economic development.

RUTH S. MORGENTHAU is Adlai Stevenson Professor of International Politics at Brandeis University and Visiting Scholar in the

Hunger Program at Brown University. She has served on the United States Delegation to the United Nations and to the Food and Agriculture Organization. She is the author of the prize-winning *Political Parties in French-Speaking West Africa* (1964) and of numerous articles in journals and edited collections on African politics and rural development. She is also the President of the International Liaison Committee for Food Corps Programs (CILCA), an organization that helps farmers in poor countries move toward self-sufficiency.

SAYRE P. SCHATZ is Professor of Economics at Temple University. He is the author of three books on African economic development, including *Nigerian Capitalism* (1977), the editor of another, and coauthor of *Postimperialism: International Capitalism and Development in the Late Twentieth Century* (1987). He has written more than forty journal articles on economic development.

ROBERT WASHINGTON is Associate Professor of Sociology at Bryn Mawr College, Pennsylvania. He has written articles on social and cultural forces in Africa and among Afro-Americans for several sociological and anthropological quarterly journals and annuals. His field work includes stays in Kenya and South Africa.

SATYA YALAMANCHILI is on the staff of the Eastern and Southern Region of the World Bank. He has published articles on debt issues in Africa, on agriculture in Ethiopia, and on industrial policy in India.